BIRTHMARKS OF EUROPE

Birthmarks of Europe

The Origins of the European Community Reconsidered

EDELGARD MAHANT
Glendon College, York University, Canada

Routledge
Taylor & Francis Group
LONDON AND NEW YORK

First published 2004 by Ashgate Publishing

Reissued 2018 by Routledge
2 Park Square, Milton Park, Abingdon, Oxon OX14 4RN
711 Third Avenue, New York, NY 10017, USA

Routledge is an imprint of the Taylor & Francis Group, an informa business

A Library of Congress record exists under LC control number: 2003056926

ISBN 13: 978-0-815-38782-4 (hbk)
ISBN 13: 978-1-351-16244-9 (ebk)

Contents

Acknowledgements

In thanking those who helped with a project which has taken over five years to come to fruition, there is always the danger of forgetting someone. So let me begin by apologising to anyone whose name I may forget to mention. You are hereby thanked just as much as those who are mentioned below!

In chronological order, Prof. Andrew Moravcsik of Harvard University, and Ms Sophie Tzoutzi, a PhD student at York University, gave me invaluable assistance in conceptualizing the project in its beginnings. As for collecting the material, the staff at the European Archives in Florence and at the Quai d'Orsay Archives in Paris went out of their way to be helpful.

The Delegation of the Commission of the European Community in Ottawa provided a generous research grant which enabled me to do the archival research for this book. Glendon College's research fund provided three small research grants which enabled me to employ an amazing team of graduate and undergraduate students to bring the writing and formatting process to its conclusion. Alexandre Brassard took on the job of formatting the references, a task which Müzeyyen Öksüz took over and completed with amazing patience, dedication and attention to detail, while Alexandre gave her his continuing after sales service, as he likes to call it. Glen Norton carefully proofread the final product, catching all those little mistakes and incongruities that those of us who are enthusiastic about our subject tend to miss.

Last, but certainly not least, I would like to thank Dr. Jake VanderKooy and PhD candidate Tuna Baskoy, who read chapters and gave me valuable comments. Also in the same last-but-not-least-category, I must thank my family, my husband Parkash, my son Paul and my daughter Sheila, whose wedding and the birth of whose first child all occurred within the five year gestation period of this book, and all of whom, as a result, received less attention than they merited.

Edelgard Mahant
Glendon College, York University

List of Abbreviations

AA	Auswärtiges Amt
ACP	African, Caribbean and Pacific Countries
BDI	Bundesverband der Deutschen Industries
BSE	Bovine Spongiform Encephalopathy
CAP	Common Agricultural Policy
CDU	Christlich Demokratische Union
CGPME	Confédération Générale des Petites et Moyennes Entreprises
CGT	Confédération Générale du Travail
CNIP	Centre National des Indépendants et Paysans
CNPF	Conseil Nationale du Patronat Français
CSU	Christlich Soziale Union
DGB	Deutscher Gewerkschaftsbund
DIHT	Deutscher Industrie- und Handelstag
EAEC	European Atomic Energy Community
EC/EU	European Community/European Union
ECSC	European Coal and Steel Community
EDC	European Defence Community
EEC	European Economic Community
EPC	European Political Community
EPP	European Peoples' Party
EU	European Union
Euratom	European Atomic Community
FDP	Freie Demokratische Parrtei
FNSEA	Fédération Nationale des Syndicats d'Exploitants Agricoles
FO	Force Ouvrière
GATT	General Agreement on Tariffs and Trade
GB/BHE	Gesamterdeutscher Block/Block der Heimatvertriebenen und Entrechteten
GDP	Gross Domestic Product
IGC	Intergovernmental Conference
ILO	International Labour Organisation
IR	International Relations

MRP	Mouvement Républicain Populaire
NATO	North Atlantic Treaty Organization
NGO	Non-governmental organization
OECD	Organization for Economic Cooperation and Development
OEEC	Organization for European Economic Cooperation
SEA	Single European Act
SFIO	Section Française de l'Internationale Ouvrière
SMP	Single Market Programme
SPD	Sozialdemokratische Partei Deutschlands
TEU	Treaty on European Union
UDSR	Union Démocratique et Sociale de la Résistance
WEU	Western European Union
WTO	World Trade Organization

1 Introduction

To paraphrase Winston Churchill, when it comes to the study of European integration, seldom have so many built so much upon so little. This statement is not meant to belittle the scholarship of those who toil in the vineyard of European integration, much less to belittle the achievements of the Union itself, but to point out that the European Union and its predecessors have attracted an extraordinary degree of scholarly attention. Without speculating unduly on the causes of this phenomenon (the attractions of European travel? the national origins of the scholars involved? the intellectual attraction of a new kind of institution and the theoretical possibilities thereof, gaining 'new insights into the wider prospects for multilateral inter-governmental organizations'? (Strange, 1996:163)), it is worth pointing out that this degree of scholarly attention has led to a proliferation of historical and theoretical interpretations as each generation and each group of scholars tries to make its mark. It would seem presumptuous to add to this accumulation of scholarship were it not for the fact that as the Union itself develops, some theoretical interpretations become less applicable, while others need to be refined or reinterpreted to take account of new developments.

This book contends that ideas and values play a significant role in the shaping of political institutions. Accordingly, the European Union, since its birth as the European Economic Community, has been shaped by a specific set of ideas and values which were prevalent among French and German elites at that time, that is in the middle of the 1950s.

Before beginning such an endeavour, it is necessary to review some of the theories and theoretical frameworks that have attempted to explain the founding and the development of the European Union and its predecessors (henceforward, the European Union for short), notably those theories which seek to explain the development of the Union in terms of some of the theories of international relations. These theories, as they relate to the European Union, can be classified according to two different typologies. The first typology is based on the source, that is the institution, which first inspired the theorist to design his/her theory. A number of such theories use European integration as the primary example, in many cases even as a model in the normative sense of that word (Chryssochoou, 2000) and continue by developing general theories of international integration

(Haas, 1958; Lindberg, 1963; Pentland, 1973), which may or may not be then tested against the example of other geographical regions (Axline, 1994; Higgett, 1998; Haas, 1964) or universal international organizations (Haas, 1964 on the International Labour Organization; Sewell, 1966 on the World Bank). The second type of study tries to apply and refine theories of international relations by applying them to the case of the European Union. Studies of this kind have been more common in recent years (Moravcsik, 1998; Hoffmann and Keohane, 1991).

The second major typology separates studies according to the motives which they ascribe to the political actors who have led the process of European integration. The major division here is between those who see a process driven primarily by material interests and those who see a process driven primarily by ideas. But whose interests? And whose ideas? Here again there is a bifurcation, between those who write of the interests and ideas of states and those who write of the interests of groups and individuals. This double classification produces the matrix presented in Table 1.

Such a rough and rigid categorization, of course, simplifies as much as it clarifies. The categories themselves are far from unambiguous. Take the concept of ideas. Though there are a number of recent and not-so-recent converts to the importance of ideas in shaping national and transnational policies, there is considerable confusion as to what constitutes an ideational influence. Some see ideas as causal beliefs, concepts as to what consequence 'b' will result from action 'a' (Goldstein and Keohane, 1993). Indeed, March and Olsen (1998) have labelled the idea that self-interest motivates the actions which lead to change in international political 'orders' the 'logic of consequence'. Such a concept of ideas could blend into another category, that of material self-interest, since the notion that such or such an action will make a person, or a group or a state richer or more powerful is hardly an idea pursued for its moral value. On the other hand, the anticipated consequence may be something that is wider than the material self-interest of the individual or group; it may be a normative goal (peace, the reduction of poverty) or a non-material benefit (a sense of identity).

• Or ideas could mean an ideology, that is a set of ideas applied to political situations. Goldstein and Keohane call ideologies world views, but that phrase does not convey the sense of political purpose implied by an ideology. At yet other times, ideas become a synonym for norms or principled beliefs (Goldstein and Keohane, 1993). What is more, institutions are often lumped in with ideas, as if institutions were no more than reified ideas. Garrett and Weingast (1993), for example, devote the empirical section of an article entitled 'Ideas, Interests and Institutions: Constructing the European Community's Internal Market' to a discussion of decisions of the European Court. While courts can and do develop norms as well as enforce them, the decisions of courts which the litigants have agreed to accept are surely in a different category than are moral precepts, such as the condemnation of slavery or the rightness of international peace. Yet the literature on the ideational factors often does not make this distinction. Lieshout (1999: 29-30), on the other hand, makes the point that institutions can play an autonomous role and contribute to international events, but he limits his analysis to geopolitical factors. More recently, the concept of identities as ideas has appeared in the literature. While the identities of individuals and the influence of great leaders has been the subject of study since ancient times, writers have now added the identities of states to the values national leaders defend (Ruggie, 1998). The idea that the state, not its leaders or elites, could have an identity separate from that of its leaders is surely an anthropomorphism of Hegelian proportions.

The concept of identity in turn relates to that of roles, an idea developed by James Rosenau and Kal Holsti (Rosenau, 1980; Holsti, 1970). Roles can refer to the state an individual sees her/himself as representing (the Canadian foreign minister, for example, could see Canada as a peacemaker) or to the role played by individuals within a national, transnational or international political system. Thus Jacques Delors as President of the European Commission saw himself as a builder of a supranational Europe (Ross, 1995).

Though it may seem obvious that the categories of ideas and self-interest are not mutually exclusive or that it is not always possible to make a sharp distinction between the interests of individuals, groups and states (did not a wise man once say that what was good for General Motors was good for the United States?), academics defend their particular corner of this intellectual patch with vigour. Ruggie (1998) and Parsons (2000) make a strong case for the importance of ideas in shaping the world political system after 1945 and the European Union (EU), respectively. Moravcsik (1998) is just as firm in his defence of the role of governments, which in turn represent the interests of powerful groups within their states. And, of course, they can all marshal strong empirical evidence to support their position.

Table 1: A Schematic Table of Some of the Principal Theories of European Integration[1]

Motivating factor	Actors	European Union as primary inspiration	International Relations theory as primary inspiration
Material interests as expressed by:	States/ structures	Inter-governmentalism	Realism/neo-liberalism
	Groups/ individuals	Neo-functionalism	Functionalism/ Liberalism/ Neo-liberal institutionalism/ Marxism
		The 'Additive' Model	
Ideas and norms	States/ Structures	Federalism	Regime theory/ Social constructivism
	Groups/ individuals	Consociationalism/ Multi-level governance theory	Post-structuralism/ Constructivism

The division between theories based on the EU as a primary example and those derived from international relations theory generally may seem incongruous. Yet it can have some heuristic value, for at least two reasons. Academics and persons involved in the European institutions have repeated many times that the EU is *sui generis*, neither a state nor an international system. Not surprisingly, therefore, analysts have borrowed theories from both international relations and comparative politics to explain its dynamics, though the former appears to predominate. By attempting to relate theories of international relations to European integration, we can determine the extent to which the EU does function like an international system. If, on the other hand, these theories do not 'fit' the

1 Table as conceived by Ms Sofie Tzoutzi.

EU, we have further evidence that the EU is a political, but not an international system. This categorization can also help us to make at least a rough and ready judgement as to the extent to which theories of European integration, as against theories of international relations more generally, emphasize the importance of ideas in the shaping of the political process known as European integration. Europeans have often claimed that the 'European idea' means that European integration is more ideational than most of the other international processes of the contemporary world. A glance at Table 1 suggests that this is not necessarily the case.

A full commentary and explication of Table 1 would require a separate book, not least because of the voluminous literature on European integration and the theories of international relations. So the next section will be limited to a few examples of some of the writers who have espoused some of the theories listed on the table, concentrating on those who have been primarily inspired by European integration.

Intergovernmentalism is the EU inspired equivalent of realism and neo-realism. Given the fact that the EU is supposed to be more than just an intergovernmental organization, this approach has relatively few adherents. Hoffmann and Keohane (1991) and Pedersen (1998) fall into this category. (The observant reader will have noticed that Mr. Keohane changed camps between 1991 and 1993.) *Neo-functionalism* was the first of the major International Relations (IR) theories to be based primarily on the European example. Haas (1958) and Lindberg (1963) are the classical examples. Pentland (1973) added a useful analysis, while Ross's study of the European Commission (1995) provides a recent example. *Neo-liberalism* and *neo-liberal institutionalism* are not approaches which began with European integration, but they have inspired widespread analysis of the EU, notably the voluminous writings of Andrew Moravcsik, which found their culmination in his magisterial analysis of five major European Union decisions (1998). Sterling-Folker (2000) makes the case that constructivism, neo-liberal institutionalism and neo-functionalism are theories which are so much alike as to be almost the same. Her case is more convincing with respect to constructivism and neo-functionalism than it is with respect to neo-liberal institutionalism. She points out that 'institutional innovation' may occur 'because actors want to obtain the pre-given collective interests more than their identities, interests or preferences are shaped and constrained by the non-systemic collective social practices in which they have been engaged'. She makes the error, mentioned above, of treating the decisions of institutions as norms, rather than legal obligations.

European *federalism* has been out of favour for some years; in Britain it has even been derided as that 'F' word. It is, therefore, not surprising that most of the work of European federalists dates from the period before 1970. Brugmans (1969), Spinelli (1966, ch.1 and 1972, ch.11) and Etzioni (1963) provide examples; Burgess (2000) is one of the few recent advocates of federalism. Federalism relies on the constitutional unification of the constituent states. Since this is unlikely in the short or medium term, writers of a federalist persuasion now sometimes describe the European Union as a 'quasi-federal system' (Dehousse as cited in Pierson, 1996). Theories based on the supposition that it is the ideas of groups and individuals, not material interests, which shape international events and institutions, known by terms such as *post-structuralism* and *social constructivism*, have recently become fashionable among academics; it seems especially so since 1990. Most of these approaches were not designed especially for the study of European integration, but have been applied to integration in recent years (Parsons, 2000). Based on similar premises as to the importance of ideas and identities are theories of *consociationalism*, (Chryssochoou, 1997) borrowed from comparative politics, and theories of *multilevel governance* (Hooghe, 1996). Consociationalism is based on the idea of cooperation among elites. It is assumed that elites enjoy a sufficient minimum of a common political culture, that is norms and values, to negotiate and make agreements that the wider public, which presumably shares at least some of these norms, will then be willing to accept (Chryssochoou, 1997). Consociationalism is thus applicable to both federal states and the European Union. It by-passes the issue of sovereignty, but requires the public to accept the presence of more than one national and/or regional identity.

This book adds another category (See Table 1) which I call the *additive* model. (*Integrative* might be a more apt term, but since the discussion is about European integration the use of this word could cause some confusion.) My principal argument is that major political changes cannot be implemented successfully unless the participants leading that process are inspired by *both* ideas and material self-interest. On an intuitive level, such an argument is immediately appealing, for two reasons. First, as humans most of us see ourselves as moral beings. It stands to reason that an action to which a negotiator or national leader devotes a lot of time and effort would be morally defensible as well as materially satisfying. This is true even when powerful combinations of geopolitical necessity and economic advantage coalesce to form a compelling case for a government's participation in a regional economic arrangement (Mahant and de Vanssay, 1994). Secondly, in most international negotiations, especially those of the multilateral kind, there are winners and losers on different points. While leaders can justify losses by pointing to gains in other areas, they can also justify them by showing that they were right, that is that the rightness of the cause justifies some material sacrifices. Such an argument constitutes more than *ex post facto* rationalisation. Leaders as well as publics derive satisfaction from a belief in the rightness of their cause, and as sometimes rational beings can sacrifice short term gains for long-term or overarching causes.

I do not make any claims of originality for this model. Careful scholars have long realized that both material and moral impulsions are the necessary drivers of successful political action. E.H. Carr (1946: 89-94), often classified as an unabashed realist, in fact tried to do no more than balance the excessive idealism of Wilsonian internationalism. More recently, Martin Rhodes, writing of European social policy, points out that:

> ...from the very beginning, any attempt by the European Commission to set an agenda for harmonisation ... or promote supranational decision-making, has provoked a two-way conceptual clash between the competing philosophies of highly and loosely regulated labour markets, and between 'solidarity and subsidiarity' .... Neither of these clashes represent the pursuit of pure self-interest: they are shaped by national political traditions, patterns of economic organisation and the ideology of parties in power (1999).

Alan Milward admits, albeit reluctantly, that ideas and feelings can and do play a role in political action. He writes:

> The Single European Act was imbued with nostalgia. While it was a serious attempt to revive the concept of integration, as an extra stimulus to national income growth, it relied on the intellectual framework of the 1950s as a guide to what should be done in the new circumstances. The concept of economic growth still remained the one possible ideology that could span the widening gap in economic and political ideas between and within the member-states (2000: 431).

So while the idea that material interests and ideas combine to form successful political action is not original, it is worth investigating because the recent intellectual trend towards the ideational side, and the riposte, from various materialists and realists, has led to the false impression that this a controversy in which only one side can be right.

Ideas, however, are filtered through the personalities of national leaders, an often neglected factor in the study of international politics. Korany (1974) assumes that the personality factor may be less important in influencing decisions in established bureaucratic states such as France or Germany than it is in developing countries where the educated elite is usually small in number. Yet personality may have played a role during the negotiations leading to the Treaty of Rome because the foreign policy-making elite in both France and Germany was relatively small. This was especially true in West Germany, where the diplomatic service was just being rebuilt, and Chancellor Adenauer was thus able to dominate the making of German foreign policy. It was less true in France, where the shifting governments of the Fourth Republic were not dominated by any one personality. Nevertheless, the fact that nearly all of the participants in these governments had participated in the Resistance, where there had been much talk about a united post-war Europe and where there was a heightened consciousness of the less than glorious role some French governments played during World War II, should be kept in mind. While this book will not examine personality factors as such, they form an important part of the additive model and should be kept in mind as a factor requiring further investigation. The book will limit itself to examining the interplay of ideas and interests which influenced the negotiations leading to the Treaty of Rome (1957) and to providing some guidelines for estimating the persistence of these ideas for many years after the Treaty had been implemented.

But what were the ideas which influenced these negotiations? There were many, of course, and they were sometimes mutually contradictory. The ideas which influenced the negotiations of the Treaty of Rome include fairly vague ideas, such as the 'European idea' itself, that is the concept that Europe should be unified, an idea which became a moral value in its own right. Other ideas include ideologies such as classical liberalism (the benefit of larger, freer markets) and social democracy (the ideal of the welfare state). They also include ideas closely linked to feelings and emotions, such as the value of regional identities and regional equity, the moral qualities of rural life and the obligations of Europeans to peoples living in less fortunate continents and countries.

This book examines four sets of such ideas and the degree to which they influenced related issues during the negotiations leading to the Treaty of Rome. These four sets of ideas were selected partly because their persistence can be traced through the later history of the EC/EU. In that sense, the selection will, to some extent, influence the conclusions reached.

The four sets of ideas to be examined in this book are:

1. The European idea and its reflection in the negotiations about the institutions of the European Economic Community (EEC).
2. The ideal of a social policy which would provide the best standard of living economic conditions permitted to all of the population of the participating countries.
3. The idea that agriculture and the rural way of life have a special value, over and above any material benefits agriculture could provide to the European economy.
4. The idea that Europeans have a special moral obligation toward their former colonies in Africa, the Caribbean and elsewhere.

Let me briefly outline the principal components of each of these sets of ideas, so as to facilitate their later application to the practical issues which arose during the negotiations of the Treaty of Rome.

The first set of ideas can be loosely described as 'the European idea'. From the end of World War II until at least the 1990s a large majority of the French and German (and the Dutch, Belgian and Italian) political class believed that the uniting of Europe constituted a normative value which should be pursued even at the cost of some material sacrifices. As Paul-Henri Spaak said, 'everything which tends towards European organizations is good' (cited in Milward, 2000: 324). During the 1950s, only an insignificant number of West Germans and the hard-line Gaullists and the Communists in France dissented from this view (Rabier, 1989). Of course, this does not mean that everyone who said that he or she was in favour of the uniting of Europe necessarily supported any specific proposal, such as the European Defence Community or the European Economic Community. It does mean, however, that any opposition was phrased in the form, 'we support the unification of Europe, but...'. Moravcsik (1993) noticed the same phenomenon 35 years later when studying the French reaction to the Maastricht Treaty, and in the year 2000, the French President and the German foreign minister, devoted major speeches to their devotion to the cause of European unification (Chirac, 2000; Fischer, 2000).

The idea of a united Europe as a value in its own right can be traced back to the thinking of the leaders of the World War II underground Resistance to fascism. Resistance leaders wrote of moral regeneration and of a 'spiritual revolution' into which they wanted to lead post-war Europe. Plans for this Europe included a 'United States of Europe', a federation within which the 'old nation-states bellicose and unresponsive to the needs of their citizens were to be superseded ... by more responsible institutions' (Burgess, 1989:28-32). Thus peace and democracy were values to be achieved by means of the unification of Europe. To these, Konrad Adenauer, the first chancellor of the new West German state, added the propagation of European culture. Europe, he wrote, has the 'mission of preserving Western culture for all of humanity and of being a guardian of peace for the world' (1955: 32). Paul Reynaud, a leading French politician of the late Third and early Fourth Republic was more specific in his enumeration of European values. He wrote:

> A passion for research, the gift of invention, a generous respect of the human personality, the desire to conquer nature and to capture the forces of the universe while worshipping them, finally the collaboration of realism, ideals and the philosophical spirit, all these traits ... are those of the European man (1951:16).

This is surprisingly similar to what another Frenchman wrote in 1987. Edgar Morin then defined the essence of Europe as consisting of 'critical rationality' and a willingness to engage in self-criticism (cited in Boer, 1995:178). Boer himself adds 'democracy, freedom of opinion and constitutionalism and modernization and modernity' to the list of European values (1995:204-5).

The near unanimity on the part of the West European political classes as to the value and desirability of European integration deserves an explanation. In the years after World War II, this advocacy of a united Europe was to a large extent fuelled by a sense of guilt and a determination to make the European future better than the past had been. This sense of guilt was especially pronounced among French and German elites. The European nation-state system appeared to have failed the Europeans, or worse, to have led them astray. Excesses of nationalism had led to indescribable crimes and to destructive wars. This sentiment was at times quite overt. In 1947, the German non-governmental organization (NGO) Europa-Union heard the following in the keynote address to its first annual conference, 'since it is Germany's fault that Europe and all of mankind has reached the current unhappy situation, Germany, more than any other people, should be ready and determined to make its contribution to the unification of Europe and thereby to a lasting peace for all' (Eickhorn, 1993:15). In 1951, the same organization adopted a resolution which declared that 'The Europa-Union condemns and rejects all nationalistic aspirations in Germany'[2] (Eickhorn, 1993:25). Such sentiments were not confined to Germany. Edouard Herriot, a prominent politician of the Third French Republic, addressed the Council of Europe Assembly of 1949 by citing Paul Valéry, 'Europe will be punished for her politics' ('Voices of Europe', 1997:7). Winston Churchill addressed the Assembly in a similar vein, 'we must rise above those passions which have ravaged Europe and turned it into ruins. We must put an end to our old quarrels; we must renounce territorial ambitions... [and] render the most genuine services to our common cause' ('Voices of Europe', 1997:12). In 1951, Belgian politician Paul-Henri Spaak told the same Assembly in a slightly more subtle statement that 'we are prepared to sacrifice for the sake of Europe as a whole things to which we are attached as much as any other country ... namely a part of our sovereignty and ... even ... certain material interests' ('Voices of Europe', 1997:44). Overdrawn as it may now sound, the following excerpt from the address of a French Christian Democratic politician, Pierre-Henri Teitgen, to the 1957 annual party congress sums up all of the above points:

> In the construction of Europe, we have an excellent opportunity of bringing together the real and the ideal, for Europe means life; Europe means freedom; Europe means dignity; Europe means social justice; Europe means that peace and the brotherhood of man will at last be possible, so that the horrors we have known will not be repeated (Mouvement républicain populaire, 1957).

Traumatic events, such as World War II and its aftermath, can lead to a search for new norms (Finnemore and Sikkink, 1998). That new norm was a supranational Europe: perhaps Europeans should give up the comfort and security of patriotism for a larger European whole, and in so doing could build the better Europe to which they aspired. In this book it will be the attitudes and positions towards the institutions of the European Economic Community that will demonstrate the effect of the European idea.

Teitgen's oratory leads naturally into the second set of ideas which influenced the negotiators of the Treaty of Rome. North Americans and Europeans, who are experiencing a revival of classical liberalism, need to remind themselves that in Europe after World War II social security had a

---

2 Unless there is an indication to the contrary, all translations from the French and German were done by the author of this book.

positive image. Almost everyone, except for a few die-hard economic liberals (for example, Ludwig Erhard in Germany) and the Far Right in France (the Poujadists), agreed that a high level of social security was desirable. It was part of the post-war conception of the welfare state, the idea that the divisions between Left and Right which had marked the 1930s would and could be overcome by the creation of a non-Marxist welfare state, that after the privations of the Depression and the war, ordinary people deserved a better life and that a welfare state would assure the future of democracy in western Europe. Thus the idea that as the European economy grew and expanded, some of the resultant wealth should be devoted to social benefits was widely accepted. It had become a norm. Article 117 of the original Treaty of Rome began with the following sentence: 'Member States hereby agree on the necessity to promote improvement of the living and working conditions of labour so as to promote the equalisation of such conditions in an upward direction' (Treaty of Rome, 1962). In this book, an examination of the attitudes to questions of social security will reveal the existence, or otherwise, of this concept of social security.

In the case of agriculture, the idea that its preservation and protection should be an objective of government policy, a good for its own sake, predates the post-war period. Since the spread of industrialization in the eighteenth century, European elites, if not so frequently the farmers and peasants themselves, have rhapsodized about the supposed moral value of agriculture and more especially the family farm. From Grey's *Elegy in a Country Churchyard* to Balzac's savage denunciations of the corrupting influence of cities to Johanna Spyri's (*Heidi*) novel on the wholesome qualities of rural life to André Gide's rhapsodies about his village, West Europeans have had an often romantic notion about the uplifting aspects of life on the farm. While keeping farmers content had its political aspects – it was assumed farmers would vote for conservative political parties and keep the Communist menace at bay – it also had a moral aspect. For example, commenting on the negotiations of the Treaty of Rome, a spokesman for German agriculture contrasted the [good] values of tradition and self-reliance with the less desirable goals of 'economic efficiency and so-called progress' (cited in Mahant, 1969:307). In studying the attitudes toward agriculture, I will be looking for evidence not only of the self-interest of French and German farmers, but also of the belief in the non-material values of agriculture.

There was less unanimity on the desirability of associating the remaining French, Belgian, Dutch and Italian colonies with the European

Economic Community, but nevertheless a widespread sentiment that Europeans had some kind of an obligation to the peoples of Africa, 'a deep sense of moral, aside from political, responsibility for the former colonies and their populations' (Grilli, 1992:3). But this responsibility was not meant to be one-sided. Europeans and Africans should be or become equals in their political association. Pierre-Olivier Lapie, a French Socialist, said, 'according to the French tradition, we want the inhabitants of Africa to become civilized men and to be equal with us in the exploitation of their riches...' (France, 'Journal officiel', July 5, 1957).

However, the association of Europe with some of the member states' former colonies was not just a moral obligation. It also held economic and financial advantages for both sides. Europe could provide financial assistance for the development of the former colonies and sell them technology and manufactured goods, whereas the ex-colonies would provide Europe with a guaranteed source of raw materials (Grilli, 1992:11). Robert Schuman, the father of Europe and a leading French Christian Democrat, believed that the association of Europe and Africa would have advantages for both sides. It was an idea he espoused as early as 1950, in the famous Schuman Declaration of May 9, the date that has become known as the birthday of Europe. In the full text of that declaration, not just the oral version, which is all that is usually cited, Schuman said that with a growing economy, 'Europe could pursue one of its essential obligations: the development of the African continent' ('The Schuman Plan', 1953). In 1956, Schuman made a more explicit statement of his vision:

> The association of Europe and Africa will be a revolutionary political action with an economic basis. Thanks to it, Europe and Africa will strengthen each other in a common enterprise of general cooperation. This will be the beginning of political reform, of economic expansion, of an effective struggle against poverty, a solid base for reconciliation and peace (Comité national M.R.P., 1956).

As the second quotation from Schuman demonstrates, with respect to the association of the overseas territories the commitment to ideals was less than it was in the case of the European idea, social security or agriculture. Instead, French, and more especially German leaders, balanced talk of responsibility for democratization in Africa with references to the material and perhaps political advantages that the association with Africa might bring to Europe. Adenauer, in his memoirs, begins by stressing the useful raw materials that could be found in Africa and continues that 'the standard of living of these countries must be raised' (Adenauer, 1965, v.3:269). A speaker for the German Free Democratic Party objected to the financial contributions Germany would have to make to overseas development, but concluded that the development of Africa was 'the legitimate task of Europe' (Margulies, 1957). Maurice Faure, speaking for the French Radical Party,[3] similarly balanced idealistic and political considerations. He spoke of a 'civilizing mission ... to help the peoples of Africa', but continued by pointing to the political advantages of contributing to the development of Africa, without which there might be 'bloody disorders' (France, Conseil de la République, July 23, 1957:1697). In 1956, the German Europa-Union advocated 'an extensive plan for friendship and support' of the peoples of Asia and Africa, so that former domination may become a new friendship' (Eickhorn, 1993:38). A later German study pointed to the commercial advantages the EC could derive from the development of the Third World (Gebauer, 1980:143).

It appears, therefore, that on all four topics this book will be examining, the European leaders who contributed to the negotiations of the Treaty of Rome balanced material interests with ideals and ideas, though the mix varied somewhat from topic to topic. The approximate proportion of this mix will be one of the subjects to be investigated.

It is the author's contention that the European Union that has evolved over the past 45 years is not only a continuation, though perhaps by now a gradually diluting continuation, of the ideas of its founders, but that the ideas and interests on which the European Economic Community was based were primarily those of the French and German political elites. This is not to say that no one else's ideas and interests mattered. To mention only a few examples: the Dutch and Belgian governments played a major role in the founding of the Community, the Belgian and Italians similarly played a large role in the negotiation of the Single European Act of 1985 (Burgess, 2000), and the Italian and later the Spanish and Greek governments have been important players in the development of regional ('cohesion') policy. However, with respect to the basic institutional structure and the major programs and policies, French and German interests and ideas have continued to dominate the EC/EU.

Ideas which shape the founding of an institution may or may not be in accordance with the material interests of the founders and the groups, parties or countries they represent. In either case, the ideas, once they have

---

[3] The French Radical Party is a party of nineteenth century liberalism; there was nothing radical about it by the 1950s.

taken form in the shape of an institution, often become moral precepts not only to those who participate in the institution but to many others who accept what they hear often enough as moral guidance. These ideas are often so powerful that they may persist even as material interests change. The best-known historical example is that of American trade policy, which continued to be protectionist long after the American economy would have benefited from free trade (Goldstein, 1993:82-83). Indeed this example demonstrates how ideas may take on a life of their own and become dogmas.

On the other hand, ideas may also fade as the initial idealism and enthusiasm which led to the founding of an institution fades. If this happens, material interests which were once suppressed or sacrificed may reassert themselves and make the management and development of the institution difficult. Or, the material circumstances may change and cause interests to change. Thus the government of Italy initially favoured a protectionist agricultural policy for Europe, but as Italy industrialized and the country began to import a great variety of agricultural products, Italian governments came to favour a less generous agricultural policy. Similarly, the governments of Ireland may soon abandon their advocacy of generous regional development grants, now that Ireland has become one of the wealthier members of the European Union.

I am not the first to emphasize the continuity of ideas, especially ideas which have become the *raison d'être* of an institution. Michael Burgess's latest book admirably demonstrates the continuity of European federalist thought from Monnet to Delors (2000:174-5). David Haglund (2001) analyses the persistence of the Franco-German myth and the importance of this idea to the continuation of French European policy. This book takes the process one step further by applying these ideas to some of the issues facing the negotiators of 1955 to 1957 and by suggesting how some of these ideas have continued to affect the same issues over the course of the EC/EU's history.

The book thus examines the mix of idealism and self-interest which inspired the French and German elites who dominated the founding of the European Economic Community and makes a preliminary attempt to assess the extent to which this mixture of interests and ideas has changed over the course of the Community's history.

The book adopts conventional wisdom in one respect. It accepts that it was the ideas of the French and German political elites which dominated the negotiations of the original Treaty of Rome, and that these ideas, passed on to succeeding generations of political elites in these same two countries, have continued to dominate not just the thinking, but the institutions and policies of the EC/EU. Indeed, the belief in France and Germany as the motor of European integration has in itself become an excellent illustration of a self-perpetuating idea. A summary of the books and articles written on this topic could in themselves fill a book. So the paragraphs which follow will provide only the briefest overview of the persistence of this belief.

In May 1950, the French foreign minister, Robert Schuman, presented the European Coal and Steel Community as a Franco-German project to which others European governments could subscribe, as they wished. In 1963, President de Gaulle and Chancellor Adenauer reaffirmed Franco-German solidarity in a treaty of friendship, which followed de Gaulle's refusal to allow the UK to become a member of the EEC. Britain did join in 1973, but this has not shaken the firm belief in the existence and the desirability of a Franco-German motor. In 1984, a French official, Michael Poniatowski, wrote that it is only 'around France and Germany that Europe can be built and restored to power...' (cited in Haglund, 2001). In 1997, at a colloquium of French and German academics, both sides spoke fulsomely of the continuing need for France and Germany to be the motor of European integration. One German academic, after paying tribute to the French and German leaders who had won public support for the post-war integration of Europe, continued by stressing the symbiotic relationship between Franco-German relations and European integration and concluded by stating that:

> German reunification and the perspective of the enlargement of Europe ... present Franco-German cooperation with a new challenge within the European Union. That is why the role of our two countries as the motor of the future development of European Union is more necessary now than it has ever been (Opperman, 1997).

On March 24, 2001, *The Economist* published a three-page analysis of the Franco-German relationship, the headline of which provocatively mentioned the possibility of a Franco-German divorce. After summarizing the changes a new generation of leaders had wrought and the many difficulties the Franco-German relationship had recently encountered, the article concludes with a description of the many measures the two governments have taken to improve their relationship and the fact that public opinion in both countries now sees the other as their closest friend (for similar polls, see Leblond, 1997:241). The *Economist* article cites one of Chancellor Schröder's foreign policy advisors, who spoke of 'a certain indefinable mystique, unlike that existing between any other two EU states'. David Haglund, who has done an extensive survey of the recent literature on Franco-German relations, concludes that even though some may believe that the Franco-German motor no longer works, 'the metaphor and the myth that subtends it continue to be invoked', which he says, citing Ann-Sofie Dahl, proves that 'a myth has a degree of independence from reality' (Haglund, 2001).

In summary, the ideas of the Franco-German political elites provide a more than adequate synopsis of the ideas which have shaped the European Economic Community through its reincarnations as the European Community and later the European Union.

Plan of the Book

After a brief chapter reminding readers of the history of European integration from the end of World War II to the founding of the European Economic Community, I continue by examining in some detail the positions on the negotiations of the Treaty of Rome over the years 1955 to 1957 held by French and German elites (Chapters 3 and 4). Chapter 5 analyses the negotiations within the two governments, as each attempted to arrive at a negotiating position for the Brussels conference. Chapter 6 deals with the negotiations themselves and determines the outcome with respect to the four issues under consideration in relation to the position of the French and German governments. Chapter 7 analyses the negotiations described in Chapter 6, with a view to determining the major influences on the content of the treaty. On the basis of this analysis, Chapter 7 concludes with a framework for tracing the continuation of the ideas which predominated at the time of negotiations through subsequent developments within the European Community. Chapter 8 makes a first cut at applying the framework developed in Chapter 7 by studying some of the later developments with respect to the three issues covered earlier in the book (agriculture, social policy and relations with former colonies) and on three subsequent issues (the Single European Act, the single market programme and the Treaty on European Union). Finally a brief concluding chapter draws some theoretical implications from the findings presented in the book.

2 European Integration to 1955

The 1957 Treaty of Rome was a highpoint in the achievement of a vision, or perhaps more accurately visions, which had preoccupied a number of European political leaders since the darkest days of World War II. Even before the war was over, interest groups formed for that purpose began advocating a united Europe. Understandably, the politicians were at first preoccupied with providing the basic necessities of life for their peoples, an aim which could only be achieved if the political structures which the Nazi onslaught had destroyed or discredited were put back in place. Except in the case of Germany, these political structures were recreations of the nation-states which had existed before 1939 (Burgess, 1991). This meant that the unification of Europe could not begin *tabula rasa*. Rather it had to overcome the sovereignty of the recreated nation-states.

As mentioned in the previous chapter, post-war plans for the integration of Europe and the overcoming of national sovereignty formed an important theme of the political ideas of the leaders of the French and German Resistance to fascism/Nazism during World War II. (European integration played an even more important part in the ideas of the Italian Resistance, but it is not the topic here.) Even at this difficult time, French Christian democrats wrote of including Germany within a future European federation – though others also wrote of the guardianship (*la tutelle*) of Germany. Some members of the French Resistance considered the unification of Europe to be so important that they formed a *Comité français pour la fédération européenne*, which issued a declaration in June 1944. This declaration called for a European federal government which, among other tasks, would control economic and commercial policy, maintain armed forces, prevent the establishment of authoritarian governments and administer the colonies of the various European nations (Hamon and Keller, 1997:85; Mahant, 1969:19-22).

The German resistance movement developed similar ideas. What is especially interesting is that whereas the French Resistance conceived of a post-war European federation largely in institutional terms, the German leaders wrote of a *Staatenbund* or confederation. Carl Goerdeler, who would have become chancellor if the July 20, 1944 plot to assassinate Hitler had succeeded, wrote that economic and commercial unification should precede political unification, an idea echoed in the memorandum another German resistance leader, Dr. Hans Schönfeld, sent to the Bishop of Chichester. Schönfeld wrote that 'economic interdependence' should become the 'strongest possible guarantee against ... European militarism' (Ritter, 1958:575; 'Zwei', 1957).

Some Resistance leaders attached so much importance to the future unification of Europe that in May and again in July 1944, when travel in Europe was surely very difficult, Resistance leaders from eight countries (including one German representative) met in Geneva to plan for the future integration of Europe. The May meeting issued a declaration on which the July meeting elaborated (Mahant, 1969:23-24). The May declaration specifically mentioned that a European federation would allow the German people to participate in European life without their becoming a danger to others and that a federation would facilitate reconstruction without the creation of national autarchies. The May declaration described the institutions of the planned European federation:

> The federal union must possess ... (1) a government responsible not to the governments of the various member states, but to their peoples, by whom it must be elected and over whom it must be able to exercise direct jurisdiction within the limits assigned to it; (2) an armed force at its orders, which excludes all other national armies; (3) a supreme tribunal, which will judge all questions relative to the interpretation of the Federal Constitution... (Delzell, 1960).

The July declaration added that local problems were to be solved locally in accordance with national traditions (Pegg, 1952).

In short, a number of Resistance leaders were thoroughly dedicated to the concept of a united Europe, and in their discussions they anticipated many of the issues which were to confront the participants in the European integration process for the next sixty years. While most of the Resistance leaders insisted on the need to control and limit the authority of states, the July 1944 declaration also foreshadowed the idea of subsidiarity (Burgess, 1991).

Governments and individual politicians who were in exile during World War II also talked about a future united Europe, though for the most part their ideas were not as detailed as those of the Resistance leaders. The Belgian Socialist Paul Van Zeeland, the French Christian Democrat Maurice (not the more famous Robert) Schumann and General de Gaulle wrote of the need for a future united Europe, while the French civil servant Jean Monnet and the Belgian politician Paul-Henri Spaak presented more detailed plans. Monnet wrote of the need for a European federation and an economic community whereas Spaak pondered the need for majority voting among the participating governments (Hamon and Keller, 1997:81-82).

Once the war was over, the European governments had immediate priorities which forced the postponement of action on European unification. External political developments also played a major role. The Cold War division of Europe meant that European unification would in fact mean the unification of Western Europe, and Cold War security considerations as well as the economic might of the United States meant that American views and attitudes would play some role in whatever action European governments decided upon.

Thus from 1945 to 1950, the efforts to unite Europe ran in four different streams. One stream consisted of the NGOs discussed in the following paragraph. A second consisted of the European-wide efforts to deal with immediate economic needs. The third consisted of the West European governments' reaction to the advance of Soviet control over Eastern Europe. A fourth is to be found in the relentless efforts of French governments to find guarantees of permanent security against a German *relance*.

While the governments of France, Italy, Belgium and Holland tried to deal with the immediate problems of their peoples, a number of these people formed NGOs which advocated the unification of Europe, and West Germans followed as soon as their freedom of association was restored. There were a great number of such organizations, and many of the participants were soon, or were already, playing acting roles in their governments: Robert Schuman and Paul Reynaud in France, Konrad Adenauer in Germany, Alcide de Gasperi in Italy, Paul van Zeeland and Paul-Henri Spaak in Belgium.

Many of these persons attended the May 1948 Hague Congress, where more than 750 delegates from West European NGOs met to discuss the future unification of Europe. The Congress studied European unity from several angles, and while it accepted the long-term goal of a European federation, its recommendations were for the gradual establishment of an economic union, military and defence cooperation and the creation of a consultative assembly consisting of delegates from the existing parliaments (Fursdon, 1980:15; Mahant, 1969:30).

Economic needs meant that the establishment of a number of committees to distribute scarce raw materials, such as coal, and to transport them was an essential part of the European recovery effort. The American sponsored Marshall Plan of 1947, followed by the creation of the Organization for European Economic Cooperation (OEEC) continued these efforts. While both Americans and Europeans hoped that the OEEC would become a means for the unification of Europe, the OEEC – much later, in 1961 – became the Organization for Economic Cooperation and Development (OECD), and thus this was a stream which diverged and did not join the European river.

Security concerns at first were not as pressing as economic ones, but soon became so, especially after the Soviet-supported *coup* in Prague in February of 1948. In March 1947, France and Britain signed a mutual defence treaty (the Treaty of Dunkerque) followed in March 1948 by the Brussels Treaty linking France, Belgium, Holland, Luxembourg and Britain. While this Treaty led directly to the creation of the North Atlantic Treaty Organization (NATO) a year later, it also forms a part of the history of European integration. One could say that the Brussels Treaty split into two rivulets, one leading to NATO and the other to the Western European Union and the Council of Europe.

The fourth stream was that of French policy. French governments, notably foreign minister Georges Bidault, continued to demand the dismemberment of Germany, even of the Western zones, as well as the dismantling of German factories. Their pleas fell on deaf ears, and soon American pressure for the economic reconstruction of West Germany intensified. More specifically, the limits on German production of coal and steel were increased several times and in 1949, the dismantling of West German factories stopped (Fursdon, 1980:44; Mahant, 1969:29). The time for a new French policy had come. And nearly everyone involved, including the American Secretary of State Dean Acheson, agreed that it was up to the French to act (Gerbet, 1983:105).

German foreign policy was less influential than that of France in shaping events, partly because the Federal Republic of Germany was not a sovereign state. It did not even have a foreign minister and only had a fledgling foreign office. The Chancellor, Konrad Adenauer, served as his own foreign minister. So what foreign policy there was, was shaped by his dominant personality. In European policy, Adenauer had two main objectives. One was to have Germany readmitted to the community of nations as an equal, which meant giving Germany some element of sovereignty while reducing the sovereignty of the other European states to the level that the Germans had. Adenauer's second aim was not ever again to allow German nationalism to run amuck. Binding Germany into Europe was Adenauer's solution to this problem (Hendriks and Morgan, 2001:18-44; Hitchcock, 1997).

The European leaders who had met at the Hague continued their determined quest for a European organization which would assume at least some of the sovereignty of the nation-states. The vital link between the Hague Congress and the governmental efforts to unite Europe was Robert Schuman, the new foreign minister of France, who in a July 1948 speech to the assembly of the Brussels powers suggested an economic union and a consultative assembly. Some historians credit Georges Bidault, the outgoing French foreign minister, with this initiative (Jílek, 1997). The assembly appointed a subcommittee which examined various suggestions coming from both governments and private organizations. Based on the suggestions of this subcommittee and after some behind the scenes negotiations between Robert Schuman and Ernest Bevin, the British foreign minister, the five governments of the Brussels signatory states agreed on the basic structure of a new organization (Jílek, 1997). They then invited the governments of Ireland, Sweden, Norway, Denmark and Italy to join them. These ten governments agreed on the Statute of the Council of Europe, which they signed on May 3, 1949, and which came into force later that year (Fursdon, 1980:16-17; Mahant, 1969:31).

The Federal Republic of Germany at first had only observer status in the Council of Europe, and it was not an original recipient of Marshall Plan aid. This fact gave the governments of France an exceptional opportunity to shape the early European institutions to their liking. But not entirely. The British government did not share the continental Christian Democrats' enthusiasm for European institutions which would take over some of the sovereignty of the nation-states. And so the Council of Europe began as an intergovernmental organization consisting of a Consultative Assembly chosen from the parliamentarians of member states, an assembly that was not even supposed to talk about issues relating to defence or economics (a provision which the Assembly soon ignored) and a Council of Ministers which could take decisions only by unanimity. The European federalists, led by Paul-Henri Spaak, the Belgian foreign minister, at first attempted to make the Council of Europe more supranational from within, but this effort failed as it encountered the opposition of some of the governments (Palayret, 1997).

Thus the intergovernmental institutions of the Council of Europe were a disappointment to those Europeans who had hoped for an organization that would somehow transcend the sovereignty of the nation-states. On the other hand, the Statute creating the Council of Europe included a ringing endorsement of the European idea and European ideals:

> Reaffirming their devotion to the spiritual and moral values which are the common heritage of their peoples and the true source of individual freedom, political liberty and the rule of law... Believing that, for the maintenance and further realisation of these ideals and in the interests of economic and social progress, there is a need of a closer unity between all like-minded countries of Europe... Have in consequence decided to set up a Council of Europe... (Statute, 2002).

This dichotomy between the limited institutional achievements and the ideal described in the Council of Europe's Statue was a reminder of how much Europeans still needed to do to achieve genuine union.

May 1949 was also the month of the creation of the Federal Republic of Germany, and it soon became evident that restrictions on German industrial production, and specifically the production of steel which the allies had imposed after the war would need to be lifted, so as to allow the Germans to support themselves and thereby at least indirectly contribute to the defence of Western Europe. Indeed, and the timing is certainly interesting, representatives of the governments of France, Britain and the US were to meet on May 12-13, 1950, to discuss the lifting of the controls of German industrial production. Perhaps it was to deal with such an eventuality that, as early as 1949, the European Movement, also meeting in London, had suggested a pooling of the basic industries of the European countries (Gerbet, 1983:103-104; Hitchcock, 1997).

A 'note' found in the archives of the French foreign ministry, imprecisely dated May 1950, on ministry letterhead but unsigned, gives an interesting insight into French policy at this time.[1] The writer states that the French policy of restraining German economic growth and of allowing French industry to benefit from this circumstance had failed. This failure and the American pressure under the Marshall Plan to allow Germany to support herself, the need to keep Germany out of the Soviet zone of influence as well as a concern about the threat to French security an unrestrained West Germany might pose, led the government of France to advocate the creation of the European Coal and Steel Community (see also Hitchcock, 1997 and Thiemeyer, 1998). This was the famous Schuman Declaration of May 9, 1950, the day which is still celebrated as the birthday of 'Europe'.

The Schuman Plan was clearly a French proposal (Schwabe, 1988b). It was based on a memorandum which Jean Monnet, the head of

---

1 The only other identifying mark on the document are the page numbers 039-042 stamped in the upper right hand corner.

the *Commissariat du plan* had sent to Schuman, then still foreign minister, on May 3, 1950 (Hamon and Keller, 1997:115). The Minister's introduction to the Declaration stressed its French origins:

> It is ...time... for a bold, constructive act. France has acted, and the consequences of her action may be immense. We hope they will... France is now taking the first decisive step towards the construction of Europe and is associating Germany in this venture... Out of all this will come forth Europe, a solid and united Europe (cited in Fontaine, 2000:13).

Chancellor Adenauer had sent his enthusiastic approval, but he had been consulted only on the previous day, May 8, and his reply arrived only on the morning of May 9 (Fontaine, 2000:12-13; Carstens, 1993:199-200; Schwabe, 1988a:131). The text of the declaration itself made clear the central role which Germany and France were to play:

> The coming together of the nations of Europe requires the elimination of the age-old opposition of France and Germany. Any action taken must in the first place concern these two countries... The pooling of coal and steel production should immediately provide for the setting up of common foundations for economic development as a first step in the federation of Europe... By pooling basic production and by instituting a new High Authority, whose decisions will bind France, Germany and other member countries, this proposal will lead to the realisation of the first concrete foundation of a European federation... this common High Authority will be charged [with] securing ...the supply of coal and steel on identical terms to the French and German markets (Europe, 2000).

Six governments[2] agreed to take part in the negotiations for such a coal and steel community, though the government of the Netherlands made some reservations which clarified the fact that it would not be committed until it had seen the final text of the agreement (Fursdon, 1980:62). On April 18, 1951, the same six governments signed the Treaty of Paris, creating the European Coal and Steel Community (ECSC), and by 1952, the Treaty was in force. Much modified since, the Treaty of Paris is still a part of the *acquis communautaire* and as such constitutes a part of the as yet uncodified constitution of the European Union.

More importantly, the ECSC established the basic institutional structure which the succeeding European communities (EEC, EAEC, EC and EU) have adopted – and adapted – to this day: that is the supranational

2 France, Germany, Italy, Belgium, the Netherlands and Luxembourg.

High Authority, which in later versions came to be called Commission, a Council of Ministers, a parliamentary assembly, a court and a bureaucracy which works under the direction of the Commission. This structure represented a compromise between the ardent desire of some leaders for a supranational authority and the equally ardent determination of other, or even the same leaders, to maintain some degree of national control over the European institutions. The institutional structure was supposedly inspired by the Tennessee Valley Authority, while the French academic Paul Reuter suggested the term High Authority as the name for the new supranational institution (Lovett, 1996; Stirk, 1996:123-124). Besides reflecting the contradictory desires for supranationality and sovereignty, this institutional arrangement also reflects a strain in French political thought which can be traced back as far as Rousseau and forward into the constitution of the Fifth French Republic, namely that it is possible to make a distinction between institutions representing a community overall ('the general will' or the President of the Fifth Republic) and institutions which represent the diversity of that same community ('the will of all' or the parliament of the Fifth Republic).

However, world events overtook the incipient European institution before it could begin its work. Already in May 1950, Winston Churchill, then leader of the opposition in the British Parliament, suggested the creation of German army units, which could be incorporated in a European army (Gerbet, 1983:102). Then in June 1950, North Korean troops attacked South Korea, and we know now what many suspected at the same time, that this attack had the at least tacit support of the Soviet leader, Stalin (Zubok and Pleshakov, 1996:55-63). As a result, American pressure for the rearming of Germany or the Germans became irresistible. Yet, only five years after World War II, many continental Europeans, most especially in France, the Netherlands and Italy, found the thought of Germans in uniform, much less a German army, unbearable. As recently as December 1949, Robert Schuman had called the idea of European army with German contingents the product of a 'fertile imagination' (Hitchcock, 1997). Yet in response to the US pressure, René Pleven, the Prime Minister of France, on October 24, 1950, proposed the creation of a European army on the model of the Coal and Steel Community. (For details of the American pressure and the French response, see Fursdon, 1980:67-88 and Stirk, 1996:127).

Though there was significant opposition to rearmament in Germany and major opposition in France (Fursdon, 1980:90-94; Ruane, 2000:18), negotiations proceeded at an intense pace, and on May 27, 1952, the same six governments which had created the Community signed a treaty which envisaged a European Defence Community. The rapidity with which this agreement had been negotiated meant that there had to be concessions to various points of view and that as a consequence the resulting draft treaty was full of ambiguities and even contradictions. Major issues, such as by whom and how the decision to mobilize the armed forces would be made, were left unsettled (Mahant, 1969:36). There were differences as to the degree to which the various national armies were to be integrated into the European army. All German soldiers were to belong to the European army, whereas the French were able to keep part of their army under national control so as to deal with their colonial responsibilities. (France was fighting a war in Indochina even as the Defence Community was being negotiated.)

All six governments faced difficulties when it came to ratifying such a treaty. The Belgian and Dutch governments had to amend their national constitutions. The Germans had to deal with a constitutional challenge in front of their constitutional court. Italian governments, always in danger of defeat, decided to hang back and wait for the French. In France, the issue of the Defence Community dominated politics for over two years and caused divisions within every political party, including the pro-European Christian Democrats (MRP). The French National Assembly held two debates on the EDC, but the governments, as prone to defeat as those of Italy, dared not put the Treaty to a vote. After the shock of the French defeat in Indochina in June of 1954, a new Prime Minister, Pierre Mendès-France, decided that France must be rid of the cancer of this divisive debate no matter what the cost is in terms of loss of American support. On August 30, 1954, after Mendès-France had put the issue of the EDC to the National Assembly, Edouard Herriot, another member of the Radical party, proposed that the vote be put off indefinitely, thus in effect killing French ratification of the Treaty. The Prime Minister declared that he would abstain on that vote. Once it became clear that the fate of the government was not at stake, the fate of the Treaty was all but settled. The Assembly voted for Herriot's motion with a majority of 319 to 264 (and 12 abstentions) (Fursdon, 1980: 286-297). Every major political party (except the Communists, who were opposed) were divided on that vote, which was followed by a raucous scene as anti-EDC deputies sang the *Marseillaise* while pro-EDC members banged their desks in an effort to drown them out (Bédarida, 1992).

But what resulted was not the permanent disarmament of Germany that so many of the EDC's opponents had desired. Instead, the British and American governments proposed the creation of West German armed forces. While these armed forces were to be limited as to the kinds of weapons they could own or use, Germany was to join the Brussels Treaty, or Western European Union, as well as NATO, and the West German government was to be given sovereignty over most of its affairs, wiping out all but a few of the remaining powers of the three occupying governments (France, the UK and the US). The French government, weakened by the outbreak of yet another colonial war, now in Algeria, did not resist these plans. In May 1955, the Federal Republic of Germany joined NATO and became a sovereign state.

One of the arguments made against the EDC had been that an army could not exist without a government to control it. And so, in September 1952, the foreign ministers of the six ECSC/EDC countries asked the parliamentary assembly of the incipient Coal and Steel Community to draft yet another treaty, this one to create a European Political Community. For this purpose, the ECSC Assembly was to be made more representative by the inclusion of some of the six nations' delegates to the Council of Europe's Consultative Assembly. However, this attempt to make the resulting Ad Hoc assembly representative of the political currents in the member states failed. Communists, who represented an important political force in France and Italy, were excluded, and the German Social Democrats, the country's second largest political party, chose to boycott the Assembly, which was made even more unrepresentative by the fact that those chosen to sit there tended to be the national parliamentarians who were most inclined to favour European integration (Mahant, 1969:39).

These parliamentarians did what they were asked to do; they produced a draft treaty purporting to create a European Political Community. In March 1953 the draft treaty was ready. The EPC had the appearance, but the appearance only, of a federal constitution. There was to be a People's Chamber, elected directly by the citizens of the member states, a Senate representing the national parliaments, an Executive Council, which would be responsible to the legislature, and a Court of Justice. The one institution that did not fit into this pattern was the proposed Council of National Ministers; yet it was this Council which held practically all the power, including that of raising revenue (Mahant, 1969:40).

It is indeed surprising that an assembly packed with federalists (Burgess, 2000:69) would produce such a weak constitution. The answer is that the EPC draft treaty was drafted for one and one reason only, to save the Defence Community, and the opponents of the Defence Community were not to be won over by a federalist constitution.

The draft treaty contained an interesting provision. On the suggestion of Johan Beyen, the Dutch foreign minister, Article 82 envisaged the creation of a common market, although the negotiations for this common market were to begin only after the European Political Community had been in existence for one year (Article 84).

While these various projects were under discussion, the success of the Coal and Steel Community inspired other politicians to suggest the integration of other economic sectors. Sicco Mansholt, the Dutch minister of agriculture, and Pierre Pflimlin, a French Christian Democrat, suggested the creation of a 'Green Pool' or agricultural community while others suggested the creation of European Health Community or 'White Pool' and the creation of a European transport authority. The French governments invited a large number of European governments to discuss these ideas; the resulting conference met in Paris from December 12-13, 1952, but the proposals did not progress past the discussion stage (Gerbet, 1987:66-68; *Keesing's Contemporary Archives*, 1953:12932).

There was a pause in integration schemes as Europeans waited to see whether France would or would not ratify the EDC. By July 1954, perhaps anticipating the failure of EDC, Dutch, Belgian and German officials began to put flesh on Beyen's idea of a common market. The ideas they discussed included the free movement of goods, persons, capital and services, a competition policy, the harmonisation of economic and social policies and a readaptation fund to help small business and agriculture (Küsters, 1982:65).

After a defeat of the EDC, there was a flurry of schemes to further European integration. Most of the discussions took place behind closed doors and attracted little attention, as the more high profile issue of the rearmament of Germany was settled. A brief summary will give a flavour of some of these discussions.

The French government promoted the idea of the integration of the arms manufacturing industries. This idea found little sympathy among the other European governments and was quietly dropped in March 1955 (Küsters, 1982:88-94). In the margins of the October 1954 negotiations on the rearmament of Germany and the revitalisation of the WEU, Antoine Pinay, at that time foreign minister of France, and Adenauer agreed that there should be further economic and cultural cooperation between their two countries. This agreement sparked a discussion between the French and German peak industrial organizations, the *Bundesverband der Deutschen Industrie* (BDI) and the *Conseil national du patronat français* (CNPF). Their discussions envisaged cartel-like arrangements with guaranteed contracts for the exchange of industrial and agricultural goods as well as common investment projects in the French overseas territories. Neither idea was taken up by the two governments (Küsters, 1982:67-78).

Jean Monnet, still President of the High Authority of the ECSC, was preoccupied with the idea of further sectorial integration of specific industries. He envisaged a transport and an energy community, preferably by extension of the mandate of the ECSC, and a separate European atomic energy community. Beyen opposed sectoral integration and continued to promote the idea of a common market. Spaak, Belgium's foreign minister, took an intermediate position. He was willing to accept sectorial or general integration, as long as whatever was done continued the process of European integration. Towering above all three was Adenauer, equally determined to promote integration, but concerned primarily about the geopolitical consequences of whatever scheme was adopted.

Side-lining Monnet, Spaak and Beyen agreed that they would suggest both further sectorial integration as well as a common market. On April 7, 1955, Franz-Josef Strauss, then a German federal cabinet minister, travelled to Paris for talks with Pinay, still the foreign minister in a Faure government, and on April 30, Pinay travelled to Bonn. The leaders of the two governments agreed that any further integration must be built on Franco-German agreement, but they did not produce concrete suggestions for further European integration (Pinay 1955; Küsters, 1982:103-105). On February 23, 1955, when Edgar Faure became Prime Minister of France, his investiture speech promised a study of the European integration of the transport and energy (classic as well as nuclear) sectors. Faure also made a vague reference to the tempting dream of a European common market of 200 million inhabitants (France, 'Journal officiel', 1957:8681), but the French government seems not to have followed up that idea.

Declarations of the necessity of Franco-German cooperation notwithstanding, Spaak and Beyen continued their discussions, and on May 20 submitted to the other three governments and released publicly a joint Benelux memorandum advocating the creation of a common market, the harmonisation of social policies as well as the integration of the conventional energy, atomic energy and transport sectors (Küsters, 1982:106-109).

Two of the three governments reacted by drafting their own memoranda. Within the German Foreign Ministry, Carl Friedrich Ophüls, a convinced European of the Adenauer school, drafted a memorandum in which he advocated a united Western Europe for geopolitical reasons. In a bipolar world, he wrote, the power of China and the USSR needed to be balanced by the power of the USA and a united Europe (Thiemeyer, 1998). However, the note which the German government sent to the other ECSC governments was written by the Ministry of Economic Affairs, and that only after an official of that ministry had invited representatives of the various factions, those who favoured institutional integration (the Foreign ministry), those who wanted free trade with minimal institutional supervision (the Erhard group) as well as various intermediate factions to his country home, where the congenial atmosphere allowed the various groups to adopt a compromise position (Küsters, 1982:116-199; Auswärtiges Amt, 1957; Gerbet, 1987:78-82). The resulting German memorandum stressed the advantages of freer trade, rather than calling for a specific European community (Mahant, 1969:53). An Italian memorandum accepted the Benelux suggestion of a common market, but added a call for the free convertibility of currencies, a readaptation fund, a common investment policy and the free movement of labour (Mahant, 1969:53-54). Only the French government did not put its ideas in writing, and the archives of the French foreign ministry do not include a copy of Pinay's negotiating mandate for the Messina Conference. Interestingly, on May 25, Edgar Faure, the Prime Minister, spoke of the need for a new supranational institution even if it was not called that. 'If the term supranational is abhorrent, it [the new institution] nevertheless needs to be given powers of decision' (Gerbet, 1983:198).

On June 1 and 2, 1955, the foreign ministers of the six Coal and Steel Community countries[3] met in Messina on the island of Sicily to name the new head of the ECSC's High Authority and to discuss the various proposals for further integration. Beyen opened the discussion by presenting his ideas for the gradual creation of a common market, accompanied by energy, transport and atomic energy communities. He gave two political reasons for his position: the need to absorb Germany and the need to build Europe ('la construction européenne'). Walter Hallstein spoke of the need for Europe to maintain its position in the world, on the political as well as the 'spiritual' level. He continued by stressing the need for strong European institutions. Pinay spoke of the need to succeed. The European cause could not stand another failure. For this reason, he preferred sectorial to general integration. He also insisted on the need for social harmonisation (France, 1955).

---

[3] To be entirely correct, one should say that there were five foreign Ministers and Walter Hallstein, Adenauer's foreign policy advisor, since Adenauer, who was still acting as foreign minister as well as being chancellor, could not attend a conference that it would have taken days to reach and days to return from.

After negotiations which lasted far into the night of June 2 and early into the morning of June 3, the ministers agreed in principle to appoint a committee of experts, headed by a 'political personality'. This committee would study the integration of the transport, conventional energy and atomic energy sectors and the creation of a general common market. The study of the common market was to include the gradual suppression of barriers to trade and the harmonisation of financial, economic, monetary and social security policies; there were also to be escape clauses and a re-adaptation fund to help areas or industries which might find themselves in difficulty. There was no mention of agriculture or the overseas territories (Messina Conference, 1958). In the history of European integration, the adoption of the Messina resolution has become known as the 'European *relance*'.

Concluding Comments

Even without the *relance*, European integration had made considerable progress by 1955, more than the small number of relatively minor European institutions would suggest. First and foremost, the idea that European integration was good and nationalism and national sovereignty were not so good had become deeply ingrained in the political culture of France and Germany. Even opponents of the Coal and Steel Community and of the other earlier schemes for European integration felt compelled to say that they were for a united Europe, but against these particular proposals. This was true, for example, of Michel Debré, that faithful companion of General De Gaulle, as well as of the German Social Democrats ('Ad Hoc', 1953). A united Europe had become a value in its own right.

On the international level, European integration had become a policy espoused by the American administrations of Presidents Truman, Eisenhower and Kennedy. It is ironic that whereas European leaders, such as Adenauer, were promoting the idea of Europe as a 'third force' between the Soviet Union and the US, American representatives were promoting the integration and even the federation of Europe. The opening of American archives for this period has removed any doubt on this score (Ellwood, 1990).

On the institutional level, the ECSC had established the basic institutional framework that was to be the model for further supranational communities. And the Council of Europe, which had been such a disappointment to European federalists, had adopted its European convention of Human Rights and created the European Commission and Court of Human Rights, which were to become the instruments for the creation of a common standard of civil rights throughout Western Europe, and much later all of Europe.

The Messina Conference added another plank of what was later to become the Community method of making decisions and advancing integration. It outlined the components of a common market treaty but it did not commit the governments to negotiating such a treaty. Instead, the six governments agreed to appoint experts headed by a 'political personality' to 'work out' treaties, which were then to be submitted to the foreign ministers (Messina Conference, 1958). This procedure foreshadowed the agreements to agree by a certain deadline, which have become a hallmark of European-level decision-making.

So by June 1955 all three of the elements which were to shape not only the European Economic Community but also its successors were in place: the European idea as a value in its own right, the basic institutional structure and the community method of decision-making. All three of these contributed in no small part to the Treaty which the six governments were to negotiate over the next two years.

3 French Elites

> ...the ideas of economists and political philosophers...are more powerful than is commonly understood. Indeed, the world is ruled by little else. Practical men, who believe themselves to be quite exempt from any intellectual influences, are usually the slaves of some defunct economist. Madmen in authority, who hear voices in the air, are distilling their frenzy from some academic scribbler of a few years back. I am sure that the power of vested interests is vastly exaggerated compared with the gradual encroachment of ideas (Keynes, 1951:383).

So wrote John Maynard Keynes, an economist, in 1935. It may be that Keynes overstated the case. Successful political action must be based on a combination of ideas and values while taking due account of existing interests.

This chapter will attempt a systematic analysis of the ideas of some of the French elites and the degree to which they blended ideas and interests as they discussed and lobbied with respect to the negotiations which led to the signing of that part of the Treaty of Rome of March 25, 1957 that created the European Economic Community. (There were in fact two Treaties signed on March 25, 1957; the other Treaty led to the creation of the European Atomic Energy Community, which is not the subject of this book). The ideas and interests expressed are drawn primarily from the time period beginning with the Messina Conference of June 1-2, 1955 and ending with the debate in the French National Assembly, in July 1957, which culminated in a vote authorizing the government of France to ratify the Treaties of Rome.

The elites whose views will be examined include all the political parties which were represented in the National Assembly, but not necessarily the Senate, before and after the elections of January 1956, and the principal interest groups representing industry/employers, labour and agriculture. The attitudes of the elite with respect to the four subject areas discussed in Chapter 1 – European institutions, agriculture, social policy and the association of the overseas territories – will be examined. In each case, I shall be looking for ideas and values specific to that subject matter as well as ideas and values relating to the integration of Europe. But in addition to ideas and values, I will also be considering the interests French elites defended, i.e. the interests of France as a nation-state and those of western Europe as a political entity.

Since this and the following chapter will explore attitudes towards the new European Economic Community (EEC) with a view to determining how these attitudes helped to shape and set conceptions of an integrating Europe, it will inevitably miss several aspects of the discussions. Political parties and interest groups are engaged in a constant struggle (or is a minuet?) for influence and the finite amount of power within the state. Any issue becomes a part of this struggle and sometimes becomes intertwined with the internal workings of the groups. The Mendésist wing of the Radical Party, for example, felt that it had to justify its killing of the EDC by opposing the EEC (see Chapter 2). Within the Christian Democratic MRP, on the other hand, party leaders emphasized Europe as a unifying theme since the party was divided on other key issues facing the French government, most notably the war in Algeria (Letamendia, 1993:103-114; Mahant, 1969:135). This is a dimension which, though interesting, does not advance the study of the subject of this book.

This chapter explores the ideas and interests of French elites, strictly with respect to the about to be created European Economic Community. Of what mixture of interests and ideas did these attitudes consist? The next subject, the extent to which these ideas and interests shaped the new community, is a topic to which I will return in Chapter 5.

The Institutions of the European Economic Community

The principal issue here was the degree of supranationality which the institutions of the European Economic Community (EEC) should enjoy, and supranationality in turn usually referred to majority voting within intergovernmental institutions and to the freedom of European institutions to act independently of national governments. But there were other controversies about the institutions of the EEC, notably whether it should have a directly elected parliament and whether economic and social groups should be formally represented within the institutions of the new community.

The institutions of the EEC were usually discussed in conjunction with another topic, that of the 'European idea' – that is, the concept that the unification of Europe represented a value in its own right. Generally speaking, those who professed a belief in the European idea were also those who favoured supranational institutions. Indeed, these two concepts were so closely linked that it is impossible to distinguish between them. The two concepts, the belief in the idea of Europe as a moral value in its own right, and the advocacy of supranational institutions will, therefore, be examined together.

The failure of the EDC had dampened the enthusiasm of those French elites who advocated the European idea. During 1955 and 1957, only three political parties and one major interest group openly touted the European idea. Of the three political parties, the one which did so most openly and enthusiastically was the Socialist Party (then still known by its anachronistic acronym, SFIO).[1] Robert Marjolin, a member of foreign minister Christian Pineau's *cabinet* and later a French negotiator in the negotiations leading to the Treaty of Rome, wrote that the 'salvation of France' required progress in the unification of Europe by means of the creation of a customs union (Marjolin, 1986:247). Writing in the March 1957 issue of the socialist journal *Demain*, party leader and recent Prime Minister Mollet advocated the creation of a 'genuine European political community' (Cited in Pineau and Rimbaud, 1991:263). The UDSR[2] took a yet stronger position. It advocated creation of a federal Europe and, in November 1956, described the concept of the nation-state as outmoded (*depassé*) (cited in Mahant, 1969:151 and 353). André Sanglier, a deputy belonging to the Radicals, a party normally associated with cautious centre-of-the-roadism, was somewhat more enthusiastic. He waxed passionately: 'building Europe means preserving the equilibrium of the world by saving Western civilization, based on spirituality...' (*Journal officiel*, 1957:203). The Mouvement Républicain Populaire (MRP), that bastion of Europeanism and supposedly Catholicism, had been badly burned by its enthusiastic advocacy of the EDC. It, therefore, took an almost cautious approach to the EEC. Maurice Schumann spoke of a 'dose of supranationality', while Alain Poher warned against 'grandiose projects' (cited in Brunet, 1993:233-250).

At this time, the most enthusiastic expression of the European idea came not from an ideologically motivated political party but from an interest group. The French agricultural groups expressed their enthusiasm for participating in an endeavour which would 'progress beyond and include nation-states'. Hélène Delorme and Yves Tavernier go so far as to

---

1 Section française de l'Internationale ouvrière.

2 *Union démocratique et socialiste de la Résistance* – This moderate socialist party is remembered mainly for the fact that is founders included one François Mitterrand.

suggest that French peasants (*paysans*) might already have seen themselves as citizens of a future Europe (Delorme and Tavernier, 1969:141).

Those who professed to believe in the European idea insisted nevertheless that becoming part of Europe would be good for France. There was no more talk of sacrificing sovereignty, as there had been in the immediate post-war years. Europe, the MRP, the Christian trade unions and the UDSR insisted, would help France to reform its poorly functioning institutions and to revive its sputtering economy (Mahant, 1969:133-135, 152 and 203). Marjolin wrote of the 'needed rebirth [of France] in the framework of a unified Europe' (Marjolin, 1986:255). Socialists and the MRP agreed that a united Europe provided the best means for absorbing the supposed ambitions of a resurgent Germany, which thus would not become an economic or even a military threat to France (Brunet, 1993:233-250; Guillen, 1992:505-516; Schreiner, 1993:273-290).

Those who opposed French acceptance of the EEC Treaty used arguments very similar to those who supported the Treaty. They also insisted that France was weak and needed to reform itself, but the EEC's opponents argued that France needed to be stronger before it could face German and international competition. The Gaullists[3] wanted France to be strong before it participated in a unifying Europe, while Mendès-France warned of German hegemony in a united Europe (Mahant, 1969:93 and 96; Marjolin, 1986:291).

As for the composition and powers of institutions of the EEC, three points of view, two of which contradicted one another, dominated the views of French elites. The Socialists, Union Démocratique et Sociale de la Résistance (UDSR) and MRP were firm advocates of supranational institutions. Alfred Coste-Floret of the MRP went so far as to advocate a small community, of no more than six countries, because other governments, such as those of Britain, would not accept supranational institutions (Mahant, 1969:117-118). The MRP and the Socialists also advocated a directly elected European parliament (Brunet, 1993:233-250; Mahant, 1969:131 and 169). Mollet and Pineau claimed that European institutions would do a better job of protecting French interests than the French had done themselves (Guillen, 1992: 505-516), and the socialist party's ultra-European, André Philip, insisted on majority voting in the

3 The political movement which had been formed to implement the ideas of General de Gaulle split and reformed itself several times during the life of the Fourth Republic (for details, see Williams 1964:135-137). Here all factions will be referred to as Gaullist without distinction.

EEC's Council of Ministers, raising the possibility that France could be outvoted (Mahant, 1969:170).

However, there were many among the French elites who, even if they were willing to accept a European common market, did not want it to be run by supranational institutions. The groups representing industry and agriculture, the *Conseil Nationale du Patronat Français* (CNPF) and the *Fédération Nationale des Syndicats d'Exploitants Agricoles* (FNSEA) were especially insistent on this point. They had great faith in the ability of the institutions of the French state to protect them. If there was to be any voting within the EEC, it should be unanimous, so that France could not be outvoted (Mahant 1969:189-190 and 226-227; Delorme and Tavernier, 1969:20-27). The Radicals, the quintessential party of the Third Republic and thus of an earlier age of nation-states, could not imagine that France could be outvoted. Édouard Daladier feared that if France was outvoted she 'would be reduced to the rank of a province...' (cited in Mahant, 1969:145). The French agricultural groups claimed that they favoured a 'United States of Europe,' but that they wanted the French government to continue to protect them (Delorme and Tavernier, 1969:141-142)!

Unlike the *patronat* and the agricultural representatives, the French labour unions were not so sure that they could trust the French state to protect them. The Christian trade unions advocated strong European institutions, whereas the Communist unions, of course, rejected the idea of any European community. The socialist unions took a cautious stand in favour of whatever position the Mollet government had adopted (Mahant, 1969:202-207 and 216-218).

Whether or not they favoured a supranational EEC, practically all of the French elites agreed that the EEC's institutions should include representation of economic and social groups. The conservatives,[4] the MRP, the *patronat*, the unions and the agricultural groups all agreed on this point (Brunet, 1993: 233-250; Mahant, 1969:104, 189 and 207; Delorme and Tavernier, 1969:27). They wanted the EEC institutions to include an economic and social council, similar to that which existed in France, and the Christian unions even wanted this council to have real powers of decision (Mahant, 1969:205-206). The French elites' insistence on this point has no obvious explanation. Perhaps, in a time before high

---

4 In this chapter, the term 'conservatives' will be used to describe politicians affiliated with the *Centre national des indépendants et paysans*, an electoral and legislative alliance of non-Gaullist conservatives, which co-ordinated the activities of most of the moderate French Right from 1951 to 1958 (Williams, 1964:150-159).

speed trains and Internet, Brussels or Luxembourg seemed far away from Paris, and guaranteed representation must have seemed a good substitute for the access which interest groups enjoyed in Paris. In the words of one conservative politician (Jacques Vasser), 'I fear that for a long time yet the national spirit of competition will prevail over the European community spirit' (France, 1957:3269).

What was almost entirely lacking from the statements of the French elites was any conception of a common European interest, over and above the interests of France and the French. There are a few scattered references to the values of Western civilization or the danger that the Atlantic world faced from the USSR. Beyond that, the conservative politician and former prime minister (the Fourth Republic had many former prime ministers) Antoine Pinay, spoke of the need for larger economic areas, a point on which other conservatives agreed with him, and the Socialists Pineau and Mollet, along with the Radical, Maurice Faure, spoke of the need for larger economic areas, so as to allow the European economy to grow and the standard of living to rise (Guillen, 1992:505-516; Mahant, 1969:100). This was about as close as anyone came to the idea of a common European interest.

Social Policy and Social Harmonisation[5]

A belief that living standards could and should continue to rise and that the resulting benefits should be redistributed by means of state-sponsored social welfare programs formed an important part of the post-war consensus in Western Europe. Not surprisingly, therefore, both advocates and opponents of the EEC, but especially the former, expressed a belief in the need for 'social progress' and continually rising standards of living for the people overall.

The MRP, the socialists and the Christian trade unions insisted on their belief that the social progress they advocated could be achieved by means of a united Europe. In resolution after resolution and in speech after speech, the MRP insisted that the creation of the EEC would lead to 'an improvement in the standard of living'. The local party in Maine-et-Loire claimed that the EEC was the 'only means of raising the standard of living in Europe', and at the party's 1956 congress, a speaker was applauded

5 For the sake of brevity, I shall be referring to the harmonisation of government-mandated social security measures as social harmonisation, though the phrase is perhaps not as felicitous as it might be.

when he said that 'we are not building Europe in order to have armies; we are building Europe so that the people can live comfortably' (cited in Mahant, 1969:123-124). In a similar vein, the socialists believed that only a European union would 'allow the European model of social democracy to come into being' (Guillen, 1992:16). The Mendésist wing of the Radical party, on the other hand, while also professing a belief in an 'advanced social policy' feared that in an integrating Europe, German style economic liberalism would prevail; such liberalism would cause greater inequalities among the people of France and cause French social benefits to fall (Mahant, 1969:147; Brunet, 1993). The Communist party also insisted that German social security benefits were much lower than the French, and that in a common market, French benefits would fall to the German level (Mahant, 1969:172).

But the socialists and the MRP believed that the converse of their optimistic arguments was also true. Not only would a united Europe help to raise standards of living; the policy of improving social benefits across Europe would contribute to the unification of Europe. The MRP envisaged a European social policy based on the French model, since the leaders of the MRP, like almost every other French person who discussed the issue, firmly believed that French social security policy was more progressive than that of the other five countries (Mahant 1969:125). A socialist, Gérard Jacquet, gave the idea of a common European social policy more thought. He envisaged a minimum standard of social security which would apply to all EEC member countries (Mahant, 1969:166). A representative for the Christian trade unions went further. Georges Levard envisaged an authority which could make social and economic policy for the entire EEC:

> We are not interested in returning to that true common market which existed in Europe before 1914... Liberal Europe which did not blush at the poverty of men... the common market which interests us is that which has a well defined mandate for economic and social progress and which has the necessary means to coordinate the use of Europe's resources to that end (Levard, 1957).

In the phraseology of the times, the creation of a common European system of social benefits was known as 'social harmonisation', and nearly all French elites agreed that social harmonisation would serve the interests of France and its people. Those, such as the Gaullists and the Communists, who opposed the EEC, did not oppose the principle of social harmonisation; they claimed that the Treaty of Rome did not include enough social harmonisation or that the Germans would not raise their social benefits to the French level (Mahant, 1969:95 and 172). The main French conservative party, the CNIP, also insisted on social harmonisation, but most of its members argued that the proposed treaty provided for a sufficient degree of social harmonisation. Conservatives and farm groups also wanted to harmonize the fiscal systems of the common market countries, a position similar to that of the *patronat* (Mahant, 1969:106, 180-181 and 223; Girault, 1989).

The leaders of the MRP and the socialists believed that social harmonisation would benefit France in two specific ways. A generous social policy of ever increasing benefits would undercut support for communism both within France and in the rest of Europe. In the menacing words of one MRP speaker, Fernand Bouxome, if the working class could not find their place in Europe, they would find it outside, that is by supporting the ideology of the Soviet Union (Mahant, 1969:124). The double meaning of the word Europe in this context is worth noting. Europe to this MRP speaker meant not only a united Europe but also a concept, one which presumably included democracy and tolerance and other virtues not characteristic of Soviet communism.

The socialist periodical *Le Populaire* claimed that a higher standard of living would cause the people of western Europe to reject communism (Mahant, 1969:165). Some MRP speakers hoped that the upward harmonisation of social benefits would restrain the rapid growth of the German economy. (These were the years of the German economic miracle.) In 1957, an anonymous author writing in the MRP's party organ, *Forces Nouvelles*, wrote:

> Would the dynamism of the German economy be less dangerous if it developed without rule or hindrance... The setting up of the Common Market will increase the costs which weigh on German prices: harmonization of social costs, the raising of tariffs with non-member countries, financial contributions to the Investment Bank and the Investment Fund for the overseas territories... (Comité national M.R.P., 1957:5).

Hardly an expression of Franco-German reconciliation.

Nor did French elites appear to have a conception of a common European interest in a common European social policy. It was not, as Küsters (1989:300) claims, as if social harmonisation was the *patronat*'s route to the integration of Europe. When the CNPF asked that one national government not be allowed to change its social security benefits unless all the others agreed to do so, this was not an expression of a common

European interest (Mahant, 1969:181-182). Such statements were an expression of a lack of faith in the government of France, which the *patronat* feared would make concessions to the demands of French citizens. Valery Giscard d'Estaing, then a young conservative deputy, blamed the weakness of the French economy on that economy's structure, that is the strength of the trade unions (which in fact were not all that strong in comparison with those in Germany (Küsters, 1989:365)). One of the few expressions of a common European interest came from the Christian trade unions, who urged trade unions to organize Europe-wide so as to counteract the influence of European industry (Mahant, 1969:203).

The representatives of only two of the smaller French political parties, the Radicals and the UDSR, dared openly say that French social benefits might not be that much higher than were those in other countries. Maurice Faure, a Radical and the chief negotiator for France, of course, defended the degree of harmonisation achieved in the Treaty of Rome. Other Radicals agreed, pointing out that the problem might only affect some industries. Some Radicals even hoped that the creation of the EEC would exert downward pressure on French social security benefits (Mahant, 1969:141). Pleven, representing the UDSR, believed that in a common market there would be a natural alignment of social security benefits (in an upward direction) and that, in any case, the French economy was stronger than many of his compatriots believed it to be. Other UDSR representatives hoped that the EEC would lead to higher productivity and thus make a higher standard of social security possible (Mahant, 1969:152; Küsters, 1982). The *patronat* was two-faced on this issue. While in public they continued to demand harmonisation of social security benefits, Georges Villiers, the long time head of the CNPF, told a German diplomat that the moderate degree of harmonisation achieved in the Treaty was adequate since 'the transition period was long enough to achieve a certain degree of equalisation' (Auswärtiges Amt, 1957).

Before I leave the subject of social harmonisation, it should be pointed out that the so called problem of social harmonisation was really an issue of the overvaluation of the French franc, which, for political reasons, the weak governments of the last years of the Fourth Republic dared not devalue. This was a problem of which many among the French elite, notably professional economists and the *patronat*, were aware, but they seldom dared to mention it (Mahant 1969:184). So they thundered on about the higher costs of French industry and the need to raise the costs of other nations' industries, an argument which makes no economic sense at all, while many of them knew full well that with one or two exceptions, such as the length of the working week and equal pay for men and women doing the same work, German social benefits were in fact no lower than the French ones. And even in the case of equal pay, this was a principle which in practice did not yet apply throughout most of French industry.

Agriculture

The glorification and sentimentalisation of rural life discussed in Chapter 1 was – and perhaps still is – more pronounced in France than in any other European country. For the MRP, the family farm embodied many of the 'human and social values' which the party elite liked to think were typical of Christian democracy (Teitgen, 1957:277). Jacques Vasser, a conservative, saw yet another value in agriculture; it contributed to the country's 'social equilibrium' (France, 1957:97), meaning that farmers were less likely to vote for left-wing parties, such as the Communists.[6] The farmers themselves were divided on this issue. While the mainline interest groups supported the traditional small holders, a dissident group of so-called young peasants favoured a more commercial approach to farming, with larger, competitive holdings (Mahant, 1969:255-226).

That said, there is survey evidence which indicates that the 'European idea' of peace, good will and prosperity by means of a united Europe had penetrated into rural France. Delorme and Tavernier (1969:107 and 141) claim French peasants believed that peace could be achieved by overcoming national barriers, and more specifically some among them were willing to have the national government delegate powers to a European community of states.

But there was more than the European idea to the agricultural groups' support of a united Europe, and more specifically a common market. By the 1950s, French agriculture had largely recovered from the disruptions of World War II. France was once again producing a surplus of most agricultural products, such as the basic grains and wine. Not surprisingly, therefore, the prices French farmers received for their produce were lower than they were in West Germany, where the conservative CDU government of that highly industrialised country could afford to support farm prices (Mahant, 1969:225-226; Delorme and Tavernier, 1969:17-23). Conservative politicians in France spoke directly about the need to gain

6 Vasser was wrong. During the 1950s, voters in very small communities and farmers were more likely to vote Communist than were city dwellers (Williams, 1964:509).

access to the German market for agricultural products (Mahant, 1969:103). The MRP and the farmers' associations themselves were less openly self-interested in their commentary. They spoke and wrote of the need for a common European market for agricultural products (Mahant, 1969:126; Delorme and Tavernier, 1969:80). Indeed, the MRP had plans for a specific European agricultural policy, which would include minimum prices, long-term contracts for the sale of agricultural products and an investment policy (Mahant, 1969:127). The MRP also believed that free trade would reduce the price of manufactured goods to farmers, so that farmers would gain doubly, higher prices for their products and lower prices for their purchases (Mahant, 1969:127). Once again, the MRP's policy of reconciliation with Germany was based on more than altruism.

The French agricultural groups believed that a common European agricultural policy would be good for France because the export of agricultural products could help to offset what at the time seemed to be a chronic French balance of payments problem, which in turn was due to the various colonial wars, most notably those in Indochina and Algeria, that the French government had and was engaged in (Mahant 1969:228). The MRP added that European prices for agricultural products should be set at a level higher than the prices prevailing on world markets (Mahant 1969:126).

The agricultural groups in France foresaw that their country would soon be producing agricultural surpluses. Based on this knowledge, they developed specific plans as to what measures a common agricultural policy should consist of (Küsters, 1989:340). It should provide for protection against third countries and provide for the 'highest possible' coverage of European needs by European products. Furthermore, and this was a policy espoused especially by the producers of wheat and sugar, Europeans overall should be responsible for the financing and disposal of European – that is French – agricultural surpluses. Wine and beef producers were less certain of the degree to which they could increase exports within a European common market – there was Italian and Dutch competition to worry about – and they, therefore, wanted a European policy to leave open the possibility of controlling national imports (Delorme and Tavernier, 1969:83 and 90; Küsters, 1989:349).

The agricultural groups also did not have the complete faith in Europe that their advocacy of a common European market would appear to suggest. They wanted escape clauses which would allow the French government to cut off imports in case of import 'surges', and, as mentioned above, they wanted the European institutions to take unanimous decisions with respect to the agricultural policy, so that the French government would be able to continue to protect French farming (Delorme and Tavernier 1969: 25-27).

Among the French groups and political parties, it was only the socialists who advocated a common agricultural policy for the benefit of Europeans, rather than just for the benefit of the French. André Philip wrote of a European agricultural policy under which European authorities would be able to buy, stockpile and sell 'in the common interest' of Europeans (Mahant 1969:169).

The Overseas Territories

The 1950s was a time when European (and North Americans) attitudes to the areas of the world which later became known as the Third World were evolving, from those of paternalism to those of a common obligation to help the less fortunate. This dichotomy is evident from the discussion of the relationship of the colonies of France (and Belgium, Italy and the Netherlands) to the future European Economic Community. At the 1956 party congress, an MRP deputy, Jean Jacques Juglas, spoke of France's 'humanitarian mission' in Africa, which a united Europe could help fulfil (cited in Girault, 1989:355). Socialist deputies, and especially the ministers Mollet and Pineau, were more likely to speak of the degree to which EEC countries other than France could aid the development and raise the standard of living of the African colonies (Guillen, 1992:509; Mahant, 1969:167). A particularly prescient MRP deputy, René Charpentier, also foresaw that the food surpluses a European agricultural policy might produce could be used as food aid to developing countries (cited in Mahant, 1969:127).

By the 1950s, the 'European mystique' was more powerful than that of France as an African country (Frank, 1992:170). Europe could help Africa develop, but according to the MRP and the SFIO, Africa was also an important source of economic strength and political support for Europe (Brunet, 1993:233-250). In a strange twist of logic, Pineau argued that it would be colonialism if France tried to keep its colonies for itself, but that a European African association would be source of strength for a declining Europe (Pineau as cited in Pineau and Rimbaud, 1991:231). The charge of colonialism was directed at the Poujadists and the Mendésists who argued that France should keep its valuable African colonies to support its own greatness (Mahant, 1969:83 and 148).

Pineau's point of view was exceptional. The overwhelming majority of those in France who discussed the association of the overseas territories and the EEC viewed the topic from a nation-state centred point of view – that is, they viewed the association as an advantage for France. Even the Gaullists, who opposed the creation of the EEC, supported the association with the overseas territories, for had General de Gaulle not said – and this was in 1950 – 'Unless we force ourselves to look at the matter coolly, we might almost be dazzled by the perspective of what German values and French values, extended to Africa could do together' (cited in Manin, 1966:78). While some conservatives and Gaullists and surprisingly, the communist trade union confederation, the CGT, claimed that Africa was more important to France than was Europe (Mahant, 1969:95, 105 and 217), the usual argument was that European aid in developing the African colonies would enable France to keep the French Union, the name the constitution of the Fourth Republic had given to the French empire (Williams, 1964:293; Küsters, 1982:382). This was a powerful argument, since France had recently lost Indochina to a colonial war, Tunisia and Morocco had just become independent and the Algerians were fighting a war for their independence. If France could not keep the French Union, perhaps Europe could help her to do so.

This point of view could be found right across the political spectrum, from the conservatives to the socialists. Emmanuel Temple, a conservative, argued that European investment would help France to keep its Africa and 'to accomplish her mission' there (cited in Mahant, 1969:105; also Küsters, 1989:382). The MRP and Radicals argued that not only would European investment help France to keep its Africa colonies, it would also prevent the spread to Africa of communism and Soviet influence and thus contribute to the security of France (Girault, 1989:355-356; Mahant, 1969:128-129 and 137).

The Socialists and the Socialist dominated trade union federation, the *Force Ouvrière* (FO), argued that the French Union would derive political and economic advantages from the European association with the overseas territories. The economic advantages would include lower prices for manufactured goods and a larger markets for the colonies' tropical products, to which the agricultural groups added the advantage of a market for French agricultural products (Mahant, 1969:167-8, 210 and 226). The *patronat* agreed with the Socialists on the importance of European investment in Africa (Auswärtiges Amt, 1957; Girault, 1989:365; Küsters, 1989:301; Guillen, 1992:508-9; Mahant, 1969: 187-8). Emphasizing political rather than economic factors, a Radical, Jean Masson, pointed out that France would be stronger within Europe if she entered with her colonies, and a few members of the MRP even argued that France, strengthened by Europe and Eurafrica, would be able to win the war in Algeria or at least bring it to an honourable conclusion (Girault, 1989:367; Mahant, 1969:130), while the Socialist trade unions hoped that a united Europe would help France resolve the Algerian problem by providing 'welfare, social justice, economic prosperity, security through peace and dignity through liberty' (cited in Mahant, 1969:211).

In France, there was very little dissent with this glorious vision of the future Euro-African partnership. The Communist party did provide one dissenting voice, as it argued for the independence of the colonies as a means of ending their current exploitation (Küsters, 1989:38; Mahant, 1969:173) – though it was not so clear cut on Algeria – and some members of the business community worried about German and other European competition in what had been a protected market for French manufactured goods (Küsters, 1989:301). In a similar argument the Socialist finance minister, Paul Ramadier, called the idea of Eurafrica an illusion; he would have preferred France to keep the colonial markets and the franc zone to itself (Guillen, 1992: 505-516:508).

Thus most of the French elites saw the association with the overseas territories primarily in terms of the national interests of France and the French. Only a few Frenchmen spoke up for the common interests of Europe, or at least Europe as represented by the six member states of the EEC. In December 1956, Robert Schuman addressed an MRP party assembly:

> The association of Europe and Africa will be a revolutionary political action with an economic basis. Because of it, Europe and Africa will strengthen each other in a common enterprise of general cooperation. This will be the beginning of political reform, of economic expansion, of an effective struggle against all poverty, a solid base for reconciliation and peace (cited in Mahant, 1969:128).

Several Radicals and some members of the MRP pointed out the advantages that other Europeans would derive from the association with the African colonies: markets and a secure source of raw materials (Küsters, 1989:381). Even Maurice Faure, France's chief negotiator and also a Radical, claimed that France had made sacrifices by giving the other European countries access to her colonies (Mahant, 1969:128-9 and 139-140). The UDSR, which was in a parliamentary alliance with a group representing some of the African deputies, saw a common European-

African bloc as a third force in world politics, one which would save Africa 'from the devouring Russo-American rivalry' (cited in Mahant, 1969:154). The MRP believed that a united Europe needed Africa, just as the French Union needed a united Europe to survive (Girault, 1989:355), a profoundly conservative argument which set a goal of preservation above that of progress. In a more forward looking frame of mind, some French industrialists hoped that cooperation on common European projects in Africa would lead to cooperation with German industrialists in other areas (Küsters, 1989:382).

Concluding Comments

In terms of frequency at least, the one interest French elites stressed in their discussions of the proposed European economic community was the interest of France as a nation-state. In terms of world politics and foreign policy, the EEC would make France more secure by containing Germany, by reducing the threat of communism and the Soviet threat and by helping France to maintain the French Union. With respect to domestic politics, a united Europe would provide the context in which France could revive its sputtering political institutions and reduce the threat of political extremism on the right and the left (Gaullism, Poujadism and communism), which threatened to strangle the democratic institutions of the Fourth Republic. On the economic level, the common market would help to invigorate the French economy and reduce the country's apparently chronic balance of payments problem. Such a revitalized French economy would, in turn, be able to provide the social benefits which would lead to social peace and harmony and would allow the French economy to compete with the German one.

After the interests of France, French elites were about equally concerned with their own interests and with grander concepts, such as the idea of the uniting of Europe as a value in its own right. Among the political parties, the hope that a prosperous united Europe could undercut support for political extremism was a hope which inspired the Socialists and the Christian democrats (MRP). *Sotto voce*, some of the business groups hoped that a uniting Europe would restrain the growth of social welfare spending in France. Some business groups also looked to expanding markets. Agricultural groups and others hoped that the other member countries of the EEC, notably Germany, would provide a valuable market for French agricultural products. The French labour unions, divided into three major and some minor confederations, looked enviously at the strength of the almost monolithic German trade union federation and hoped to benefit from that strength in a uniting Europe.

After the debacle of the European Defence Community, the European idea got somewhat less attention during the debates on the EEC than it did in earlier years. The Socialists, some of the Radicals and to a lesser extent the MRP still advocated the European idea, as did the agricultural interest groups and Christian trade unions. Significantly, groups such as the Gaullists and the Mendésists, who opposed the common market and the Treaty of Rome, still claimed to believe in a united Europe. Their argument was that the time was not yet right, or that this was not the right approach to the building of Europe. Only groups which were considered beyond the pale of mainline politics, specifically the Poujadists, spoke against the concept of a united Europe. The Communist party, while it did not claim to support a united Europe, nevertheless did not speak against that concept either. It contended itself with condemning the Treaty of Rome as being not in the interests of France or the French working class.

While French elites were perhaps shy of advocating the European idea as such, they had, for the most part, internalized the idea of Europe as a value in its own right. As this chapter shows, nearly everyone who discussed the European Economic Community, including the Communists and the Gaullists, did not oppose the idea of a united Europe, only the particular manifestation of it, that is the EEC, which was being presented to them.

What is even more surprising is that there was such widespread acceptance of a united Europe as a positive value that both interest groups and political parties accepted it equally. One might expect that interest groups, by definition, would first and foremost espouse the interests of their members. And so they did. But they did so while also advocating the idea of Europe. Indeed, in the case of the French elites, the interest groups were as likely to espouse Europe as were the political parties. And the only determined opposition to the EEC came from political parties, not from interest groups.

Marcussen and Roscher (1999) identify five elements of the Europe as a value concept: Europe as a community which benefits its nation-state members, Europe as a community of values, Europe as a third force between communism and capitalism, Europe as a part of the Western world and Europe as a part of a community of western values (*l'Occident* in French or *das Abendland* in German). Among French elites, the first of these concepts dominated, though the Socialists especially also saw Europe as a third force. Conservatives, the MRP, the Socialists, the agricultural groups and the Christian unions also occasionally espoused European values.

It followed that, for the most part, French elites envisaged a united Europe with institutions which were characterized by a limited degree of supranationality and which would create a common market for industrial and agricultural goods, would provide some kind of assistance for the French colonies and would help France to maintain and expand its recently created welfare state. These hopes and expectations were leavened by a limited dose of European idealism, an idealism which provided the comfortable feeling that uniting Europe was the right thing to do.

4 German Elites

This chapter analyses the ideas and interests German elites expressed as they discussed the negotiations leading to the signing of the Treaty of Rome of March 25, 1957. So the time period covered is as it was in the previous chapter, that is June 1, 1955 to July 1957, when the Bundestag voted its approval of that Treaty. The elites studied include all the political parties represented in the Bundestag and the major interest groups representing industry and commerce, labour and agriculture.

More so than in France, where national elections had been held in January 1956, in Germany, where elections where due to be held in the autumn of 1957, domestic politics and positioning intruded into the debate about the European Economic Community. Thus the Social Democrats' conversion from an anti- to pro-European position was at least partly motivated by a desire to don the apparently so successful electoral policies of the Adenauer government (Mahant, 1969:274; Rhenisch, 1994:55). Similarly, the main interest group representing German industry moderated its criticism of the Treaty of Rome because it wanted to allow the Adenauer government to look good and successful. The business community preferred to have the Adenauer government re-elected; they were, therefore, willing to say little publicly about their dissatisfaction with the Treaties of Rome, which that government had negotiated (Rhenisch, 1994:123 and 296). Agricultural groups, similarly, muted their criticism of the Treaty because they did not want to see the urban-based SPD win the election.

1957 was also twelve years after the end of World War II. Twelve years had been long enough for many, if not all, of the memories of the collaboration with the Nazis practised by some of the French business community to fade. It was not long enough even to begin to wash away the collective guilt of the Germans (Simonian, 1985:47). There was thus a great reluctance to express openly nationalist positions and considerable enthusiasm for a united Europe and the European idea, an enthusiasm which was at least in part a consequence of this collective guilt. The enthusiasm permeated all sections of the German society, from the political parties to the economic elites to public opinion (Paterson, 1974:120). Germans hoped thereby to gain the acceptance of Germany and the Germans as equals in international society. Europe had become a kind of magic word, a means of escape from the past, a means for a 'provisional and insecure nation' to find a means 'to a larger more secure and morally positive identity' (Almond, 1955:21 and 87). In the words of one German writer, 'the very word Europe had a fascination like no other because it seemed to hold all hope for the future' (cited in Simonian, 1985:33).

One would expect, therefore, that ideas rather than interests played a predominant role in the determination of the position of German elites. One might even expect to find a most unusual phenomenon, a willingness on the part of groups representing economic interests to make sacrifices for the greater good, not of their country in the short run, but for the long-term future of that country and its international position. If this was indeed the case, it would have given the other major government involved in the negotiations, that is the government of France, an unusual opportunity to shape the European Economic Community to its own liking. (The extent to which French and/or German interests and ideas shaped the fledgling European Economic Community will be discussed in Chapter 5.) Here I will discuss the degree to which ideas and interests shaped the views of German elites.

As in the previous chapter about French elites, the attitudes of the German elites with respect to the four subject areas discussed in Chapter 1 – the European idea and European institutions, agriculture, social policy and the association of the overseas territories – will be examined. In each case, I shall be looking for ideas and values specific to that subject matter as well as to ideas and value relating to the integration of Europe.

The Institutions of the European Economic Community

As expected, Germans from all the groups studied espoused the European idea and common European values. Adenauer himself identified his version of the European idea with what he perceived to be European values. He made references to concepts such as 'European thought, Western thought, Christian thought,' and one of his associates, Franz Etzel, wrote of the 'spiritual unity of this old historical area...' (Mahant, 1969:233 and Etzel, 1955). It is worth noting that the latter reference occurred in an article which dealt with the economic aspects of the proposed common market. State Secretary Walter Hallstein,[1] Adenauer's closest foreign

[1] Until June of 1955, Adenauer served as his own foreign minister. He then apointed Heinrich von Brentano as Minister of Foreign Affairs. However, Walter Hallstein, who had attended the Messina conference for Adenauer, continued to look after the European integration dossier, becoming Germany's head negotiator

policy advisor, who represented him at the Messina Conference, saw the sovereign nation-state as outmoded. For Hallstein, as for Adenauer, a united Europe represented the way of the future (Becker, 1992; Schreiner, 1993).

While these are the kind of sentiments one might expect from speakers for the CDU, references to the European idea occurred across the political spectrum. The Social Democrats (SPD) came to the realization that if they were to be serious contenders as a governing party, they needed to be mainstream, that is, accept the European idea (Küsters, 1989:229-230). Herbert Wehner, a prominent member of the Social Democratic Party, was enthusiastic about the Messina Declaration and was soon lecturing members of his party about their 'European tasks' (Paterson, 1974:122). Spokespersons for the political party representing refugees (its designation was GB/BHE) opposed the European Economic Community, but felt compelled to say that their party supported the integration of Western Europe (Mahant, 1969:261).

Even representatives of economic interest groups stressed the idealistic and political reasons for their support of a united Europe. Members of the German business community were especially likely to stress their commitment to the ideal of a united Europe, to the point where several of their spokesmen expressed a willingness to make economic sacrifices to achieve the ideal of a united Europe (Bührer, 1995; Mahant, 1969:286-287). The leader of the Federation of German Industry (BDI), Fritz Berg, went further. He wanted Germany to be the pioneer of the creation of a united Europe (Bührer, 1993). The main German trade union federation, the DGB, similarly stressed its support of Europe and its willingness to make economic sacrifices for the achievement of that ideal (Mahant, 1969:294).

However, the willingness to support the European idea in principle did not always translate into support for supranational European institutions. On this subject, there was a wide variety of opinion among German elites. Within the CDU, for example, many leading members of the party, such as Heinrich von Brentano, Hans Furler and Fritz Hellwig, supported supranational institutions with real powers of decision as the only true expressions of Europeanism. Ludwig Erhard, the Economics Minister, on the other hand, was suspicious of supranational institutions, lest they become *dirigiste* and interfere with the running of the economy

---

and in 1958 the first President of the Commission of the European Economic Community. Hallstein was a senior civil servant (a Secretary of State) and not an elected politician.

(Mahant, 1969:240). But Erhard also wanted the European institutions to be strong enough to enforce a tough competition policy (Mahant, 1969:248). Hellwig, in a foreshadowing of what much later was to become known variously as subsidiarity or multi-level governance, spoke of a happy medium, where national, supranational and international institutions would all have their own spheres of authority (Mahant, 1969:247).

Outside of the CDU, there was less enthusiasm for supranational institutions. The refugee party was suspicious of European institutions and of France. Its representatives wrote about the organic nature of nation-states in almost Gaullist terms (Mahant, 1969:262). Suspicion of France, though expressed in much more discreet language, was also found within the SPD. In a press release, the party claimed that the CDU government had been taken in by the French government, which successfully used a recalcitrant National Assembly to gain concessions. In the Bundestag debate on the Treaty, the SPD's Willi Birkelbach accused the government of having made concessions which amounted to subsidies to the French economy and that such subsidies constituted an indirect subsidy of the French war effort in Algeria (Mahant, 1969:273 and 401).

German business was ambiguous on the subject of supranational institutions. At first, spokesmen for business were happy that the new institutions were to be much less supranational than the ECSC had been. But later representatives of German business expressed a wide variety of views. Suspicions of France led to fear of common institutions which might try to impose French economic policies of high taxation and social spending. On the other hand, some among the business community hoped that common institutions might curb what were perceived as the excesses of lax French economic policies (Bührer, 1995; Mahant, 1969:277-8 and 284-5; Rhenisch, 1994:84, 88-89, 124, 183, 190-1). The head of the German trade union confederation, Ludwig Rosenberg, favoured supranational institutions, but the DGB also insisted that unions be represented within the new European institution (Deutscher Gewerkschaftsbund, 1957; Mahant, 1969:295). German agriculture was mute on the subject of supranational institutions, but made extravagant demands for representation within any new institutions (Mahant, 1969:305).

No doubt in an effort to promote their democratic credentials, German elites paid special attention to the parliament (then known as Assembly) of the new European communities. CDU speakers wanted the Assembly to have the widest possible powers, including the power to vote economic directives. The CDU also advocated the direct election of a European parliament, a revolutionary idea in 1957. The SPD was not to be left behind in its advocacy of Europe-wide democracy. It wanted the Assembly to have some control over both the Commission and the Council of Ministers of the new communities, and it wanted the three communities (ECSC, EEC and EAEC) to have only one common parliament. Foreshadowing the much later debate about a European democratic deficit, one SPD speaker after another insisted that the European parliamentary assembly must have control over any areas of government activity ceded to the European level, since otherwise the national parliaments would have lost control to non-elected European institutions (Mahant, 1969:240, 270 and 399; Paterson, 1974:128: Schreiner, 1993).

Only two other institutions attracted widespread comment from German elites. There was ambiguity, on the part of both business and labour, with respect to the proposed readaptation fund and investment bank for Europe and the investment fund for overseas territories. Even within the pro-European CDU, Fritz Hellwig expressed the suspicion that the readaptation fund would be just a means of subsidizing French industry with German money (Mahant, 1969:241). Hermann Abs, a prominent banker and an advisor to Adenauer, did not want any investment fund to interfere with capital markets (Rhenisch, 1994:88). Later, when the terms of the Treaty were published, the German business community concluded that the readaptation fund was small enough not to do much harm and that the Bank would in any case work according to market principles (Mahant, 1969:278-9). The German unions were divided. Some union leaders favoured the readaptation fund because it might be able to help German workers, whereas others suspected that the money would primarily be spent in other countries (Mahant, 1969:298).

With respect to the economic and social committee, demanded by practically every sector in France, German business as well as Erhard's Ministry of Economics were opposed to the creation of such an institution because they feared that in an institution consisting of half employers and half labour representatives, on the model of the German system of co-determination, the employers might be at a disadvantage (Küsters, 1989:409-410). However, when it emerged that the economic and social committee was to consist of representatives from various sectors of the economy, including agriculture and consumers, German business leaders reluctantly accepted the committee as an institution within which they might be able to have some influence (Rhenisch, 1994:169, 183 and 191-2). The German unions, on the other hand, wanted an economic and social committee consisting equally of labour and business, and they were disappointed when the final composition was very different from that model. The unions had also wanted the committee to have the power to initiate legislative proposals, another wish that was not granted (Mahant, 1969:298). German agriculture wanted representation within the economic and social committee, but, like German business, it also sought the creation of special advisory committees dealing only with its topics of interest (Mahant, 1969:305). There was no provision for any such committees in the Treaty of Rome, though many such committees were created in years to come. (On comitology, see Dinan, 1999:227-229).

Over and beyond the specific institutions of the new community, West German elites believed that they had one special national interest to protect: the reunification of what remained of their country, that is of the Federal Republic of Germany, of the German Democratic Republic and of Berlin. This was a politically delicate issue. No politician could afford to say that any proposed policy would make reunification more difficult or unlikely. Politicians opposed to the EEC, that is the FDP and the refugee party, were most likely to say that European integration would make the prospect of reunification more unlikely, which indeed is what the Social Democrats had argued when they opposed the ECSC and the EDC (Mahant, 1969:252-3 and 260-1). The right wing of the Christian democratic movement, most notably the CDU's Bavarian sister party, the Christian Social Union, made a related argument when they said that Germany was a central European country, which should not throw all its weight to the West (Knipping, 1992; Mahant, 1969:238). This was less of an argument for reunification than it was one for an autonomous German foreign policy, one not overly reliant on NATO and the US.

Adenauer and the CDU claimed that European integration was a necessary step on the road to reunification because: (1) Germans had to show that they had overcome their nationalist past before other governments would support reunification; (2) Western, especially American support, was essential to reunification; (3) a stronger Western Europe was more likely to succeed in negotiations with the Soviet Union (Mahant, 1969:236). In 2003, these arguments may sound prescient; in 1956-57, they seemed to postpone German reunification to a very far away future. So to meet the concerns of those in its own coalition parties as well as the SPD and the trade unions who expressed repeated concerns about reunification, the government assured Germans that at the very least the Treaty of Rome would not deepen the division of Germany (Mahant, 1969:295; Paterson, 1974:120 and 127). This meant that there were, in principle, to be no tariffs or trade restrictions between the Federal Republic, on the one hand, and Berlin and the German Democratic Republic on the other, which in turn meant that there needed to be some kind of control as to the origin of goods coming from those two jurisdictions (Couve de Murville, 1957).

German elites, however, also perceived wider Western and European interests. Anti-Communism was a powerful theme among French supporters of European integration, since communism and the Soviet Union were as much a domestic as they were a foreign policy threat. In the Federal Republic of Germany, making Germany a committed and unwavering member of the Western bloc was Adenauer's primordial foreign policy goal, and a united Europe was a part of that goal. To achieve this greater aim, Adenauer was willing to impose economic sacrifices on German elites and the German people (Becker, 1992; Mahant, 1969:231-4). But many Germans, including Adenauer, also believed that the Western bloc led by the US either might not last, or that American and European interests might not always coincide. They, therefore, wrote and spoke about a so-called 'Third Force,' an economic and political bloc, which could defend European as against American and against Soviet or Communist interests and values (Knipping, 1992; Rhenisch, 1994:227). A united Europe, Adenauer and some other CDU leaders believed, could become such a Third Force. In short, in addition to protecting Germany's economic interests and supporting the European idea, German elites were also thinking in terms of the traditional geopolitical balance of power.

Social Policy and Social Harmonisation

The topic of the harmonisation of social benefits attracted much less attention among German elites than it did in France. There was first of all little enthusiastic commentary on the concept of the welfare state and the ideal of higher social benefits. This may reflect a tinge of American business style liberalism; on the other hand, it may also be that since Germans had a long tradition of government-provided social welfare (going back to Chancellor Otto von Bismarck in the 1880s), the idea that social benefits should increase as national income may have been taken for granted. It just did not require further comment. After all, the social market economy had become part of the canon of West German politics. The only person who seems to have mentioned the ideal of rising standards of living for all was Economics Minister Ludwig Erhard, who was himself firmly opposed to social harmonisation. Yet he spoke of a 'moral duty to raise standards of living,' which would in turn contribute to political stability (Germany, 1956). The German business community agreed, saying that a larger market would automatically lead to a higher standard of living (Rhenisch, 1994:187).

German elites tended to see the specific measures of social harmonization demanded by French negotiators primarily in terms of the interest of the German economy overall. However, these interests were perceived in different ways. A small number among the German elites, notably the trade union leadership and some members of the SPD, accepted social harmonisation as a good thing because they believed it would cause German social welfare benefits to rise to the perceived higher French levels (Loth, 1989; Paterson, 1974:127; Richter, 1957). Both unions and management also were suspicious of the French system of government-legislated, and thus by extension possibly treaty mandated, social benefits; they preferred the German system of determining such benefits through collective bargaining (Mahant, 1969:317).

A more common reaction was that of the business community, some leading members of the SPD (notably Willi Birkelbach) and Ludwig Erhard. They accepted that French social benefits were higher than the German, but objected to harmonisation on the grounds that such harmonisation would raise costs and make the German economy less competitive (Couve de Murville, 1957; Mahant, 1969:255; Paterson, 1974:127; Rhenisch, 1994:101-2, 119 and 154-7). To which an anonymous writer in the Free Democratic Party's news bulletin added nastily that the German standard of living would fall if Germans had to adopt the 'French rhythm of work' (cited in Mahant, 1969:254).

A less common reaction was that if all factors were considered – for example, if religious holidays as well as annual holidays were counted – the total cost of French and German social security was not all that different. And if that was the case, according to some leaders of the German industrial federation BDI, and the German chambers of commerce (DIHT), then the issue became: which social security system was to be the model, the German or the French? The Germans, naturally, preferred the German (Bührer, 1995; Rhenisch, 1994:225).

Once the text of the Treaty of Rome had been published, German elites found that the degree of social harmonisation their government had promised to implement was less than they had feared. They thought that they could adapt to what the Treaty provided, though some business leaders still had reservations about the idea of equal pay for men and women doing the same work (Mahant, 1969:280; Rhenisch, 1994:199-201 and 225).

But the most common German reaction to the idea of social harmonisation was what the French call *la fuite en avant* or flight forward;

in other words, if social policies were to be harmonised in accordance with French wishes, then other policies should also be harmonised in accordance with German wishes. In the case of some leading members of the CDU, notably Adenauer, Brentano and Furler, this flight forward consisted of the belief that economic integration would eventually lead to a common European social policy (Mahant, 1969:244). A large number of the German business community argued that if there was to be social harmonisation, there should also be a common monetary policy (Mahant, 1969:243 and 280; Rhenisch, 1994:87, 193 and 212). Behind the call for a common monetary policy lay the fact that, under the Bretton Woods system of fixed exchange rates prevailing at that time, the French franc was seriously overvalued, but the weak governments of the last years of the Fourth Republic dared not to devalue the currency (Mahant, 1969:184-5). German business leaders expected that a European monetary policy would be as rigorous and consistent as they believed the German one to be, and thus problems, such as the one that had arisen in France, would not arise under a European monetary policy.

In addition to a common monetary policy, German business called for a harmonisation of fiscal policies (Bührer, 1993; Mahant, 1969:280; Rhenisch, 1994:112 and 198). So, ironically, both French and German business wanted to harmonise fiscal policy, believing that they would benefit from the other country's provisions. The German agricultural groups had their own demands for harmonisation. Besides those demanded by industry, they asked for the integration of capital and labour markets and the harmonisation of feed grains prices (Mahant, 1969:305-6).

So the flight forward envisaged by the German elites could have taken European integration very far indeed. To varying degrees, German elites foresaw a common social and monetary policy as well as the harmonisation of fiscal policies, in short a common European economy.

Agriculture

The Germans, like the French, had romantic notions about agriculture. At the 1957 annual meeting of the agricultural cooperative movement (*Raiffeisenverband*), a speaker praised the values of tradition and self-reliance perpetuated by farm life and contrasted these values with 'economic efficiency and so-called progress' (cited in Mahant, 1969:307). But agriculture was much less important to the German economy than it was to the French economy, so that such notions had less influence on politics overall.[2] On the other hand, the political importance of German agriculture was great. A majority of German farmers voted for the CDU/CSU, the agricultural vote made up 12.5 per cent of that party's votes, and 1957 was an election year in Germany. So one could expect the CDU government to lend an ear to the demands of German agriculture.

It is no exaggeration to say that hardly anyone in Germany liked any aspect of the agricultural provisions of the Treaty of Rome. As a heavily industrialized country, West Germany could afford to subsidize its agriculture to a considerable degree. German marketing boards paid farmers higher than world prices for most agricultural products, prices which thus were higher than those received by farmers in the other five countries (Küsters, 1989:350-352). This kind of protection would not be affordable in countries such as Italy and France, where agriculture contributed a large proportion of the labour force, and was unnecessary in the Netherlands were agricultural producers were commercially competitive. Therefore, the German agricultural interest groups disliked the idea of a common agricultural policy because any European policy was almost bound to be less generous than the German policy it would replace (Loth, 1989). Like the French business community, they therefore demanded harmonisation of all kinds of policies before they could accept free trade in agricultural products (see previous section). In the end, the agricultural groups gave the Treaty of Rome a lukewarm acceptance only because the alternative, a city-based SPD government, would have been worse than a CDU-negotiated common agricultural policy.

German industry did not like the agricultural provisions being discussed any more than did the agricultural groups. They criticized the agricultural provisions of the Treaty as *dirgiste* and protectionist. They feared that having to buy French or Italian products would harm Germany's trade relations with other countries. According to Wilhelm Beutler, of the BDI, German industry could sell agricultural machinery and equipment in return for purchases of agricultural products (Couve de Murville, 1957). But under the provisions of the Treaty of Rome, said a spokesman for the German Chambers of Commerce (DIHT), the people of the other member countries would have 'to eat every last grain of French cereal' before they could buy food elsewhere (cited in

2 In 1954, 19.7 per cent of the German labour force worked in agriculture; for France the figure was 28 per cent (Friedrich, 1969:91). French agriculture also contributed to the French balance of payments by exporting, whereas Germany was a net importer of agricultural products.

Mahant, 1969:282). To which trade union leaders added that if Germans had to buy food from other European countries, rather than on the world market, food prices would go up and before long there would be agricultural surpluses, as European farmers responded to the higher prices (which, of course, is indeed what happened). The German unions had an alternative solution: the 'rationalisation' of agricultural production, that is larger more productive farms which presumably would produce food for lower prices, and the inclusion of agricultural products in the planned customs union, which was expected to put further downward press on food prices (Mahant, 1969:295). This was a solution which risked the wrath of farmers and which neither the French nor the German government was thus likely to accept.

Political parties added their negative comments to those of the interest groups. Some political leaders, such as Erhard (from the CDU) and the leaders of the FDP objected that the provisions of the Treaty were too protectionist and would force Germans to buy French agricultural products at higher than market prices. Erhard especially objected to the idea of long term contracts for the purchase of agricultural products, an idea which did not make it into the Treaty (Mahant, 1969:256; Rhenisch, 1994:169). Those members of the CDU/CSU who depended on agricultural votes or felt close to that industry objected that the policy outlined in the Treaty of Rome did not provide enough protection for German agriculture. The minister for food, Heinrich Lübke, tried to find compensating arguments. He pointed out that the rising standards of living the common market was supposed to bring about would lead to an increase in the demand for food, in the long run and that in the short run, free trade should reduce the price of agricultural equipment (Mahant, 1969:246).

Thus, while there was widespread dissatisfaction with the agricultural provisions of the Treaty of Rome, German elites felt compelled to support European integration and, therefore, to make the best of the unsatisfactory agricultural provisions.

The Overseas Territories

German interest groups and political parties were no more enthusiastic about the proposed association with the overseas territories than they were about the proposed special provisions for agriculture. There was nary a hint of sympathy for the poor people of the Third World. Only Adenauer occasionally spoke of the good Europeans could do in Africa, of the schools and hospitals they could build there (Mahant, 1969:244).

Otherwise, most of the German elites agreed that the principles of liberalism and democracy should extend to the former colonies of European countries. The FDP thought that the governments of the newly independent countries and former French colonies of Tunisia and Morocco should have been consulted about the provisions of the proposed association (Mahant, 1969:255). Leaders of all three major parties – the CDU, the SPD and the FDP – agreed that eventual independence should be the objective of any policy with respect to the existing colonies (Mahant, 1969:55 and 274). When the Treaty of Rome was undergoing the process of approval by the Bundestag, the SPD and the CDU drafted a common resolution expressing their belief that colonies should become independent countries. However, the leaders of the parliamentary parties could not agree on the exact wording of the resolution, so that in the end the Bundestag adopted a CDU/CSU resolution calling for the 'political autonomy' of the overseas territories, while the SPD moved its own resolution calling for their independence (Paterson, 1974:128-129).

Only the agricultural interest groups dissented from this democratic consensus. They argued that the association with the overseas territories constituted an 'adulteration of the European idea'. They also feared that the inclusion of the overseas territories would have a negative impact on the status European farmers could hope to enjoy within the new community since the status of the producers from the colonies 'will always' be 'completely different from that which the European farmers must have...' (both citations from Mahant, 1969:304). These quotations are from a telegram which the agricultural groups sent to Adenauer on February 19, 1957, that is during the last stages of the negotiations of the Treaty of Rome, and the telegram contains no further information as to what this difference in status might have meant.

Most of the comments the German elites made about the association with the overseas territories perceived the issue from the point of the national interest of the Federal Republic and the Germans. And here the commentators could find little to cheer about. The business community, the FDP and even the trade unions pointed out that the association would cost Germany money because the government would have to contribute to an investment fund for the overseas territories (Couve de Murville, 1957; Mahant, 1969:255, 282-3 and 296). German farmers feared competition from cheaply produced agricultural products, and the manufacturers of non-ferrous metals had similar concerns about competition from minerals produced in the overseas territories (Mahant, 1969:304; Rhenisch, 1994:215). The unions feared immigration from the overseas territories (Mahant, 1969:296). Erhard, officials in the Ministry of Economics and the business community objected to the creation of a preferential trade area for the overseas territories. They would have preferred world-wide free trade (Küsters, 1989:423-424; Mahant, 1969:283; Rhenisch, 1994:166 and 225-6). Fritz Hellwig and other leading members of the CDU as well as business leaders objected that a special association with former French and Belgian colonies would harm both Germany's trading and its political relationship with other developing areas, such as Latin America (Mahant, 1969:245; Rhenisch, 1994:166-7 and 225-6).

Leaders of both the CDU and the SPD and of the business community warned that Germany might be tainted with the brush marks of French colonialism and that to avoid such a fate, foreign aid money should go to all needy countries equally, not just to the former colonies of France and Belgium (Mahant, 1969:245, 272 and 283). SPD speakers said that any association with colonialism would constitute an abuse of the European idea (Küsters, 1989:425). The trade union leadership added that a preferential trade area might increase the cost of tropical goods, luxuries which had so recently reappeared on the German consumer market (Mahant, 1969:295).

Only a few Germans could find anything positive to say about the proposed association with the overseas territories. Adenauer spoke of access to African raw materials and African energy, such as oil and hydroelectric power. Yet the CDU magazine, which usually treated Adenauer with the greatest of deference, greeted his ideas about the association with the overseas territories with the sarcastic headline 'Adenauer has Visions' (Mahant, 1969:245). Other CDU speakers consoled themselves that the sacrifices made for the overseas territories would be worth the reward, reconciliation with France and closer ties with other Western countries (Küsters, 1989:425). A speaker for the small German Party (a regional party from the Hanover area) was one of the few who showed genuine enthusiasm for the association with the overseas territories. He had been a member of a European parliamentary delegation which had toured the French colonies, and he came back convinced that the peoples of these territories favoured the association with these territories and that democracy had a promising future there (Mahant, 1969:259).

A very few Germans saw a wider European interest in the association with the overseas territories. Adenauer believed that the European Economic Community would increase 'European influence in underdeveloped regions such as Africa, where, she might pose, for historical reasons as a privileged partner, assuring that the poorer countries would not be pushed back into a new era of colonialisation' (Knipping,

1992). Some German industrialists, whom a group of French business leaders had invited to a meeting about the common market, came back convinced that Africa represented not only a good source of raw materials for Europe but also a potential market for European-produced consumer goods (Rhenisch, 1994:67-68).

In spite of such occasional bursts of enthusiasm, most German elites had only negative comments about the association with the overseas territories. Even CDU deputies and ministers could not find anything better to say than that the association was a necessary sacrifice that Germans had to make in order to get the government of France to accept the European Economic Community (Mahant, 1969:245).

Concluding Comments

As expected, the idea of a united Europe received overwhelming support from German elites. Among those who were actively and prominently involved in politics in the mid-1950s, hardly anyone spoke up for the idea of the sovereign nation-state or opposed a united Europe on principle. This support in turn translated into nearly unanimous support for the idea of a European common market and then the Treaty of Rome. The Free Democratic Party was the only significant group which opposed the ratification of the Treaty, and that move can be at least partly explained in terms of political opportunism. In an election year, when both major political parties supported the Treaty, the FDP could distinguish itself by pointing out those measures in the Treaty of Rome about which many Germans felt some unease.

But in spite of this widespread support for a united Europe almost as a value in its own right, most of the German elites had a highly developed concept of their own interests and of the interest of their country, the Federal Republic of Germany. Most German business leaders, for example, believed that a common agricultural policy, an association with the former colonies and probably also the harmonisation of social policies, were all measures which would not promote the economic interests of German business. The leaders of the agricultural groups also knew that any European agricultural policy was likely to be less economically advantageous for them than the existing German policies. However, all of them were willing to accept, and in the case of business leaders even to promote, a European common market, because they saw a wider national interest, that of Germany being accepted as a member of the European and the international community. Hence the frequent use of words such as sacrifice. That said, it was, of course, also true that German business expected to benefit from a wider European market. Indeed, their argument was: the wider the market, the greater the benefit. Most of German business would like to have seen a larger free trade area, as proposed by Britain, rather than a customs union limited to six countries (Mahant, 1969:280). In Carl Friedrich's words, 'businessmen found the courage to accept the proposed experiment, a courage which was to be rewarded by a remarkable degree of forward movement and industrial progress' (Friedrich, 1969:52).

Most of Germany's political leaders had, by 1955, decided to accept the main outlines of the foreign policy shaped by Adenauer, and this foreign policy included a vision of a Europe united in a particular fashion, that of a supranational community to which the member states would cede some of their sovereignty. Supranationality in turn meant a small community of six countries, since other governments, such as those of Britain and the Scandinavian countries, were not yet ready to accept the concept of a supranational community. So in summary, being a good European meant giving up sovereignty and accepting supranationality, and to achieve supranationality, the German government had to accept a small community of just six member states and perhaps to make other economic sacrifices. One could thus argue that German elites saw support of the European idea and European unification as being in their own and their country's interest, so that it becomes impossible to disentangle material and geopolitical interests from values and ideals.

So as the negotiations for the Treaty of Rome progressed, French negotiators heard that their German counterparts were willing to make sacrifices. If the French did not hear this from the negotiators themselves, they certainly heard it from the German press and saw it in reports from their diplomats in Bonn (Couve de Murville, 1957). One would expect, therefore, that the Treaty as concluded would reflect a French, rather than a German, vision of Europe. But did it? This is a topic to which I turn in the next chapter.

5 National Elites and the Negotiation of the Treaty of Rome

This chapter continues the penetration to the core of the topic of this book. Chapters 3 and 4 analysed the attitudes of national elites toward the negotiations of the first Treaty of Rome. This study begins an examination of the extent to which the ideas and interests of national elites in France and Germany may have influenced the negotiations and the contents of the Treaty which created the European Economic Community. Where to begin such a discussion is a dilemma. Does one begin with the position of the governments, from whom the idea of the creation of a common market undoubtedly came? (At least that is where it originated in the spring of 1955.) Or does one begin with the position of the national elites, since democratic theory requires us to assume that the position of the governments was at least to some extent shaped by that of the elites who elected them?

This chapter will use a bit of both approaches, but the second one, that of democratic theory, will predominate. The chapter begins with a guide to the reader in the form of a chronological table which will list and describe briefly the principal landmarks of the negotiations, from their beginnings in the summer of 1955 to the signing of the two Treaties of Rome on March 25, 1957. The next section will examine the extent to which the non-governmental elites were in direct contact with the two governments and their negotiators. The following section examines the decision-making process within the French and German governments. How did the two governments arrive at their negotiating positions? Who participated in the making of key decisions? When were those decisions made? What factors appear to have influenced the decision-makers? Determining how each of the two governments determined its own negotiating position will set the stage for the next chapter which will deal with the negotiations themselves.

A Capsule Summary of the Negotiations Leading to the Treaty of Rome

June 3, 1955 – The Messina meeting of the six foreign ministers agrees to appoint a committee of experts, which will study the further integration of Europe, the study to include the idea of a common market. The conference press release states that the committee is to be headed by a 'political personality'.

June 18, 1955 – The six governments agree that Paul-Henri Spaak, the Foreign Minister of Belgium, will be the political personality who will lead the study mentioned in the Messina decision. Spaak in turn convinces the governments to hold the negotiations in Brussels (Ministère, June 18, 1955).

July 9, 1955 – At its first full meeting, the committee of experts decides to appoint a steering committee as well as a number of committees and sub-committees. For the time being, a British representative joins the representatives of the six governments in these meetings (Küsters, 1982:145).

September 6, 1955 – The six foreign ministers meet in Noordwijk (the Netherlands) and decide to tell the committee of experts to continue its work.

November 29, 1955 – The French government resigns after losing a vote in the National Assembly.

January 2, 1956 – National Assembly elections in France; the parties of the centre and moderate Right and Left lose, and the extremes (Communists and Poujadists) gain votes.

January 31, 1956 – A new French government led by the Socialist Guy Mollet and with a Socialist Foreign Minister, Christian Pineau, is formed.

February 11-12, 1956 – At a meeting of the six foreign ministers, Christian Pineau says that he cannot commit his government to the common market until he has consulted French interest groups.

March 3, 1956 – A brief meeting between Adenauer and foreign minister Pineau, followed by a meeting between German foreign minister Brentano and Pineau. Adenauer talks about the 'European idea'; the communiqué only mentions that the two peoples should 'encourage the development of an economic community…' (Ministère, March 3, 1956).

March 7-9, 1956 – A meeting of the heads of the six delegations in Brussels studies a first draft of the report of the committee of experts (since known as the Spaak Report). The report is then circulated to the six governments.

April 21, 1956 – The revised Spaak Report is released.

May 29-30, 1956 – The six foreign ministers meet in Venice and decide to negotiate two treaties based on the contents of the Spaak Report. Spaak is asked to lead these negotiations, and each government is asked to name one head of delegation.

June 15, 1956 – After Maurice Faure, the head of the French delegation, travels to London to consult with the British government, the British decision to withdraw from the negotiations is confirmed.

June 26, 1956 – The Treaty drafting conference first meets in Brussels (Küsters, 1982:260).

July 9, 1956 – The heads of delegation meet in Brussels; this marks the beginning of the second half of the Brussels negotiations.

July 26, 1956 – The heads of delegation meet in Brussels to hear a French declaration of intention to proceed with negotiations of both Euratom and the common market. Shortly thereafter Donnedieu de Vabres replaces Olivier Wormser as head of the French common market negotiating team (Küsters, 1982:298).

September 16, 1956 – At a series of meetings in Berlin, Maurice Faure meets with Chancellor Adenauer and Ministers Brentano and Erhard. They all agree that they want to continue the process of European integration (Ministère, Sept.16, 1956).

Early October 1956 – The Brussels conference produces a first draft of the EEC Treaty.

October 20-21, 1956 – The foreign (and some other) ministers of the six governments meet in Paris to discuss some of the issues the Brussels conference had not been able to resolve.

November 6, 1956 – Chancellor Adenauer, Prime Minister Mollet and Foreign Minister Pineau meet in Paris and resolve several of the issues that the October meetings had left unresolved.

December 13, 1956 – The six foreign ministers meet 'in the margins' of a NATO meeting in an effort to resolve some of the outstanding issues.

January 15-22, 1957 – The French National Assembly debates and approves in principle the government's plans to negotiate treaties creating an economic and an atomic energy community.

January 26-28, 1957 – The six foreign ministers meet to consider revised drafts of the two treaties and to resolve unresolved issues with respect to agriculture and the overseas territories.

February 4, 1957 – The six foreign ministers continue their meeting of January 28 to resolve outstanding issues.

February 18-19, 1957 – The six heads of government and foreign ministers meet in Paris to discuss outstanding issues, notably the association of the overseas territories with the EEC. However, several issues remain unresolved.

March 25, 1957 – The six heads of government and foreign ministers gather in Rome to sign the treaties creating the European Economic Community and the European Atomic Energy Community. But because the assembled gathering had to decide on some last minute issues not yet resolved, the ministers in fact sign blank documents which consist of the titles of the two treaties only.

January 1, 1958 – After ratification by the six governments, the two Treaties of Rome enter into force.

Contacts Between Negotiators and Elites

It is extraordinarily difficult to determine the extent to which interest groups and other domestic forces may influence any specific set of international negotiations. A government's negotiators may want to show that they are responsive to domestic opinion, but at the same time, they want to demonstrate that they are not 'in the pocket' of any so-called 'special' interest groups, forgetting that all interests are by definition particular to that group, and therefore, presumably, 'special'. Many contacts between groups, governments and negotiators will take place behind closed doors, or over the phone, or in informal settings such as restaurants. This is especially true of France, where the system of *pantouflage* between public and private administration (which in turn draws from a common source, the *grandes écoles*) facilitated contacts between groups and government (Simonian, 1985:61).

In the 1950s, the situation was different in Germany where interest groups colonized various ministries. Thus the agricultural groups maintained close contacts with the Ministry of Food, Agriculture and Forestry (hereinafter referred to as the Ministry of Agriculture), the refugee groups with the ministry responsible for refugees, and trade unions with the Ministry of Labour. Business and employer groups had to choose between the Chancellor and the Ministry of Economics. They, of course, lobbied both, but their influence seems to have been greater with the former.

Even more difficult to gauge is the extent to which the influence of groups and political parties flows directly to the negotiators through direct contact on specific issues. This influence may be, to some extent, indirect, in the sense that the party's or group's position may be anticipated by the negotiators or may be passed on by the media. Thus the reports of German diplomats in Paris and Brussels include a number of analyses of the position of the French political parties represented in the National Assembly, since it was the Assembly which had killed the EDC, and, therefore, it was important for all the delegations to anticipate the likely reactions of the French political parties. Similarly when, in January 1957, the French deputy, Leopold Senghor, spoke out against the association of the French overseas territories with the EEC, the German consul from Dakar sent a long report to the Foreign Ministry (AA, Jan 18, 1957).

Here I take the position that evidence of contact between political parties, groups and the negotiators deserves special attention, even though these groups could have influenced the negotiators via several other routes and contact does not necessarily denote influence. There is some, though limited, evidence of contact between French negotiators and interest groups. It is almost as if the persons who wrote Foreign Ministry notes for posterity, or perhaps those who selected what would go into the archives, were careful to maintain the illusion of a French state which rises above the particular interests of specific groups and interests. So archival references to consultation with or even thoughts about interest groups are few.

In the Wormser papers, and therefore presumably written by Wormser, there is an analysis of the negotiations to date, written for Pineau and dated February 8, 1956. There the author stresses the need to reassure the unions because they may fear the common market project (Ministère, Feb. 8, 1956). At the meeting of the six foreign ministers in February 11-12, 1956, Pineau was careful to tell his colleagues that he was consulting French interest because he wanted to 'avoid a failure' (Comité, Feb.11-12, 1956). Similarly, at the Venice conference at the end of May, Pineau pointed out that he had referred the issue of the common market to the French Economic and Social Council before he consulted other ministries (Conférence, May 29-30, 1956). Writing from Brussels, the head of the German negotiating team, Carl Friedrich Ophüls, claimed that the French *patronat* had sent a special messenger (not just a message) to the Venice conference, to inform the French delegation of its approval of the association of the overseas territories with the proposed common market (AA, June 21bis, 1956).

Robert Marjolin, who was the active head of the French negotiating team while Maurice Faure looked after the politics in Paris, spent the weeks before the opening of formal negotiations on June 26, 1956, consulting business, agricultural and professional groups so as to assure himself of their support during the negotiations (Küsters, 1982:297-8). There is little in the Foreign Ministry archives about contacts with groups after that time. The leader of the *Confédération Générale de Petites et Moyennes Entreprises* (CGPME), which opposed the European Economic Community in its entirety, asked to see the Minister only after the Treaty was signed and was then allowed to speak only to the minister's *chef de cabinet* (Ministère, April 12 and May 16, 1957).

German groups were not so fortunate. A letter of August 1955, from the association representing the German construction industry to the

Ministry of Foreign Affairs, expressed great interest in the proposed European transportation network (mentioned in the Messina resolution but dropped from the plans by the time of the Venice Conference). The letter received a curt reply, informing the association that for the time being the negotiations were only open to governmental representatives (AA, Aug.12, 1955). On June 21, 1956, Carl Friedrich Ophüls, the second in command of the German delegation, suggested that business groups and unions be consulted only by means of an arms lengths procedure, whereby experts who were not themselves members of the delegation would speak to such groups. He seems not have received a reply (AA, June 23, 1956).

Though business groups had informal access to the Chancellor's office, and used that access to assure him of their support during the negotiations (AA, June 1956), it was late autumn 1956 before Alfred Müller-Armack of the Economics Ministry and the negotiating team met with some interest group representatives, but supposedly only for the purpose of informing them about the negotiations. In December, when another representative of the business groups (Beutler) asked to have his group included in the negotiations, since, according to him, Belgium and the Netherlands had made such arrangements, the officials in the foreign ministry agreed that this was out of the question; they differed only on whether to give interest groups documents from the negotiations or to allow them to get such documentation from cognate groups in other countries. It was January 1957, when the main outlines of the Treaty were already in place, when some German interest groups, including the BDI, were consulted about the negotiations. At that point, the negotiators agreed also to consult representatives of farming and the trade unions, though it is not clear whether such consultations took place. As late as February 1957, the agricultural groups were asking the Chancellor's office for access to the negotiators, and they were once again referred to the Ministry of Agriculture (Küsters, 1982:260, 275-6 and 426; AA, Dec. 14 and 17, 1956; AA, Jan. [date unspecified] and Feb. 2, 1957).

The groups representing German agriculture, who for the most were supporters of the governing Christian Democrats, showed great perseverance and cleverness in gaining access to the negotiators, if not necessarily the negotiations. They began in August 1956, when the head of the main agricultural interest group, Dr. Andreas Hermes, asked to speak to a senior foreign ministry official. A briefing note for said official (Karl Carstens) asks him to keep the discussion to very general topics and to seek to postpone substantive discussions to a later date (AA, Aug. 24, 1956). On October 23, 1956, the agricultural interest groups once again asked for a meeting with foreign ministry officials. They were told to go and speak to the Ministry of Agriculture, which they did do (on October 26), but on October 29, they were once again knocking on the door of the Foreign Ministry, asking to be 'instructed' about the 'political issues' relating to the common market. They were then granted a meeting, which took place on November 3. The discussions soon turned from general political issues to the common external tariff on agricultural products and the price of fodder and potatoes. The leaders of the agricultural groups specifically expressed their opposition to the idea of a free market.

The agricultural groups returned to the fray in January 1957, upon hearing that business groups had met with the German delegation. This time a foreign ministry official advised that their request be treated without urgency ('*dilatorisch*') since the groups had had plenty of chance to be consulted. A ministry official accordingly drafted a letter to the groups, in which he advised them that if interest groups were to be consulted about the negotiations, consumers and unions as well as farmers would be included (AA, Oct. 23, 1956; Oct. 31, 1956; Nov. 6, 1956; Jan. 1957 [day unspecified]; Jan.17, 1957). This last statement constituted a not too subtle attempt to intimidate the agricultural groups, since unions and consumers were likely to advocate more imports and lower food prices.

It is now time to cross the divide between groups and government and to look at the process of determining the national negotiating position as it occurred within the two governments.

Determination of the National Negotiating Positions

If it is difficult to determine what happened between groups and government, it is equally difficult to trace the determination of the national negotiating positions. If the archival record is to be believed, the German government was in a constant state of internal warfare, with ministries fighting it out over various European issues, while within the French government there was one national negotiating position, with only the occasional polite hint of dissension. This, of course, was not the case. There *were* differences within the French government, and within the German government Adenauer's strong will and dominating influence usually prevailed over the positions of the various ministry officials and ministers. It helped that the German foreign ministry was a recent creation, so that most of the senior bureaucrats were Adenauer's personal choices (Lee in Deighton, 1955). It also helped that there were a number of senior bureaucrats, more so in Germany than in France, who really believed in the building of a new Europe, over and beyond the nation-states. Marjolin in France and Hanns von der Groeben and Ophüls in Germany were of their number.

In France, there was not only the sharp division among political parties, discussed in Chapter 3, but also a division between politicians and officials, with the former generally taking a stronger pro-European position than the latter. Indeed, a number of the senior administrators showed great scepticism toward the idea of a common market, as, privately, did Pineau, who became foreign minister in January 1956. According to Lynch (1997:171-2), the Foreign Ministry was so opposed to the idea of a common market that Wormser dreamt up a Machiavellian scheme whereby France would appear not to be supporting both Euratom and the common market, and would then look good by allowing only Euratom to be created. Also, an unsigned note of October 10, 1955, addressed to the Prime Minister, asks him to keep Pierre Pflimlin and Félix Gaillard (both ministers) in line, so that they do not create difficulties for the negotiators, presumably because of their excessive European enthusiasm (Ministère, Oct. 10, 1955). It was because of such differences that the French delegation did not receive its initial negotiating instructions until October 1955.

However, differences within the ministry persisted. On March 30, 1956, a bureaucrat from the Directorate for Economic and Financial Affairs wrote an analysis, it seems to no one in particular, warning that 'entire regions' of France could become the scene of 'economic and social turmoil' if France were subjected to free trade (Ministère, March 30, 1956). Girault credits lobbying by Jean Monnet's recently created Action Committee for a United States of Europe for convincing some French officials to shed their scepticism (Girault in di Nolfo, 1992; Küsters, 1982:254, 271, 294 and 299).

The French negotiating position toward the negotiations did not come unreservedly positive until Pineau appointed a strong supporter of Europe, Robert Marjolin, as his *chef de cabinet*[1] in May 1956. (Marjolin's position on Europe was not the reason for his appointment.) Prime Minister Mollet had already put two pro-Europeans, Emile Noël and Donnedieu de

1 The French word *cabinet* refers to the small group of close advisors which a minister appoints outside of the regular civil service hiring procedure. It needs to be distinguished from the British 'cabinet' which refers to the ministers themselves as a group. Here *cabinet* will be italicized when it is used in the French sense.

Vabres, in charge of his *cabinet*. There was also some support from the ministries of finance (Bernard Clappier was particularly supportive) and overseas territories. Together these three bureaucrats and their supposed masters were able to persuade most of the rest of the government. When the French cabinet formally approved the negotiations in September 1956, there was still hesitation from some ministers, but the decision was to go ahead if the French conditions could be met (Lynch, 1997:178).

Shortly after the beginning of the preliminary negotiations in Brussels, the French government created an Interministerial Committee on Issues of European Economic Cooperation, chaired by Alexandre Verret. The Committee was based in the Prime Minister's office, and the three Prime Ministers who held office during the course of the negotiations took a personal interest in its work. Robert Marjolin describes how opposed to the common market most members of this committee were and how Verret repeatedly had to appeal to Emil Noël and through him to the Prime Minister in order to overrule the sceptical bureaucrats (Marjolin, 1986:285-6 and 298). By 1956, this committee consisted of forty representatives of various ministries and parts thereof (Küsters, 1982:271). It became so large that it required a secretariat of three and sprouted an executive committee of eleven and a sub-committee of thirteen to study the issue of the overseas territories (Ministère, July 20, 1956). According to a report from the German embassy in Paris, the Verret committee met on September 4, 1956, with the participation of the Prime Minister, the Minister of Finance and Maurice Faure, the head of the French negotiating team in Brussels. The Committee, nevertheless, concluded that a common market should not be created in the near future (AA, Sept. 5, 1956).

After the draft Spaak Report became available to the governments, an interministerial meeting of senior bureaucrats met for the purpose of drafting instructions for the French delegation. Not surprisingly, the ministry of agriculture insisted on a common agricultural policy. The ministry of social affairs stressed need for harmonisation of social benefits, even a European minimum wage, and raised the issue of the freedom of movement for Algerian workers already resident in France. Everyone agreed that the situation should be reviewed after five years, that is before the completion of the common market (Ministère, May 12. 1956).[2]

Arriving at the French negotiating position was complicated by the fact that the French government could not count on the support of the

---

2 This document is reproduced on a poor quality microfilm, so dark as to be almost illegible. Parts of lines are missing and the date could be May 12 or 13.

National Assembly, so that the government had to constantly negotiate with the political parties of the moderate left, the centre and the moderate right. Without their almost unanimous support, it would be impossible to get a treaty adopted by the National Assembly, where the Communists, the far right Poujadists and the hard-core Gaullists (there were also more flexible dissident Gaullists) held over 200 of the 596 seats. Another complicating factor was that the more extremist parties usually voted as a bloc, whereas the moderate parties split on many important issues. On the question of the institutions of the EEC and Euratom, for example, Pineau promised the Gaullists that the new communities would have institutions which were completely separate from those of the supranational ECSC (Küsters, 1982:296), a promise which in the end the next government was not able to keep.

Bureaucratic opposition to supranational institutions was also strong. On October 11, 1955, a bureaucrat warned that the creation of supranational institutions could create problems similar to those created by the dreaded EDC (Ministère, Oct. 11, 1955). Once the Spaak Report had been circulated, someone in the Directorate for Economic and Financial Affairs of the Foreign Ministry (presumably Wormser) wrote a number of alarmist memos, addressed to no one in particular, but warning of the consequences of the creation of supranational institutions. In the most alarmist of these 'notes', the writer warned that supranational institutions might lead to a common foreign policy and even the alignment of domestic policies. A common political authority might in turn lead to '*une véritable rébellion*' against the supranational authority, and once the authority was created there would be no way of turning back (Ministère, April 21, 1956) – a position which surely lacked some consistency.

With respect to social harmonisation, there was little difficulty in arriving at the French position, since practically all parties, interest groups and bureaucrats agreed that other European governments should raise their benefits to the supposedly higher French level. Specifically, the French position was that in all six countries, there should be legislation guaranteeing men and women the same pay for the same work, that paid holidays should have the same legal minimum length as they had in France, and that employers should be required to pay overtime premiums if a worker worked more than forty hours a week. These conditions were included in the negotiating position that the government sent to its delegation in October 1955. The cabinet reiterated them in its position on the Spaak Report. In July 1956, the French Economic and Social Council repeated these demands in its commentary on the draft treaty, and the cabinet insisted on them in September 1956, before it agreed to negotiations on the basis of the Spaak Report (Lynch, 1997:172-8; Küsters, 1982:299-300; Marjolin, 1986:287-88). Nevertheless, there was at least one bureaucrat who thought price disparities were a result of the distorted exchange rate (Ministère, April 25, 1956), while another unnamed bureaucrat found it necessary to warn the then Prime Minister Edgar Faure (no relation to the negotiator Maurice Faure) that France would suffer 'serious inconveniences' if social harmonisation were abandoned (Ministère, Oct. 10, 1955).

Wormser tried to reinterpret the data collected for an earlier study of the effects of OEEC-wide freer trade and found that nearly every French manufacturing industry would suffer if there was no social harmonisation (Ministère, March 26, 1956). The anonymous note writer in the directorate for Economic and Financial Affairs insisted that there had to be the same precision with respect to the harmonisation of social legislation as there was with respect to the creation of a customs union (Ministère, May 3, 1956 and June 23, 1956). Only one French diplomat expressed reservations about the need for social harmonisation. Maurice Couve de Murville, the ambassador in Bonn, pointed out that as the German standard of living rose, social harmonisation would become unnecessary (Ministère, Jan. 23, 1957). Marjolin, in a conversation with the German ambassador, claimed that the three basic French demands on social harmonisation were merely a sop to the National Assembly and public opinion; it was, he said, a '*question de présentation*' (AA, Oct. 26, 1956).

There was a similar degree of agreement with respect to agriculture. Most French interest groups, political parties and bureaucrats agreed that there should be special provisions for agriculture, notably some kind of European priority in the purchase of agricultural products, protection for European farmers and, ideally, a European agricultural policy. Such a policy was included in the French negotiating position of October 1955 and the comments on the Spaak Report in May 1956. The chief negotiator, Maurice Faure, promised just such a policy to the National Assembly in January 1957, before the Assembly approved the EEC in principle (Küsters, 1982:350; Lynch, 1997:174; Marjolin, 1986:287).

The French negotiating position was almost as clear cut with respect to the overseas territories as it was with respect to agriculture. The Economic and Social Council as well as the business community agreed that the French overseas territories should be associated with the common market, preferably in a manner which would not jeopardize French markets there and that all the member states should contribute the investment capital the overseas territories needed for their development (Küsters, 1982:301). Association for the French overseas territories was one of the conditions Pineau posed at Venice, and it was included in the cabinet's conditions in September 1956.

However, while agreeing on the need for the association if there was to be a common market, not all insiders agreed that the association would be beneficial to France. On March 30, 1956, a bureaucrat from the Foreign Ministry warned of 'unspecified' economic and political consequences if the markets of the overseas territories were opened to others (Ministère, March 30, 1956). On April 21, in another anonymous memo, the bureaucrat (presumably the same person) warned that a European common market could not co-exist with the French-led economic system which was now all that gave a 'certain cohesion to what was left of the French Empire' (Ministère, April 21, 1956; quotation marks in original). On September 27, he warned that France could lose its overseas markets and that, at the very least, the French government should consolidate and rationalize the franc zone before attaching it to Europe (Ministère, Sept. 27, 1956).

Within the ministry of France Overseas, the so-called 'modernizers' were especially interested in European assistance in developing the overseas territories, as against the 'traditionalists' who wanted to keep the French hunting grounds (*chasse gardée*) to themselves or feared European competition there. A study by the ministry made alarmist predictions as to the number of francs and jobs France stood to lose if other Europeans could trade with the overseas territories. Outside the Ministry, Paul Ramadier, Mollet's Minister of Finance, shared the fears of the traditionalists. There appeared to be one means of allaying these fears. European investment funds for the overseas territories, according to French commentators within and without the government, would help to raise the standard of living in the overseas territories and thus increase purchasing power, so that the market could expand to include French as well as other European goods (Girault in di Nolfo, 1992; Lynch, 1997:177-8 and 198-204).

The elected representative of the overseas territories, who met in the form of an advisory assembly called the Assembly of the Union, which met in Paris, voted in favour of the association 100 to 43. This support lent some legitimacy to the French position (Pineau and Rimbaud, 1991:273-4).

In Germany, the situation was almost exactly the reverse of what it was in France. Unlike the French, the German government could count on the support of the major interest groups and political parties to support European integration, but within the government the German negotiating position was the subject of constant bureaucratic and even political warfare. The Ministry of Foreign Affairs and the Ministry of Agriculture each had its own position, while the Ministry of Economics was the site of an internal dispute, with the Schuman Plan (read ECSC) division somewhat favourably disposed toward the common market, whereas the Minister, Ludwig Erhard, and at least one other division would have preferred an OEEC-wide free trade area (Müller-Armack, 1971:111-12). Before long, divisions also appeared within the Ministry of Foreign Affairs, so that at one point one division was accusing another of trying to monopolize control of the negotiations (AA, Nov. 20, 1956). The problems intensified toward the end of the negotiations, when the federal states became involved, demanding that they be consulted, a consultation which they were soon granted (AA, Nov. 17, 1956, Dec. 5, 1956 and Jan. 24, 1957). The bureaucratic and political infighting was so intense that even memos from Adenauer could not still the conflict. Even now, close to fifty years later, one can almost feel the sharpening of pencils and the aura of tension when the call went out for a *Ressortbesprechung* (an interministerial meeting at official level).

The conflict among the two divisions of the Ministry of Economics and the Foreign Ministry began before the Messina Conference. On May 22, 1955, representatives of all three groups, including Minister Erhard and the man about to become foreign minister, Heinrich von Brentano, met at the country house of a senior official from the Ministry of Economics (Alfred Müller-Armack). The von der Groeben group from the Ministry of Economics wanted a common market with free movement of goods and factors of production, common rules of competition and institutions which could govern such a market. The Erhard group wanted free trade under GATT with minimum interference from institutions. The Foreign Ministry, represented by Ophüls and Brentano, wanted to build on the supranational institutions of the Coal and Steel Community. The three groups came to a compromise, dubbed the Eichenscheider decisions, after the country house where the meeting took place. These decisions glossed over some of the differences and thus soon led to further confusion, to a point where, when the pre-conference began in Brussels, Walter Hallstein, the leader of the German delegation, opened the meeting with a statement of German support for the common market concept, since a recently published statement from the Ministry of Economics had cast some doubt on the German position (Küsters, 1982:116-118, 141-2 and 145). The

Schuman Plan section of the Ministry of Economics won a temporary victory when it was designated the lead section for the pre-negotiations, but the Foreign Ministry had the last laugh when the Chancellor's office gave it the lead for the substantive negotiations which began in June 1956, though an official from the Ministry of Economics, von der Groeben, was chosen by Spaak to head the committee which negotiated and drafted the common market treaty (Küsters, 1982:273-4).

Erhard continued his rearguard fight for more free trade and less common market after the publication of the Spaak Report. A memo from Adenauer, expressing his clear preferences for a supranational Europe (AA, January 19, 1956) did not put an end to the dissension, which continued throughout the negotiations (Küsters, 1982:225). In September 1956, when the chief French negotiator, Maurice Faure, made a visit to Berlin and Bonn, Erhard complained about the degree of social harmonisation demanded by the French. At a meeting with Adenauer the next day, Adenauer expressed enthusiasm about the European idea. Faure pointed out that Erhard had 'unfortunately used very different language' on the previous day (Ministère, Sept. 16-17, 1956).

In October 1956, Erhard and Franz-Josef Strauss, the Minister for Atomic Energy, who only days earlier had been named Minister of Defence, insisted on attending the meeting of the six foreign ministers, to the horrified amazement of foreign office officials (AA Oct. 18, 1955). As late as December 1956, Erhard was conducting separate negotiations with the British with the hope of creating an OEEC-wide free trade area (AA, Dec. 10, 1956). When the treaty was all but complete, Erhard publicly called it an over-armoured tank and labelled the Eisenhower administration romantics for supporting it, a statement which led to a protest from the French government. In the absence of Adenauer, his chief of staff Hans Globke promised to inform his boss immediately of what Erhard had said. This, however, was not sufficient for the French ambassador, Maurice Couve de Murville, who asked his ministry that he be authorized to give Erhard a 'frank explanation' of the French position, so that Erhard would be given to understand that his position 'was compatible with the policies of neither the German nor the French government' (AA, March 15, 1957; Küsters, 1982:423; Lynch, 1997:180).

With such public displays of intra-German differences, it is not surprising that the French government followed developments within the German government closely. The French archives contain a number of reports about the differences among the German governing parties, and in 1955 and in 1956, the French embassy in Bonn seems also to have had information from closed meetings, such as those of the German cabinet and the executive of the governing Christian Democratic party. These reports stopped after Couve de Murville replaced Louis Joxe as ambassador to Germany.

The first German interministerial meeting with respect to the common market negotiations occurred on June 20, 1955. Ophüls, from the Foreign Ministry, made a plea for the overall political advantages of uniting western Europe. Surprisingly, there seems to have been little dissension – surprisingly, because only a few days earlier an angry representative of the Finance Ministry had called the Foreign Ministry to complain about the plan for a readaptation fund. At the meeting of June 20, the representative from the Ministry of Agriculture thanked the Messina Conference for having remembered the special position of agriculture. Ophüls asked each ministry to name a representative, of not too senior a level, to the Brussels negotiating team (AA, June 15 and June 20, 1955), so that by September 2, there was a delegation of eleven negotiators representing eight different ministries (AA, Sept. 2, 1955).

There was a delegation, but no negotiating position. By September 29, the Chancellor's office wrote to the Foreign Ministry and the Ministry of Economics that the cabinet was urgently awaiting a draft negotiating position. On October 10, Ophüls wrote from Brussels, offering to make a report on the negotiations to date, with a view to having the cabinet adopt a negotiating position. By November 8, things seem not to have progressed very much. The chancellor's office addressed a similar message to the same two ministries, while also reminding the Foreign Ministry not to forget that the ministries of Agriculture and Finance were also interested in the Brussels negotiations (AA, Sept. 29, Oct. 10 and Nov. 8, 1955).

By November 9, the Foreign Ministry had produced a report on the status of the negotiations for cabinet approval. Carstens sent it forward accompanied by a flurry of memos, one asking the Chancellor to speak to some of the other ministers to remind them of the importance of the success of the project, another asking that von der Groeben be given the permission to speak to the leaders of interest groups who might be opposed to the project, and yet another asking Brentano and Erhard to sign the report for submission to cabinet (AA, Nov. 9, 1955, four times). The cabinet did discuss the report, but did not come to any conclusion on either Euratom or the common market. In January 1956, von der Groeben was still asking his government for a clear commitment to the common market (Küsters, 1982:223-5).

The federal cabinet did eventually approve the Spaak Report (on May 9, 1956) as the basis for further negotiations and authorized the Foreign Ministry to enter into negotiations to that end (AA, Oct. 8, 1956), but when it came to determine a negotiating position for the second part of the Brussels conference, infighting once again dominated over the national interest. The cabinet was supposed to discuss the negotiating position on June 26. Adenauer named the German negotiating team the day before. It was to be headed by Ophüls from the Foreign Ministry; Müller-Armack, from the Erhard wing of the Economics Ministry, was to be Germany's chief negotiator for the common market. Spaak had already named von der Groeben, from the ECSC (Schuman Plan) section of the Economics Ministry, as chair of the committee on the common market. Thus all three principal factions were represented on the German delegation (AA, July 5, 1956).

The cabinet asked a committee to deal with the various aspects of the negotiating position. In the meanwhile, Adenauer approved the German position, without a full cabinet discussion. A relieved Hartlieb, of the Foreign Ministry, wrote that a full cabinet discussion was now no longer necessary. He suggested that the Foreign Ministry, as the lead ministry for the negotiations, should, after consultation with the Ministry of Economics, proceed to write a report on their progress (AA, August 16, 1956).

Hartlieb's optimism did not last long. On September 1, the Ministry of Economics hosted its own interministerial meeting. Here Müller-Armack reported that the common market negotiations were not going well, so he presented his own proposal for an OEEC-wide free trade area. Carstens, for the Foreign Ministry, disagreed with Müller-Armack's assessment of the negotiations. A few days later, Hartlieb warned of 'disastrous consequences' if the Germans pursued the idea of a Western Europe wide free trade area, since the French could not possibly accept such a proposal (AA, Sept. 11, 1956). On October 5, the federal cabinet met and decided to continue the negotiations and to support supranational institutions for the two new communities (AA, Oct. 6, 1956).

The cabinet decision did not deter Erhard, who insisted on attending the next foreign ministers meeting, even though the German Foreign Ministry as well as the other delegations, who were sending only their foreign ministers, objected (AA, Oct. 18, 1956). With Strauss and Erhard in attendance, there were at least three German positions at the October 21 foreign ministers meeting. Not surprisingly, there was no agreement on the major issues. On November 6, Adenauer and Mollet met to settle a number of outstanding issues, and they were thus left to deal with the issues that the ministers from the six countries had not been able to settle. After the meeting, Adenauer sent a short letter to Brentano, attaching the decisions that he and Mollet had made and instructing the heads of the German *and* French delegations to consider this, as yet not fully negotiated, settlement as binding (AA, Nov. 7, 1956). (For the substance of these negotiations, see Chapter 6 of this book).

On the issue of the institutions of the common market, there was a clear difference of opinion between the three groups within the German government. Erhard's group wanted intergovernmental institutions with limited powers, since he feared that common institutions might hamper free trade (Müller-Armack, 1971:117). Von der Groeben's group, also from the Ministry of Economics, wanted institutions which had the power to enforce free competition, a common monetary policy, free movement of goods, services and capital and a common commercial policy. The foreign ministry wanted Europe for the sake of Europe, with institutions which were supranational. It won a temporary victory when, on July 7, 1955, the deputy Chancellor, Franz Blücher, instructed the German delegation to negotiate for supranational institutions which specifically included majority voting (Küsters, 1982:116-118, 141-4 and 1995).

The May 9, 1956 cabinet decision to accept the Spaak Report had a definite supranational bend. It insisted that the customs union must be created within a definite time limit, and it looked forward to common economic, monetary and competition policies (AA, Oct. 8, 1956). However, this apparently unified position only lasted for a few weeks. By June 7, 1956, the differences over supranationalism had reached such a stage of acrimony that a German official from the ECSC administration in Luxembourg wrote to Brentano warning him of a scheme by Erhard to rid the German delegation of its two chief negotiators, Hanns von der Groeben and Carl Friedrich Ophüls, whom Erhard apparently found to be 'too European' (AA, June 7, 1956). By October, when Erhard's ministry was making efforts to end the negotiations, the cabinet, in its next decision on the negotiations, again opted for supranational institutions which would be able to decide issues such as the movement from one stage of the common market to another (AA, Oct. 6, 1956). In November, four senior foreign ministry officials met and decided to maintain the push for supranational institutions in spite of the expected opposition from France. In January 1957, Hartlieb wrote to Christian Calmes, the secretary-general of the Brussels conference, suggesting that the new institutions be given some autonomy to decide future issues, such as the time to move from stage one to stage two of the customs union (AA, Nov. 19, 1956 and Jan. 14, 1957).

Erhard did not share the rest of the cabinet's enthusiasm for supranational institutions. He wanted the Council of Ministers to become the major decision-making organ, he opposed the creation of an economic and social committee, and he wanted a parliament (if there was to be one) directly elected rather than chosen among national parliaments because he feared a parliament which was not responsible to its voters might be irresponsibly generous with respect to social policy. The premier of Baden-Württemberg was willing to support a supranational Commission, but only if it agreed to consultations before it made decisions, presumably consultation with the German states (AA, Jan. 14 and 24, 1957). By 1957, the Minister of Finance had joined Erhard in his opposition to supranational institutions. On March 11, 1957, Hartlieb recommended that Germany agree to majority voting on the re-adaptation fund, though this would mean having to 'face' the Minister of Finance who had insisted on unanimity (AA, March 11, 1957).

The intra-German differences were particularly sharp with respect to the subject of social harmonisation. Whereas Erhard's group opposed it ferociously, the Foreign Ministry was prepared to accept it for the sake of the overall success of the negotiations. On June 21, 1956, a small interministerial group met in the Ministry of Economics without the presence of a representative from the Foreign Ministry. They seem to have come to no common conclusion. The Minister of Transport representative emoted about German unification, while the Ministry of Finance representative worried about the continuation of German excise taxes on tobacco, brandy and oil (AA, June 21, 1956). A large interministerial meeting of twenty representatives from ten ministries and offices, on June 30, 1956, was unable to agree on a German negotiating position on social harmonisation; Erhard's representatives did not even want the Brussels conference to set up a study group on this subject, a position he reiterated at another meeting at the Ministry of Economics on July 25 (AA, June 30, 1956 and July 25, 1956).

Various interministerial meetings throughout the summer and into September 1956, were unable to agree on a German position with respect to social harmonisation. On August 16, Hartlieb wrote a long memo for Hallstein, in which he pointed out that there could be no common market treaty unless Germany made some concessions on this issue, but that concessions would not be forthcoming as long as the German negotiators were under 'precise instructions' from the ministries of economics and labour. He believed that only a decision of the federal cabinet could resolve the issue, and that to that end, social harmonisation could perhaps be presented as a German subsidy to French national security, a formulation which he hoped might satisfy the representatives of the Ministry of Economics (AA, July 25, Aug. 3, and Aug. 16 and 16bis). In yet another lengthy memo, on September 11, Hartlieb pleaded with his superiors 'not to burn all bridges' with respect to social harmonisation. He said that he had spoken to Müller-Armack, and that the latter had now shown some openness to the position of the Foreign Ministry – though, Hartlieb added, we will soon see 'whether he has really given up some of his ideas' (AA, Sept. 11, 1956).

On September 29, an attempt by the German delegation in Brussels to summarize the German position on social harmonisation for the upcoming Adenauer-Mollet meeting turned into a catalogue of the positions of the various ministries. After rejecting the similar arguments of the ministries of economics and labour, the foreign ministry writer plaintively defended his ministry against the charge that the negotiators had not taken account of the views of the Ministry of Economics. He added that the specific measures of social harmonisation demanded by the French could be resolved and that the demand for equivalent labour costs was probably just a negotiating position (AA, Sept. 29, 1956).

In October 1956, Erhard was prepared to break off the negotiations if the French insisted on their demands for social harmonisation, and this in spite of a cabinet decision of October 5, which distinguished between negotiable (equal pay for men and women, equal length of holidays) and non-negotiable demands (the 40 hour week and equalization of labour costs) (AA, Oct. 19, 1956). Without clear instructions, the German delegation was unable to respond to French demands, and the negotiations broke off (Küsters, 1982:317-19). When the Chancellor did agree to some of the French demands for social harmonisation, Erhard denounced the concession as 'economic nonsense... without any spirit of liberalism' (Küsters, 1982:332).

Though Adenauer and Mollet may have thought that they settled the outstanding issues of social harmonisation, the German negotiators found more problems to raise. The Minister of Finance had doubts about the re-adaptation fund, and a meeting held at the Ministry of Labour called for a watering down of the social provisions. This ministry advocated an anodyne statement of approximation of standards in an upward direction and close cooperation among governments with specific measures to be left to the unanimous decision of the Council of Ministers (AA, Feb. 5 and 13, 1957).

With respect to agriculture, the German minister responsible for that sector began to express his doubts at a cabinet meeting of November 9, 1955. He wanted his ministry to be more closely involved with the negotiations (Küsters, 1982:222-3). By May 9, 1956, when the federal cabinet was deliberating its position with respect to the Spaak Report, the state secretary for agriculture was alarmed at the prospect of free competition in agricultural trade (Küsters. 1982:228-9). Here the Ministry of Economics agreed with the Foreign Ministry, that agriculture needed to be included in the common market, whereas senior officials from the Ministry of Agriculture feared competition from French and Italian producers. On October 5, 1956, the Minister of Agriculture came to the cabinet meeting with a written statement in which he demanded the continuation of national agricultural policies until a common agricultural policy was in place. He also wanted the cabinet to approve any negotiating position with respect to agriculture (AA, Oct. 5, 1956). This was a position the German negotiators maintained until February 1957 (AA, Dec. [day unspecified] and Dec. 17, 1956). When the negotiators agreed on the principle of a common agricultural policy, it was the Ministry of Economics turn to be opposed; Erhard said that it would lead to a continuation of current levels of national agricultural protection (Küsters, 1982:353).

Only on the subject of the overseas territories was there near unanimity among German groups and officials. Hardly anyone, with the exception of Adenauer, wanted this association, but the German negotiators in Brussels realized that without some agreement on such an association, the French would not accept a European Economic Community. Writing from Brussels on November 16, 1956, one of the German delegates pointed out that France would and could not enter the common market without some agreement on the overseas territories (AA, Nov. 16, 1956). Still, the German negotiators tried to make the unpalatable pill as tasty as it could be made to be. They asked that the leaders of the French African colonies and recent colonies (Morocco, Tunisia) be consulted about the proposed association, and they insisted that everything be done in accordance with the Charter of the United Nations. Above all, the Foreign Ministry wanted to avoid any identification with 'outdated concepts of colonialism' (AA, Oct. 3, 1956, Feb. 14, 1957 and March 12, 1957).

Such pleas, however, did not produce agreement in Bonn, where at an interministerial discussion, Müller-Armack said that it was necessary 'to talk the French out of the idea of making the association with the overseas territories a sina quo non for French participation in the Common Market.' Representatives of several other ministries asked for a delay: get the common market started and when the French have done that, proceed with the association. Carstens, for the Foreign Ministry, argued that the association was needed to stop the spread of communism into Africa. Von der Groeben added that the French already had a special economic relationship with their overseas territories and that the question was not one of 'if' but of 'how' this relationship was to continue once the common market was established. These arguments did not convince the representatives of the other ministries. All the meeting could agree on was that the relevant section of the Foreign Ministry should study the economic effects of the association, keeping in mind the position of the various ministries, and that this study would 'then' become the basis for a common position among the various ministries (AA, Nov. 24 and Nov. 26, 1956).

The next interministerial meeting made progress only to the extent that it assigned further studies to various ministries; for example, the Foreign Ministry was to determine which territories might be included, the Foreign and Economics Ministries were to study the existing trade regimes of the overseas territories, the Ministry of Agriculture and the Foreign Ministry were to study the effect the association might have on German agriculture, and three different ministries were to study the investment fund. One gets the impression that the participants were more interested in who controlled what than they were in determining a German negotiating position (AA, Dec. 3, 1956).

Erhard attempted to at least postpone any decision on the association of the overseas territories to a later date, but his lengthy submission to the cabinet did not produce the result he wanted. On January 8, 1957, the cabinet instructed the German delegation as to the conditions of the association it considered desirable. These included investments which would benefit Europe overall as well as 'social investments', such as schools and hospitals, a gradual approximation of a trading relationship with the entire common market similar to that which each territory now enjoyed with its 'mother country', and a policy of political, economic and social development of the overseas territories. The only issue still to be resolved, according to the cabinet, was that of the agricultural products of the overseas territories. A few days later, Hartlieb wrote a lengthy memo to Erhard and a shorter one to a journalist, in which he reiterated the Foreign Ministry's position that Germany wished in no way to be associated with colonialism (AA, Jan. 7, 8 and 11, 1957). A few weeks later, the Minister of Finance wanted to re-open the discussion on the overseas investment fund, lest Germany be asked to become the principal paymaster of such an institution (AA, Feb. 14, 1957).

In the end, no responsible German wanted to be the one to scuttle the launching of this European ship. Even Erhard, who had fulminated against some of the provisions of the draft treaty, in both public and closed meetings, told the *Bundesrat* (upper house of parliament) that the various protective provisions might 'not be pretty,' but that 'we need to be realistic and politically understanding' (AA, Jan. 24, 1957) – that is, European integration would continue regardless of what Erhard thought.

So in Germany as in France, once the discussions between elites and bureaucrats and among bureaucrats were over, the European imperative carried the day.

Concluding Comments

The degree to which governmental negotiators consulted interest groups with respect to the negotiation of the Treaty of Rome is extraordinarily difficult to determine. In France, the negotiators made a show of having consulted interest groups, and the government undoubtedly did consult with them, even though the government's own records show very little evidence of such consultations, which probably means that the rather tightly knit political and economic elite in France, educated for the most part in the *grandes écoles*, met and spoke in informal meetings of which little or no record has survived.

In Germany, there is some evidence of contacts between groups and government, but since the groups were for the most part supportive of the government's position, such meetings tended to deal with details which are not as important to the theme of this book as are the fundamental issues which were in dispute in France. There was a general feeling that Germans needed to show they were European in spirit. The principal exception were the agricultural groups. Motivated less by the European conviction than the survival of German agriculture in all its inefficiency, these groups nevertheless had a strong political interest in keeping the CDU/CSU government in power, and European integration was one of the defining elements of that government's policy. So rather than undermine that government and have the dreaded representatives of trade unions and consumers, that is the Social Democratic Party, come to power, the agricultural groups did their best to protect their interests while supporting the government.

As for the determination of the governments' negotiating positions, there obviously were differences among politicians and bureaucrats within both Germany and France. But even allowing for the selective nature of the records as they have been preserved by both governments, the process in France was relatively rational and orderly, compared to the near chaos which prevailed in Bonn. In Paris, there were bureaucrats who were skeptical about the possibility of France joining a common market. Olivier Wormser was perhaps the most senior placed of these skeptics. And even in the Mollet cabinet, there were some such as Christian Pineau and Paul Ramadier, who feared for France's ability to compete or sought to preserve France's sovereign autonomy over its economy. But in the end, the European ethos and Mollet's, Marjolin's and Pierre Uri's strong convictions prevailed. The January 22, 1957 National Assembly vote approving of the negotiations demonstrated the effectiveness of the government's determination to show a united front.

Germany had a coalition government, but it was dominated by the CDU/CSU alliance. Party discipline meant that the government did not have to worry about votes in the Bundestag, and the Bundesrat was also dominated by government-friendly parties. However, the lack of dissension on the political front was only the cover on a boiling cauldron. Within the government, dissension was rife. Bureaucrats within the same ministry fought each other for position and influence. Bureaucrats from different ministries struggled to control the negotiations. And at the top, ministers within the federal cabinet disagreed about the German negotiating position. While some of these differences were ideological (Erhard versus Adenauer), others were driven by the determination to protect a specific sector (agriculture) or by a struggle for influence and position. The lack of cohesion was such that it is surprising the German negotiators were able to protect any German interests. And it is this lack of cohesion which made it possible for small sectors, such as the banana importers, to successfully insert their interest into the negotiations.

After a study of the negotiations themselves, in Chapter 6, Chapter 7 will be devoted to an analysis of the factors which led to the successful conclusion of the negotiations. That analysis will in turn shed some light on the factors which influenced the negotiators.

6 The Negotiations

It is time at last to attempt to determine the extent to which the ideas of the French and German elites reviewed above, as filtered through the national bureaucracies, shaped the provisions of the Treaty of Rome with respect to the four themes analysed in this book – supranational institutions, social harmonisation, agriculture and the association of the overseas territories. Both French and German leaders agreed that the European Economic Community was about the political unification of Europe, though the French did not say so very loudly for fear of arousing anti-European sentiment in the National Assembly (AA, Sept. 1956, [date unspecified]).

I begin, therefore, with the basic institutions of the original European Economic Community. Institutional issues had two aspects, those of the structure and of the functions of the institutions. Here I will discuss first the structure, then the functions of the institutions of the new community.

The Institutions of the European Economic Community

From the beginning of the negotiations, foreign ministers Spaak (Belgium) and Beyen (Netherlands) realized that the institutions of the community could become a subject of controversy between intergovernmental and supranational advocates. They decided, therefore, to leave the discussion of the precise institutional structure to the later stages of the pre-conference. They called it putting functions first (Küsters, 1982:195-198). When, in the fall of 1955, the delegates began to discuss institutions there was no a priori assumption to copy the model of the ECSC. Rather, the delegates tried to imagine institutions which could fulfil functions such as liasing with national governments or settling disputes between governments and institutions. However, these ideas did not take form, so that the foreign ministers' meeting of February 1956, *faute de mieux*, decided that the Spaak Report would recommend an institutional structure which was similar to that of the ECSC. There was to be a supranational commission (in fact a somewhat less supranational version of the ECSC's High Authority), a council of ministers, and a parliamentary assembly, consisting of an expanded version of the ECSC assembly, and a judicial organ. The ministers, however, retained the earlier formula which stated that the institutions should only have such powers as were needed to create and govern the two communities (AA, Feb. 12, 1956; Comité, Feb. 13, 1957; Küsters, 1982:201-202 and 249-250; Ministère, Feb. 17, 1956).

While it was clear from the beginning that the Council would consist of one principal delegate per member state, the type of voting, to what extent it would be unanimous, or if not unanimous whether it would be one country one vote or weighted voting, was a subject of lengthy discussions. A conference note summarised the situation as of February 1956; it stated that unanimity would be the rule, but then listed many exceptions of subject matters which were deemed essential to the functioning of the common market. These included safeguard measures in case of a balance of payments problem. The document suggested that the Council should be able to vote to delay measures leading to the creation of the customs union, but that unanimity would be required for shortening such time periods. The document also foresaw a gradual increase over time in the number of issues to which majority voting would apply and suggested weighted voting according to the principle whereby the three large countries should not be able to outvote the three smaller ones (Comité, Feb. 13, 1956).

However, by November the French were showing dissatisfaction with that formula. Their argument was that if France could be outvoted, why not Benelux (AA, Nov. 26, 1956 and Dec. 12, 1956)? The weighted voting formula was not adopted until December 1956, and then only in such a fashion as to make it impossible for the three big countries to outvote the three small ones. The number of votes per country stayed the same, but there was a provision that at least four countries would have to vote to adopt a measure. Thus, in a concession to the sovereign sensibilities of the smaller states, the Dutch government achieved its objective: the three small countries could not be outvoted by the three large ones (Ministère, Dec. 9, 1956). There was also a complicated pattern as to what kind of voting was required for various issues (Küsters, 1982:399-403).

The French also wanted to maintain a veto right over the movement from the first to the second stage of the common market, a right that in the end they did not achieve. This issue was linked to another one: whether the Treaty should provide for the right to secede from the community. The German and Dutch foreign ministers opposed including a secession clause because they believed it might discourage governments from making the structural adjustments needed if a common market was to succeed (Conférence, Oct. 20-21, 1956).

All the delegations agreed that the Commission should have the power of decision on a number matters which related directly to the implementation of the Treaty. This included a wide range of issues relating to import quotas, the free movement of labour and competition policy. The Commission was also to administer the re-adaptation fund (which in the final Treaty version became the European Social Fund). A French bureaucrat prepared a note pointing out that the Commission would have more power than envisaged in the French proposal to the pre-conference, but made no suggestion that this should be altered. Ophüls, Germany's chief negotiator for the common market, thought that a strong commission would help the common market to function well, but that such a proposal would likely be opposed by France (AA, June 23, 1956; Comité, Feb. 13, 1957; Conférence, Nov. 22, 1956 and Dec. 10, 1956; Küsters, 1982:404; Ministère, Feb. 24, 1956).

The relative powers of the Council and the Commission were a particular thorny issue. As early as October 1955, the steering committee of the Brussels pre-negotiations had suggested that the commission would propose, where as the council of ministers would dispose (Comité, Oct. 24, 1955). By late 1956, a clear division of opinion emerged among the negotiators, with the Dutch, supported by the Italians, favouring a strong commission, while the French and Germans wanted more authority to rest with the Council of Ministers (AA, Oct. 3 and 8, 1956 and Nov. 12 and 23, 1956), though the French ambassador claimed that the Italians were also on his side (Ministère, Dec. 28, 1956). All agreed that the Commission would be responsible for the routine administration of the new institutions (AA, Nov. 24, 1956). Finally, in January 1957, the delegates adopted the formula that was to remain the basis of EEC decision-making for more than thirty years: the Council could only act on the recommendation of the Commission, and it would need unanimity to overrule the Commission or alter its proposals (Conférence, Jan. 26-28, 1957). The Commission thus became the representative of the interests of the community overall. The budget would require the agreement of both Council and Commission, and the parliament would also have the opportunity to vote on it and express opinions (Küsters, 1982:397-9 and 407).

In February 1956, the foreign ministers envisaged a parliamentary assembly with considerable powers. Besides the power to overthrow the Commission, the assembly was to be able to approve the members of the Commission and its president. It was also to have the authority to question both the Commission and the Council, and there was to be only one assembly for all three communities (Comité, Feb. 13, 1956). However,

French opponents of the ECSC advocated a separate assembly and court for the new community, causing Robert Marjolin, the chief French negotiator on the common market, to take up their suggestion while assuring the other delegations that once the institutions were in place, the assemblies could be merged with those of the ECSC (AA, Sept. 1956 [date unspecified], Sept. 13, 1956 and Dec. 8, 1957). So until the last months of the negotiations, there was the possibility of the creation of a new European parliament, in addition to the existing assemblies of the Council of Europe, the ECSC and the WEU (AA, Jan. 11, 1957). It was only last minute lobbying by the members of the existing assemblies which prevented such a duplication and led to the creation of one assembly for the new communities and the ECSC. For the time being, the assembly was to consist of delegates from national parliaments. The Treaty foresaw the possibility of a future direct election of the community assembly, an idea favoured by the German and the Italian delegations (AA, Jan. 24, 1957; Küsters, 1982:403-406; Ministère, Nov. 12, 1955).

While opposing the creation of a common assembly, the French also moved away from the earlier consensus with respect to the powers of the assembly. By November 1956, Ophüls reported that the French delegates were questioning all of the proposed powers of the assembly, including the budgetary powers and the right to overthrow the Commission (AA, Nov. 23 and 24, 1956 and Dec. 8, 1956). There may also have been differences among the French delegates; the minutes of a meeting held on November 22, 1956, show the French supporting the assembly's power to be involved in the budget process and its power to force the resignation of the Commission (Conférence, Nov. 22, 1956).

The delegates agreed to give the assembly some limited powers. It was to be a kind of sampling of opinion within the member states. It also had the power to force the resignation of the Commission and the right to discuss the budget before the Council adopted it (Küsters, 1982:406-407).

The story of the court of justice for the new communities was similar to that of the assembly, though there was less disagreement about its functions. In February 1956, the foreign ministers envisaged a single expanded court (Comité, Feb. 13, 1956; AA, Nov. 24, 1956). After considering the possibility of the creation of a second court, the governments decided on a single court for the ECSC and the two new communities. This court in fact had the strongest supranational powers of any of the institutions. It was to settle disputes between member states, between the institutions and the member states and, most importantly, interpret national laws which involved interpretation of the treaties.

In September 1956, Belgium suggested the creation of a further institution, an economic and social committee, consisting of the representatives of the principal economic interest groups. The idea was endorsed enthusiastically by the French, who took up the cause for the creation of this committee. It was opposed by the Germans because German interest groups feared the loss of a national system (co-determination) which gave them more than just consultative powers. On this issue, however, French, Belgian and Dutch wishes prevailed (Conférence, Jan. 26-28, 1957; Küsters, 1982:308 and 411-412).

By the time the Treaty was drafted, it included several other institutions, including a European Investment Bank and a Monetary Committee. These less important institutions are not included in this study.

As for the functions of the new institutions, the Spaak Report recommended that the major issues of economic policy be left to the national governments, that policies which affected the functioning of the common market be decided by a council of ministers, acting on a proposal of the commission, and that the commission be given the authority to implement measures affecting the functioning of the common market, such as the competition policy and the regulation of the free movement of labour. Though the governments agreed that there should be gradual harmonisation of economic and monetary policies, there was no willingness to transfer such significant functions to the supranational authorities. This was true of most of the French negotiators as well as Müller-Armack and the Erhard wing of the German Ministry of Economics (Conférence, June 8, 1956; Hallstein, 1962; Küsters, 1982:262-272 and 336; Müller-Armack, 1971:107 and 118).

On the other hand, there were those such as Marjolin, who wanted the European market to be about more than a customs union; Marjolin wanted the common market to become an 'area of a common political economy,' to which Müller-Armack replied that there should be agreement on the general direction of the economic policy of the new institutions (Conférence, June 27, 1956). Marjolin's vision implied some kind of a mechanism for making a European economic policy. The Germans added that function and institution were so closely linked that when the negotiators dealt with specific functions, they should include negotiations as to the institutional means for dealing with those functions (Brüsseler Integrationskonferenz, Sept. 13, 1956). The French foreign ministry knew only too well which Germans were more likely to agree with the French as to the functions of the new institutions. On returning from a visit to Berlin, Faure wrote that there should be further discussion with the Germans as to the monetary policy provisions of the Treaty; he suggested the names of four German negotiators he would like to see on the other side of the table (Ministère, Sept. 17, 1956).

When the negotiations were over, the institutions envisaged were supranational to a significant degree, though not as supranational as some of the Belgian, German and French negotiators had wanted them to be. According to the chief Belgian negotiator, he and some of the others hoped that the new community would develop its own institutional momentum, an '*imperium communautaire*' which would eventually lead to political unification (Snoy et d'Oppuers, 1965). Similarly, an unsigned document in the French foreign ministry archives stated that the important step was to get the common market adopted by the French parliament; after that '*un système progressif*' could lead to more supranationality (Ministère, Feb. 2, 1956). Spaak also foresaw a gradual growth in the authority of the parliament as well as an increased use of majority voting, and a proposal from the French delegation stressed the role of common institutions in building momentum after the first stage of the negotiations (Comité, Oct. 14, 1955; Ministère, 1958). A document prepared by the steering committee at the Brussels pre-negotiations similarly stressed the importance of majority voting so as to enhance the efficacy and supranationality of the new institutions (Comité, Nov. 6, 1955).

So it is clear that the negotiators were interested in creating supranational institutions not only for the better functioning of the common market (though that was their primary motivation), but also to create supranational institutions for their own sake, that is for the further integration of Europe.

Social Harmonisation and Social Policy

So-called social harmonisation remained a contentious issue throughout the negotiations. Unlike the institutions, which interested all participants, social harmonisation was an issue which was raised and promoted by one delegation only, that of the French. The Messina resolution mentioned the 'progressive' harmonisation of regulations concerning working hours, overtime pay and holidays, but not equal pay for equal work by men and women. By July 1955, French demands become more specific. French negotiators wanted the harmonisation of social security legislation to go lock-step with the reduction of tariffs. As tariffs were reduced, the other governments were to align their social security legislation on the French model (Comité, July 21, 1955). At Noordwijik, in September 1955, the French foreign minister (then Antoine Pinay, a dedicated European) spoke of the *prior* harmonisation of social legislation (Küsters, 1982:158-162).

By then, French demands had increased. Their head negotiator, Maurice Faure, was now demanding a harmonisation of social legislation, so that by the time of the creation of the customs union the total costs of social security would be the same in all six countries. Faure in particular demanded that other governments implement equal pay for men and women, a factor which he said especially disadvantaged the French textile industry (Comité, Sept. 28, 1955), and that this be done during the first stage of tariff reduction (French memorandum of Oct. 14, 1955 as cited in Ministère, June 23, 1956). France also wanted to retain a system of import tariffs and export subsidies it had recently instituted (Küsters, 1982:303-304).

Over the course of the eighteen months of negotiations, French demands became more specific. They included the immediate harmonisation of three aspects of social security: equal pay for men and women doing the same work, the adoption of the same length of paid holidays (eighteen days) as in France and the adoption of the forty hour week, with overtime pay for any additional hours. But when a working group of the first Brussels conference produced a report on social harmonisation, it took the position espoused by all the other delegations, that harmonisation of social policies would be an accompaniment of, not a precondition for, the creation of a common market (Comité, Feb. 18, 1956). Back in Paris, someone in the Ministry of Foreign Affairs commented that the working groups had adopted the German position (Ministère, Feb. 24, 1956).

The Spaak Report was sympathetic to the French demand for social harmonisation as a goal to be achieved, but not as prior conditions for the creation of the common market (Küsters, 1982:181). When the second Brussels conference met, the French delegation rejoined the issue of social harmonisation. It asked for the appointment of a group of experts to study the differences in social security costs (Conférence, June 17, 1956; AA, June 30, 1956). The German delegation agreed to the creation of such a study group – since they did not want to appear to be uncooperative and since in any case they considered social harmonisation to be an 'imaginary problem' (AA, July 5, 1956) – but the delegates soon disagreed as to what the group was to study (Conférence, July 12-13, 1956; Conférence, July 28, 1956; Ministère, Aug. 30, 1956). Five delegations thought that the group should study the effects of the three specific measures of social security mentioned in the Spaak Report. The French delegation wanted a total review of all aspects of social security, from family allowances to housing costs and workers' compensation (Ministère, July 23, 1956; AA, Aug. 3, 1956 and Aug. 22, 1956). Or so they said. Yet, on September 16, 1956, Faure told Erhard that France did not seek the total harmonisation of social costs, only the three measures mentioned in the Spaak Report. This did not deter Erhard from labelling French social legislation 'harmful' (Ministère, Sept 16-17, 1956). After wrangling which lasted throughout the summer of 1956, the French delegation tabled new expanded demands with respect to harmonisation. To the measures mentioned in the Spaak Report, they now added the harmonisation of 'overall labour costs'. Spaak responded by tabling his own suggestions as to the social harmonisation articles of the proposed treaty (Ministère [belge], Sept. 24, 1956).

German negotiators were opposed to social harmonisation. This was especially true of the Erhard section of the Ministry of Economics, which claimed that any attempt to harmonise costs would falsify the natural advantages which made trade beneficial for all. The Germans opposed any mechanical harmonisation of legislation, such as the 40 hour week, on the French model. And the Benelux and the Germans were able to point out that the actual differences in the specific measures sought by the French were not great. The numbers of hours worked per week varied but little between countries, and the differences between industries within France were greater than those with respect to other countries. Similarly, paid holidays were equal in number if one counted the many individual religious holidays observed by Germans. Germany had also ratified the ILO convention on equal pay for equal work for men and women, but the government said that it needed time to apply it to all industrial sectors, especially since in Germany working conditions were usually decided by labour negotiations rather than by legislative fiat (Küsters, 1982:303-308; AA, Sept. 3, 1955). Indeed, one historian of the French economy calculates that the total burden of taxation and of social benefits was, by the mid-1950s, greater in Germany than it was in France (Lynch, 1997:132). But even knowing that this might be true did not stop Hartlieb (of the German Foreign Ministry) from grumbling that the French were trying to 'burden German industry with the French social security system' (AA, July 16, 1956).

Spaak suggested a number of compromises, such as safeguard clauses for industries especially affected by the equal pay provisions or a gradual phase-in of overtime pay (Ministère [belge], Sept. 24, 1956; Conférence, Oct. 20-21, 1956). But the French remained insistent. They wanted social harmonisation *and* the import and export subsidies they would be allowed to keep until the value of the franc stabilised. And they were now linking their demand for social harmonisation to a specific institutional question: by the end of the first stage of the creation of the customs union, France and France alone reserved for itself the right to judge if there had been enough progress on social harmonisation. In other words, the French wanted there to be a unanimous vote in the Council of Ministers before the customs union could move to the second of its three stages. In Germany, Ophüls concluded that there would need to be some accommodation of the French demands (AA, June 23, 1955), though Faure also told Ophüls that the French position left some room for negotiation (AA, Sept. 7, 1956). An anonymous briefing note written for Adenauer before his September 29 meeting with Mollet (Ophüls was the likely author) suggests that compromises might be possible with respect to the issues of paid holidays and equal pay, but that Adenauer should make no commitments on the forty hour week, since the French might still come forward with a compromise (AA, [date unspecified]). However, the French proposal tabled at the Brussels negotiations on September 19 was uncompromising; wage costs were to be harmonised, so that they would be substantially equal by the time of the creation of the customs union (Conférence, Sept. 19, 1956).

This was the situation when the foreign ministers met on October 20-21, 1956. As luck would have it, this was the foreign ministers' meeting at which two uninvited guests appeared: Erhard, the German Minister of Economics, and Strauss, the newly appointed Minister of Defence; Brentano and Hallstein represented the German Foreign Ministry. (Technically this was a foreign ministers' meeting, so Erhard and Strauss were experts on the German delegation, not delegates.) Spaak presented his earlier compromise proposals and explained them at length. Agreement would in any case have been difficult, for other delegates, notably the Belgian and the Italian, were equally determined not to accept the French demands on social harmonisation. There was some willingness to accommodate the French problem with respect to the overvalued franc, but no willingness to accept social harmonisation. A compromise with respect to paid holidays, equal pay and movement from the first to the second stage might have been possible, though Erhard feared inflation in Germany might result, but there was no possibility of agreement on the forty hour week. The meeting was interrupted several times while Pineau consulted Mollet and the Germans consulted their 'experts'. The meeting broke up without reaching any agreement on social harmonisation (AA, Oct. 22,

1956; Conférence, Oct. 20-21, 1956; Küsters, 1982:313-319; Ministère, Oct. 30, 1956; Müller-Armack, 1971:115-117).

Afterwards, Marjolin assured the German ambassador that all could be resolved, that the difficult issue of the forty hour week was really only a '*question de présentation*' (AA, Oct. 26, 1956). But that was not how affairs looked at the Brussels conference. Even the optimistic Spaak now became pessimistic. Mollet did not believe that he could put a treaty without social harmonisation before the National Assembly, and the Germans were determined not to have social harmonisation. At this point, history rescued the negotiations. Adenauer was scheduled to come to Paris on November 6 to deal with various outstanding bilateral issues. Between the end of the foreign ministers' meeting and Adenauer's trip to Paris, French, British and Israeli forces attacked Egypt, and by the time Adenauer arrived in Paris, an enraged President Eisenhower told his NATO allies to withdraw their troops or the US would stop supporting the pound on international monetary markets (Nutting, 1972:180). As it turned out, the message from the British arrived while Mollet and Pineau were meeting with Adenauer.

In Pineau's memoirs there is a dramatic accounting of this incident. Mollet, after receiving the news, is supposed to have relayed it to Pineau and Adenauer, after which Adenauer said: 'And now we need to make Europe' (Pineau and Rimbaud, 1991:221-223). The minutes of the meeting tell a less dramatic story, but the fact is that Pineau was called out to receive the British ambassador, and thus on Pineau's return Adenauer was one of the first to learn the news (Ministère, Nov. 6, 1956). Shocked by the American demand and the British acceptance of that demand, Adenauer and Mollet told their officials, specifically Marjolin and Carstens, to work out a solution to the problem of social harmonisation, a solution, any solution (Küsters, 1982:328-329).

The agreed solution constituted a concession on the part of the French. Instead of a specific commitment to equalize the costs of labour, the French agreed to a formula which expressed a pious wish for an improvement in social security (Article 117 of the Treaty of Rome, 1957). The Germans and the others agreed to implement equal pay for equal work, and they agreed that there was no problem with respect to paid holidays. The provision with respect to the forty hour week was kicked to the back of the Treaty, into the protocol about the French import surcharges. In it, the other governments agreed to harmonise their overtime pay provisions with those of France. If this did not happen by the end of the first stage of the common market, the Commission could authorize France to take measures to protect affected industries (AA, Nov. 7, 1956; Comité, Nov. 21, 1956; Ministère, Nov. 7, 8 and 9, 1956; Treaty, 1962). In other words, the other five governments did not make a binding legal commitment to enact the forty hour week.

An anonymous French bureaucrat questioned this solution as not only legally unsatisfying, but also the fact that the provisions about overtime became a part of the special protocol with regard to France which was appended to the Treaty. For the time being, the Luxembourg delegation also expressed reservations; but the other five delegations eventually agreed to accept the Carstens-Marjolin proposal, which, with minor modifications, became the solution which appeared in the Treaty (AA, Jan. 16, 1957). The Dutch delegate even praised it as a 'good and elegant solution' (AA, Nov. 17, 1956; Comité, Nov. 21, 1956; Conférence, Nov. 9, 1956). The Germans and later the other delegations also agreed to allow the French government to maintain its import surcharges and export subsidies, on a temporary basis, presumably until the franc could find its true value (Carstens, 1976:599; Küsters, 1982:328-333).

Social harmonisation reappeared on the agenda of the conference in January and February, 1957. First, the delegations found they still wanted to do some fine tuning with the exact voting formula in the Council of Ministers which would decide whether there had been enough social harmonisation to proceed to the second stage of the customs union, with the French seeking a unanimous vote on this issue (Ministère, Dec. 22, 1956 and Jan. 7, 1957). The Germans then said they needed to 'reserve their position' on the entire social chapter (Conférence, Jan. 31-Feb. 9, 1957). They also, successfully, insisted on the inclusion of a reference to collective bargaining in the chapter on social policy (Conférence, Feb. 8-9, 1957). The Dutch wanted to specify that the rates of overtime pay in France which would be the base for further adjustments would be those in effect in 1956, and the French came up with a complex formula for determining which industries could be protected by safeguard clauses if the other governments did not introduce overtime after a forty hour week. Both of these provisions made it into the Treaty (Comité, Feb. 27, 1957; Conférence, Jan. 21, 1957). In the end, the Germans lifted their reservations, which in any case had probably been tactical (AA, Feb. 13, 1957).

The negotiators were also concerned with public opinion. They wanted people to like their handiwork, and there was always the French National Assembly to consider. So a reference to 'an accelerated raising of the standard of living' was included in Article 2, and Article 3 referred to the Social Fund and again mentioned the raising of the standard of living (Conférence, Feb. 26-March 1, 1957; Treaty). The Commission was also to include a section on social policy in its annual report (AA, Feb. 13, 1957). Ophüls wrote the Foreign Ministry as to how the other delegations were trying to appeal to public opinion by defending a progressive social policy, whereas he, poor man, had to defend the German reservations, which presumably were less progressive (AA, Feb. 9, 1957).

The Treaty provisions on social harmonisation were close to those Marjolin and Carstens presented to the Brussels conference on November 16, 1956. The governments agreed to attempt to achieve equal pay by the end of the first stage, and they agreed to maintain the existing equivalence with respect to paid holidays; the forty hour week, along with the French import surcharges and export subsidies, were placed in a special protocol relating to France (Küsters, 1982:375; Treaty, 1962). These provisions were a compromise between the French model of rigidly legislated working conditions and the German liberal model of working conditions which were meant to improve gradually as the result of a rising GDP and after collective negotiations between labour and management (Adenauer, 1967, vol.3:258).

Another issue of social policy, that of the readaptation fund, was less controversial than social harmonisation. All the delegations agreed to the creation of such a fund, though the German delegation, less enthusiastic than the others, sought to limit the instances in which the fund could be used, as well as wishing to reserve to national governments the overall effort with respect to unemployment and retraining (Conférence, Sept. 24-26, 1956). By December 1956, all delegations had agreed to the creation of two funds, one for professional training and one for readaptation (Ministère, Dec. 9, 1956; AA, [mid-January 1957]). Before the signing of the Treaty, these became a single Social Fund. The Germans at first insisted on unanimous voting with respect to the use of the Fund, but were willing to give this up in return for satisfactory wording defining the uses to which the fund could be put. The German insistence on unanimous voting had two causes. One was a negotiating tactic, the other was for domestic consumption. The German Minister of Finance feared that Germany would become the fund's paymaster but would have little to say about its use. Brentano told him not to worry. Since the Italians were likely to want money for retraining, whereas the French were more likely to want it for the readaptation of enterprises, Germany was not likely to be outvoted on any specific issue (AA, Feb. 8, 8bis, and 14, 1957, March 11 and 11bis, 1957).

In the end, the Fund was left to be administered by the Commission. The Council, voting by qualified majority, could set general guidelines as to how the Commission was to do this. However, the Treaty specified what the fund was to do: it was to provide up to 50 per cent of the cost of reconverting enterprises and retaining or resettling workers on projects approved by the Commission. A unanimous vote by the Council would only be required if the Fund was to be used for purposes not envisaged in the Treaty (Art. 123-128).

Agriculture

Given its future importance in the history of the Community and considering the special place agriculture occupies in European political culture (see Chapter 1), one might have expected agriculture to be a subject of major controversy during the negotiations. It was. The member states, notably France, Germany, Italy and the Netherlands had different interests when it came to trade in agriculture, but overall the subject caused less controversy, and certainly at no point caused the near collapse of the negotiations brought about by the controversies about social policy.

As discussed in Chapter 1, agriculture was the subject of a special protective regime in each of the six member countries. The 1950s had seen a number of proposals for a European agricultural market similar to that of the Coal and Steel Community (Chapter 2 of this book; Küsters, 1982:173), but the political sensitivity of the subject had not allowed any of these plans to become a formal agreement. One important factor among others was that, then as now, agricultural areas tend to be over represented in national parliaments.

The Messina communiqué did not mention agriculture, but the Brussels pre-conference discussed whether or not to include agriculture in the common market. The Dutch and Italian delegations not only wanted to include agriculture; they thought that with some special transitional measures, agriculture ought to be able to participate in the common market like any other industry (Küsters, 1982:174). According to the documentary record, the German delegation was the first to mention agriculture. In July 1955, it submitted a short memo to the pre-conference, in which it suggested the harmonisation of several policies, including monetary and agricultural policy. At the time of the Noordwijk conference, Ophüls wrote to the secretary-general of the pre-conference (Calmes), reminding him of the need for transitional measures for sectors with an organic structure, 'primarily agriculture' (AA, Sept 3, 1955; Comité, July 18, 1955). Spaak pointed out that the delegations hardly seemed ready to negotiate about agriculture; some did not even include agricultural experts (Réunion, Sept. 28, 1955).

On October 14, 1955, the French delegation submitted its position on the negotiation of a common market to the pre-conference. Included was one page devoted to agriculture. The French position was that special measures for agriculture had to begin during the first stage of the common market. These measures would need to take account of the 'special nature' of agriculture, including family farms, and should include 'a common policy of organized markets' for 'most products'(Comité, Oct. 14, 1955).

By October 24, the conference staff had produced a study of various issues, including agriculture, which needed to be resolved if there was to be a common market. The study said the committee on the common market had not taken a position as to whether agriculture was to be treated like any other industry or whether it should be given a special position; in the words of the document, the committee was 'balanced between' the two positions – or perhaps 'swung' between them, since the French *balance* also refers to a swing. The document leaned toward a free market position, pointing out that an organization of the market would be the opposite of what the term common market implied, and warned of including existing protective mechanisms which might result in 'absurd effects.' It concluded that it was important to resolve the issue of agriculture and not create the 'myth' that agriculture was a problem (Comité, Oct. 24, 1955).

A further study, submitted on November 8, reversed the earlier document's free market bias. Indeed, this document foreshadowed many of the elements of the Common Agricultural Policy adopted in 1962. It insisted that agriculture had to be included in the common market, and that there should be provisions such as fixed prices and stockpiles to cushion market effects and to protect family farms. It warned of cheap imports of agricultural products, of which some members might want to take advantage. It denied that there should be any 'abnormal preference' for the products of other members of the common market; rather it advocated playing the game according to rules. It suggested beginning the common market for agriculture with products where there was already a balance between supply and demand, so as to give the market the all important aura of success (Comité, Nov. 8, 1955). Given such contradictory background studies, it is not surprising that the meeting of November 9 could not agree on agricultural issues. Spaak suggested the creation of a committee of experts, but even on that there seems not to have been agreement (Comité, Nov. 9, 1955).

Indeed, agriculture was so divisive that Spaak, who liked to settle the easier issues first so as to get a good climate for future negotiations, seems to have kept if off the agenda of the heads of delegation meetings for the early months of 1956. There was a committee of agricultural experts, which presumably drafted the relevant section of the Spaak Report, but all that has survived of its meetings appears to be one statement from the German participant. This paper was very different from the previous ones submitted by the Germans. It pointed out that the rules of the common market could *not* simply be applied to agriculture, as if it were any other industry, called for the protection of agriculture by means of a common European policy which would be an amalgam of the six national agricultural policies, and mentioned that German agriculture had special structural problems which were costing the government up to one billion marks a year. In short, this paper called for even more protection for agriculture than envisaged by the French document the previous autumn (Comité, March 3, 1956).

The Spaak Report took a stand which was close to the French memorandum summarized above: yes, agriculture should be included in the common market, but it should enjoy some special provisions, such as minimum prices for some products. The Spaak Report, therefore, recommended a common European agricultural market, the exact parameters of which were to be recommended by the Commission within two years of the coming into effect of the Treaty (Küsters, 1982:244). However, Spaak managed to avoid further discussions of agriculture until France raised the issue in October (Conférence, Sept. 24, 1956).

On October 3, 1956, the French delegation made the inclusion of agriculture, including a common agricultural policy, which would cover both trade within the common market and trade with third parties, a condition of its participation in the customs union. The French demand, included in a detailed proposition with respect to the agricultural provisions of the draft treaty, included a policy of raising the standard of living of the agricultural population, a system of preferential purchases for community-produced agricultural products, long-term contracts for the sale (and purchase) of agricultural products within the community, special tariffs designed to raise the price of agricultural products produced within the community, and a special fund for the modernization of agriculture. Some members of the German delegation at first saw the French proposal as another *dirigiste* attack on free trade. These members of the German delegation apparently had not considered the position of German agriculture and those within the German government who supported the agricultural sector (Küsters, 1982:312-5 and 348-50).

On October 9, the common market group of the Brussels negotiation conference held its first thorough discussion of the agricultural issue. The German delegate (the minutes of the meeting unfortunately do not include names) spoke about the special position of agriculture, the way in which farmers depended on the vagaries of the harvest, the special social characteristics of agriculture, the fact that prices of agricultural products could not just be determined as they were in other economic sectors, and the need for 'protection' from the outside world. But he also spoke about the need to preserve free competition and to make foodstuffs available to consumers at reasonable prices. He concluded by recommending a mixture of free competition, the coordination of national marketing organization and a common European agricultural policy, each policy to be applicable to different agricultural products. He also advocated measures to increase agricultural productivity.

In contrast, the French position was simple. The French delegate pointed to the political importance of settling the agricultural issue and then recommended a European agricultural policy, based on the national policies already in place. He conceded that this European policy might have to be adopted at different times for different products. He also advocated long term contracts rather than minimum prices for some, unspecified, products. He made an emotional plea not to abandon European agriculture to free competition. And he advocated a common policy with respect to third countries.

The Dutch delegate wanted a free market for agricultural products, and the Italian delegate spoke of the need to export agricultural products to third countries and the need to raise the income of the rural population. The French did not like this last formulation because it seemed to imply some kind of control of the income of farmers (Conférence, Oct. 9, 1956).

The German and French positions were not so far apart. The Germans had accepted the need for a common European agricultural policy (a fact which Ophüls specifically reported on October 3 and which even Erhard admitted in a submission to the cabinet) and the need to treat agriculture differently than other industries (AA, Oct. 2 and 3bis, 1956). But the French felt that they could not afford to mention competition and the free market with respect to agriculture, a phraseology which was important to some members of the German government. And the Germans insisted on a reference to the rights of consumers to reasonably priced foodstuffs, a phrase the French would have preferred to omit. Yet, on October 22, the day after the foreign ministers' meeting had broken up over the issue of social harmonisation, Ophüls reported to a meeting of the German delegation that there had been a narrowing of the gap with respect to agricultural policy (AA, Oct. 22bis, 1956).

Even though, as pointed out above, the differences over agriculture were not just Franco-German differences, the French and German delegations saw it as their obligation to settle them. In December, von der Groeben wrote to Bonn, recommending that the agricultural questions be settled through bilateral Franco-German discussions (AA, Dec. 3, 1956). After all, this approach had worked for social harmonisation.

However, this was one issue which, at least for the time being, could not be settled by the French and Germans making a deal. In January 1957, when the negotiators began to tackle agriculture in earnest for the second time, there was widespread disagreement on many issues. There was disagreement on minimum prices, which the French insisted needed to be based on 'objective criteria', but only on the basis of unanimous voting by the Council of Ministers (in case the criteria were not as objective as they appeared to be?). There was also disagreement on how community preference for agricultural products was to be defined (Ministère, Jan.7, 1957). And delegates could not agree on how to define agricultural products. Five delegations, including the Germans and the French, wanted to include all foodstuffs, but the Italians wanted to exclude food processing, an industry in which they believed Italians to have an advantage. It took a meeting of foreign ministers to settle this issue of definition. Spaak suggested a compromise which included all products of the soil, of animal husbandry and of fisheries as well as the first processing of such products (Conférence, Jan. 22, 1957; Conférence, Feb. 4, 1957; Spaak, 1971:242). This definition became Article 38 of the Treaty. However, at almost the last minute, the French demanded that beer be treated as an industrial product, whereas wine was to be on the list of agricultural products (AA, Jan. 30, 1957; Ministère, Feb. 6, 1957). This issue resurfaced in March, just two weeks before the signing of the Treaty. The Italian delegation once again requested a reduction in the number of items placed on the special list of agricultural products which would become the subject of free trade. The Germans now wanted to add bread to the list of agricultural products. Hartlieb wrote that surely the Italians could be made to understand that their pasta, their vermouth and their linen products could be traded freely, since all the Germans and the French wanted was to add bread and beer to the list of agricultural, that is less freely traded, products (AA, March 11, 1957; Conférence, Feb. 28-March 3, 1957).

It took two meetings of the foreign ministers to settle the agricultural issues (they also discussed some issues relating to the overseas territories), and the differences were so great that Spaak considered cancelling the second meeting (AA, Feb. 1, 1957). In the end, the two meetings, the first from January 26 to 28 and the second on February 4, found compromise solutions for most of the remaining agricultural controversies. As a result, the Treaty stated that agricultural products were to be included in the common market but then established a long list of special rules for such products, including the eventual creation of a common agricultural policy. Thus both the Germans and French got what they wanted on this issue, contradictory as the solution may appear to be. The Treaty also included a provision for temporary minimum prices, which the Council could alter on a proposal from the Commission. Most of the agricultural products of the overseas territories were included in the list of agricultural products listed in Annex II of the Treaty, and thus became subject to a special transitional regime. What the ministers had agreed on by the end of their meeting on February 4 became the agricultural chapter of the Treaty of Rome, with only a few changes before the signing of the Treaties (AA, Jan. 30, 1957; Conférence, Feb. 4, 1957; Treaty).

The conference of agricultural ministers had to overcome one other unexpected obstacle. On January 8, the official responsible for trade issues in the American embassy in Paris (John W. Tuthill) appeared at the French foreign ministry, where he spoke to Olivier Wormser and expressed his concern about the creation of a preferential European market for agricultural products. Wormser told him bluntly that a treaty which did not include agriculture could not be ratified, and the Americans seem not to have persisted with their protests. At least there is no further mention of American objections, and only the French foreign ministry seems to have been the recipient of such an American warning. On January 18, Hartlieb wrote that the two Treaties 'enjoy a plentiful degree of support from the United States' (AA, Jan. 18, 1957; Ministère, Jan. 8, 1957).

In February 1957, the negotiators agreed that the common external tariff for agricultural products should be like that for most other products: the average of the existing tariffs in force in four existing customs areas (Benelux, Italy, Germany and France). However, no sooner had they made this agreement in principle, then they proceeded to list most agricultural products in a special list at the end of the Treaty which in fact exempted them from this rule (List F).

Some other agricultural issues proved more contentious. Each country had its own regime for protecting agriculture, and these would need to be integrated with one another. All agreed that there needed to be minimum prices for the major agricultural products, but no one could agree as to which products should be included, how the prices were to be set and for how long they were to remain in force. In general, the Dutch and the Italians were willing to relinquish the minimum prices after the first stage of the customs union, whereas the others wanted to maintain them (Küsters, 1982:354-6). The French also wanted there to be long term contacts for the sale and purchase of agricultural products within the Community, and the Dutch wanted a commitment for the export of products outside the Community. The Dutch and the French wanted the future community to subsidize the export of agricultural products; the Dutch made a complex proposal whereby export subsidies for agriculture were to be tied to the price of the raw materials required by farmers. There was lengthy discussion as to whether what the delegates wanted was preferential treatment for community agriculture, a term which sat well with French preferences for the protection of agriculture, or whether they should be talking about non-discrimination, a term which sat well with the German concept of a liberal trading regime (Marjolin, 1986:302).

After the February 4 agreement by the foreign ministers there were only three substantive changes to the agricultural provisions. One was the inclusion of Algerian agricultural products, on which the Germans supported the French and thus forestalled objections from other delegations (Conférence, March 9, 1957; Küsters, 1982:354-5). The other was a tightening of the commitment to a common agricultural policy. The Commission was to be obligated to call a conference to draft such a policy within two years of the coming into force of the Treaty (Conférence, March 9, 1957). The third provided for the future negotiation of contracts for the long-term sale and purchase of agricultural products within the Community. Other remaining last minute controversies – German bread, imported bananas and French beer – were not likely to threaten the completion of the Treaty. The agricultural chapter also included a lengthy canon of desirable but somewhat contradictory objectives, everything from raising the standard of living of the agricultural workforce, assuring consumers of a secure food supply at reasonable prices, and stabilising markets (Article 39).

Perhaps it was not so amazing that the delegations did come to an agreement. After all, German agriculture was even more protected than was the French, and the Germans could hardly deny community farmers what they had been giving their own (Marjolin, 1986:303).

The Overseas Territories

The negotiations about the association of the overseas territories, most former or current colonies of France, Belgium, the Netherlands and Italy, were short but particularly controversial. The issue was left to the end of the negotiations primarily because the French delegates *chose* to leave it to the last part of the negotiations – partly because, as those most interested in the issue, it took time for the French government to arrive at its own negotiating position (see Chapter 5) and partly because the French government decided not to raise this difficult issue until it could be sure that there would be a common market treaty which would otherwise be acceptable to the French government and the National Assembly. Küsters (1982:25 and 256) suggests that the French may have left the topic of the overseas territories to the end because this would be the French condition the Germans would be least likely to accept. So it made sense not to mention it until there was a treaty both sides found acceptable in other ways.

But just because this issue was left to the end to negotiate does not mean that the negotiators were not aware of it at an earlier stage. As mentioned in Chapter 2, the Schuman Declaration in 1950 already included a reference to the possible association of Africa and Europe. The issue of the need for a separate French army to deal with colonial problems had been one of the many which had brought the EDC grief. In 1953, the overseas territories still took almost twice as a high a proportion of French exports as did the other five European countries (Lynch, 1947:141). During the Brussels pre-conference, it seems that it was only the Belgian and the Italian delegates who mentioned the overseas territories. At the very first meeting of the pre-conference, held in Brussels on July 18 and 20, 1955, the Belgian delegate mentioned the need to take account of the overseas territories and the commitments that governments had toward them (Ministère, July 20, 1955). In November 1955, it was the Italian delegate who mentioned the need to study the existing jurisdictional links between the potential member countries and their overseas territories (Comité, Nov. 9, 1955). In December 1955, the French ambassador to Bonn wrote that if Germany wanted a European economic community, it should realize that it would 'have to show an interest in helping France with its African problems' (cited in Küsters, 1982:252-3).

When the first drafts of the Spaak Report were circulated in the French Ministry of Foreign Affairs, both of the anonymous bureaucrats who wrote comments on it mentioned the absence of any reference to the overseas territories (Ministère, Feb. 2 and 17, 1956). After the publication of the Spaak Report and before the Venice Conference, the French ambassador in Belgium met with Spaak in his capacity as Belgium's foreign minister to discuss the association of the two countries' overseas territories with the common market. Spaak thought that the other governments would surely welcome the association with French overseas territories, though there would need to be conditions such as the protection of infant industries and European investment in the territories (Ministère, May 26, 1956).

The other governments knew and expected the French demands with respect to the overseas territories. A telegram from the German embassy in Paris, later cited in a briefing note for the Venice conference, tells the German delegates to expect France and possibly other governments to bring up the subject of the overseas territories (AA, May 18 and 23, 1956).

The first mention by a French delegate of the overseas territories was Pineau's reference at the Venice Conference, where he made the association a condition of French participation in the common market. Pineau asked that the negotiators set up a special committee to deal with the issue of the overseas territories (Conférence, June 8, 1956; Küsters, 1982:261). Spaak agreed with him (Ministère, May 30, 1956). The communiqué issued after the Venice Conference specifically mentioned the association with the overseas territories as a subject for the future negotiations, but among foreign ministers, not the Treaty drafting conference, since, according to the communiqué, the issue was too complex for the conference ('Communiqué on the talks between the Foreign Ministers', 1959).

It was also at this time that the Mollet government began to revise its relationship with the French Union, so as to make it appear less colonial in nature. This involved a new statute governing the 'French Union' and money to be invested in the overseas territories. With precise, and probably misleading accuracy, French bureaucrats calculated that investments of 366 billion francs a year (not counting administration costs) would be required to raise the standard of living in the territories by four per cent a year (Boussat, 1993; Lynch, 1997:202; Williams, 1964:273).

On September 19, 1956, when the French government submitted a document listing six conditions for its participation in the common market, the 'solution of the problems of the overseas territories' was on the list, but with the additional comment that France would submit detailed proposals at a later date (Conférence, Sept. 19, 1956; Küsters, 1982:304). It was a condition the French delegation repeated often from that time on.

On November 14, 1956 the Belgian[1] and French delegates submitted detailed proposals for the association of the overseas territories, which the French supplemented with a further proposal of their own on November 16. The proposal included an investment fund of 175 billion French francs, gradual access for European suppliers to the market of the overseas territories, and similarly, but faster, access for the products of the overseas territories to the European market, with fixed prices for some of their staple products. European investors were to have the right to invest and establish businesses in the overseas territories of all the member states (Carstens, 1993:210-211; Küsters, 1982:382-3; Regierungskonferenz, Nov. 14, 1956).

Some of the German negotiators saw this issue as strictly a French interest, a concession in return for which Germany expected some other concessions for itself (Küsters, 1982:224; Regierungskonferenz, Nov. 16, 1956), while others believed that Germans should contribute to the security of Europe (by halting the spread of communism) and do good by contributing to the economic and social development of Africa.

And it was not only the Germans who saw the association of the overseas territories as primarily a French interest. A telegram from the French embassy in Brussels to the ministry in Paris, dated, August 28, 1956, states that Spaak told the writer that it was up to the French government to decide when the conference would discuss the association with the overseas territories. Spaak in this case would be speaking as both the chair of the conference and in his role as Belgian foreign minister (Ministère, Aug. 28, 1956).

The Germans knew that they would have to swallow this bitter pill, but they did their best to make it palatable. They tried to limit community contributions to the investment fund for the overseas territories. They tried to ensure that most of the investments made by the fund would be of the 'social' kind, that is schools and hospitals rather than roads, mines and harbours. They also wanted some say on how the money invested would

---

1 Belgium was the only country other than France to control extensive overseas territories. It ruled the Belgian Congo, Rwanda and Burundi.

be spent, but ran into French and Belgian objections of sovereign privilege (AA, Nov. 23, 1956). The Germans offered investment money in return for not having to buy the products of the French territories (so as to protect traditional German suppliers), and they refused to buy products at fixed prices or accept long term contracts, citing free market principles (AA, Jan. 27, 1957; Carstens, 1993:211). They demanded that everything be done in accordance with the Charter of the United Nations. They demanded that the peoples of the overseas territories be consulted about the association, especially the governments of the newly independent countries of Tunisia and Morocco, and that any association mention autonomy for the territories as one objective of the association (AA, June 23, 1956, Jan. 16bis, 1957 and Jan. 18, 1957). They tried to retain access to their traditional suppliers of tropical products, rather than being forced to buy from the other European countries' overseas territories.

All of the German doubts about associating with French (and other) colonialisms might have proved a serious obstacle to the conclusion of the negotiations, except for the fact that Adenauer was one of the few Germans who saw some advantage in associating the overseas territories with Europe (see Chapter 4 of this book), and his support no doubt helped the German negotiators to reach a settlement on this issue (Carstens, 1976). Indeed, Adenauer seems to have been so enthusiastic about the association that on December 8, 1956, his own foreign minister Brentano wrote to him to say that the association was fine in principle, but that many details remained to be worked out and that, therefore, it might be better to limit the wording of the Treaty to a declaration of principle in favour of the economic development of the overseas territories and their association with Europe, but to leave details to be worked out later (AA, Dec. 8, 1956).

Adenauer was not the only German who saw some advantages in the association with the overseas territories. When Erhard met with Faure on September 16, 1956, he also expressed sympathy for what France was doing for Europe as a whole by defending Suez and fighting in Algeria, but in so doing Erhard also said that he would be prepared to postpone (*allongement*), the common market project (Ministère, Sept. 16, 1956). So unlike Adenauer, who saw France's colonial responsibilities as a reason for supporting France and uniting Europe, Erhard saw these responsibilities as still another possible reason to delay a project he did not favour.

It was left to the German chief negotiator Ophüls to represent these contradictory positions during the negotiations. He told an interministerial meeting in Bonn that it was a pity technical difficulties were delaying the association with the overseas territories, since 'Europe could not survive on its own and needed backing from Africa' (AA, Nov. 24, 1956). He also asked his superiors in Bonn to allow him to continue with the project of the 'Europeanisation' of the overseas territories (AA, Nov. 17bis, 1956). On the other hand, Ophüls told another interministerial meeting in Bonn that he had no objection to helping Africa develop, but the Franco-Belgian proposal leaned too much toward getting others to share the political and economic responsibility for the African colonies (AA, Dec. 1, 1956).

An interesting background paper in the German foreign ministry archives, unfortunately both unsigned and undated, but which must, from internal evidence, have been written between January 7 and January 15, 1957, is revealing with respect to the position of some Germans who saw advantages in the association with the overseas territories. In a lengthy analysis, the document rejoices in the proposed European access to the 'African space'. It claims that Germany had for years asked for equal access to the French and Belgian territories in Africa. And it mentions Soviet propaganda in Africa, which a united Europe could work to counter (AA, Jan. 1957, Kabinettvorlage).

After the French and Belgians tabled their proposals in mid-November, initial discussions by the heads of delegation showed that there was widespread opposition to some of the proposals. The Dutch delegation was particularly opposed to the idea of using public money for infrastructure projects in the overseas territories (AA, Dec. 7, 1956). That, with the German doubts about being associated with French colonialism and the Italian fear that investment funds which could be used for the underdeveloped parts of Italy might be sent overseas, meant that the divergence among the delegates was so great as to make any useful discussion unlikely. The November 22 discussion of the overseas association ended with a warning from Marjolin that there was no point in appointing a committee to study the issue if the delegations did not agree on the principle of such an association (Conférence, Nov. 23, 1956; Ministère, Dec. 28, 1956). The French ambassador to Belgium reported that the Germans seemed the least hostile of all the five delegations, which presumably meant that there was a fair degree of hostility (Ministère, Nov. 27, 1956). Nevertheless, the next meeting, on November 29, decided to appoint a committee of experts of no more than two delegates per country which would then report to the next meeting of foreign ministers (Conférence, Nov. 30, 1956). But even this study had to be postponed twice while the delegates hammered out exactly what it was the committee was to do (Conférence, Dec. 10, 1956). And the Germans had to be allowed a third unofficial delegate as three ministries insisted on being represented (AA, Nov. 29, 1956).

The experts submitted their report quickly, on December 20. After an introduction which touted the overseas territories as reliable sources of raw material and potential export markets, the experts recommended almost exactly what the French and Belgians had suggested:

- that the trade preferences which the exports and imports of the overseas territories enjoyed with their 'mother countries' be extended to the entire common market;
- that there be a special regime for the agricultural products of the overseas territories;
- that private investors from all member states have equal access to the overseas territories;
- that there be community financing of infrastructure projects, economic and social, in the overseas territories.

However, the recommendations were followed by several pages of explanations and reservations by unnamed delegates. In short, this was a far from unanimous report (Regierungskonferenz, Dec. 20, 1956), as the first meeting of delegates to discuss it amply demonstrated. Indeed, the German delegate refused to discuss the report until after the French National Assembly had approved the common market in principle, and a stern Maurice Faure pointed out that six months had elapsed since the Venice Conference and there was still no agreement in principle on the association of the overseas territories. The other governments, he said, 'needed to state their position now with respect to this fundamental issue' (AA, Jan. 5, 1957; Ministère, Jan. 7, 1957).

On January 11, 1957, Faure travelled to Bonn to promote the association, where he met with Hallstein and two other officials. He told the Germans almost all of what they wanted to hear: that the other governments would have no political responsibility for the overseas territories, that the development of the 'colonies' would prevent the spread of communism, that in most of the French territories, with the exception of Algeria, there would soon be free elections, and that the local populations would be consulted about infrastructure projects. However, Faure did not move the three Germans who objected to the financing of infrastructure with public money from European countries and who feared that infrastructure could be used for military purposes as well for economic development (AA, Jan. 11bis, 1957).

On January 22, the French National Assembly did vote its approval, but this did not change the German position just yet. In a report dated January 30, Carstens insisted once again that Germany would not contribute to a fund for infrastructure projects, though it might be willing to contribute to individual projects on their merits (AA, Jan. 30, 1957). The Germans also wanted a guarantee that the 'mother countries' would not reduce their investments once money from other governments became available (AA, Jan. 21, 1957).

Several further meetings of heads of delegation and even of foreign ministers (Jan. 26-28 and again on Feb. 4, 1957) were unable to settle the outstanding issues with respect to the association of the overseas territories, though they did make progress on several issues; all delegations now seemed to accept the principle of an association with the overseas territories. However, the German unwillingness to invest in economic projects without having some control over the money invested could not be resolved (AA, March 12, 1957; Ministère, Feb. 5 and 6, 1957).

In an effort to impress the other delegations, the French brought Houphouët-Boigny, a National Assembly deputy from the Ivory Coast and a deputy Prime Minister in France, to a heads of delegation meeting on January 21. He spoke menacingly of the possible attraction of the incipient non-aligned movement (the founding of which dates from the 1955 Bandung conference) and claimed that the Franco-Belgian policy of economic aid to the peoples of Africa was more effective than the British policy of promoting political autonomy. Houphouët-Boigny apparently made an 'excellent impression' but not enough of an impression to move the delegates. When the Germans tried to get agreement in principle on a commercial association between the common market and the overseas territories, the Dutch delegate reserved his position (Conférence, Jan. 25, 26-28, 1957 and Feb. 4, 1957; Ministère, Jan. 25, 1957). Besides, not all African leaders were so supportive of the French position. The German consul from Dakar (Senegal) reported that Léopold Senghor, another member of the French National Assembly, had attacked the proposed association with the European Economic Community as the possible beginning of a new system of slavery, since other capitalists would not be responsible as the French had been (AA, March 4, 1957).

It was not until the heads of government met with the foreign ministers on February 18 and 19 that there was overall agreement on the outstanding issues of the association with the overseas territories. The Germans now agreed to economic as well social infrastructure projects, provided they were designated for a specific development purpose, and the prime ministers agreed on the precise amounts of money each government was to contribute to an overseas investment fund. Most of the principles previously agreed on with respect to trade were also part of the bargain. But several other issues, including which provisions would apply to Algeria, and the right of establishment in the overseas territories, were left to the delegates to settle at a later date (Conférence, Feb. 19-20, 1957; Konferenz, Feb. 20, 1957; Moravcsik, 1998:148).

The issue as to which tropical products were to be covered by the common market Treaty was so controversial that an impatient Spaak finally resorted to reading out a list of products one at a time (on February 18, 1957), inviting the assembled foreign ministers to settle the fate of each product there and then (Küsters, 1982:345; Ministère, Jan. 29, 1957). Even after this tactic, there had to be special protocols allowing Germany to import bananas and Italy coffee from some traditional suppliers. Carstens credits a single determined German businessman with the banana protocol; he insisted on continuing to import the supposedly superior quality Central American bananas as against the inferior African product. Only two weeks before the signing ceremony, a senior French negotiator, Donnedieu de Vabres, had to travel to Bonn to settle the issue of Germany's banana imports (AA, March 11bis, 1957; Carstens, 1993:211).

After the prime ministers had settled the main issues, delegates still spent many hours solving the last outstanding problems, such as the fact that Algerian workers would not have the right to free movement within the community and that the overseas investment fund would not invest in Algeria. This last item was not agreed until the day before the signing ceremony, which was also the meeting at which the delegates agreed on the German import quota for bananas (AA, March 10, 1957; Conférence, Feb. 28 – March 3, 1957 and March 24, 1957).

In the final agreement, the six governments agreed to invest 200 billion French francs in the overseas territories over five years, of which Germany and France would contribute 34 per cent each. The French territories were to receive 180 billion, or ninety percent of this amount. The Germans won the right of community control over some of the investments made by the investment fund. The Council of Ministers, voting by qualified majority, would have the final say with respect to such investments if any member states challenged the Commission's initial decision on such a project. With respect to trade, the Community was gradually to open its market to the products of the overseas territories, while these territories would continue to enjoy limited protection from European products (Lynch, 1997:205; Treaty, 1962).

Concluding Comments

Having considered the attitudes of the French and German elites on four of the subjects – the institutions of the European Economic Community, social policy, agriculture and the association of overseas territories – which dominated the negotiations for the Treaty of Rome (Chapters 3 and 4), the degree to which these attitudes were conveyed to and reflected in the intra-governmental decision-making process on these negotiations (Chapter 5) and finally having examined the negotiations themselves, I can now turn to an analysis of the degree to which ideas and interests influenced the negotiators of the two governments. This is the subject of Chapter 7.

7 Ideas and Interests

The Treaty of Rome of March 25, 1957 constitutes a complex amalgam of the interests of the six governments and of the interests of groups and firms within the six states. But it represents much more than that. The treaty would not have been possible without the ideas which influenced political leaders and elites in all six countries. Returning to the schema introduced in Chapter 1, I now attempt to analyse the extent to which ideas as well interests shaped the Treaty of Rome.

In his book *Choice for Europe*, Andrew Moravcsik (1998:88) makes a strong case for the predominance of powerful economic interests as the factor shaping the contents of the Treaty of Rome, though he does admit the limited influence of geopolitical factors such as the Cold War. While Moravcsik's facts are undoubtedly correct, his explanations are insufficient. Commercial interests of themselves cannot explain the creation of the Treaty of Rome. Only ideas can. And geopolitical interests added to ideas were crucial in bringing the project to its conclusion.

This chapter explores the ideas and geopolitical factors which influenced the contents of the Treaty. After a brief discussion of political ideologies which may have influenced the treaty drafters, I turn to the European idea itself, the extent to which the moral imperative of building a united Europe influenced elites, leaders and negotiators. Next, I discuss the ideas and values of social welfare, the intrinsic value of agriculture and the obligations of Europe to the Third World, to determine the extent to which these ideas influenced the Treaty. Lastly, I examine the geopolitical factors which made the conclusion of the Treaty possible.

Political ideologies played a limited part in the negotiations. The two ideologies which played a role of any kind are economic liberalism and Christian democracy. Those closely involved with the writing of the treaties included only three economic liberals: Erhard, Müller-Armack and Marjolin. Erhard, as we have seen, was marginalised during the writing of the treaties. His attempts to influence its content, or in the later stages to undermine it, bordered on the comical. Müller-Armack was a bureaucrat, and though his sympathies lay with Erhard, he could see the general direction of government policy, and for the most part chose to do his best to inject some liberalism into the treaties, rather than to try and change their overall direction, much less to sabotage them altogether. And as the negotiations progressed, with Müller-Armack as one of the chief German negotiators, he must surely have developed an interest in the project he was helping to build. Indeed, his memoirs show pride rather than disappointment with his work during those years; the title of his book makes this abundantly clear: *On the Road to Europe. Memories and Perspectives* (1971:100-118).[1]

Marjolin (1986:281-2), trained as an economist, states his dedication to liberalism and freer trade, but he does so in supporting the EEC as an example of such liberalism. Unlike Erhard, who described the EEC as an armoured tank of economic protectionism, Marjolin saw the EEC as a step, however gentle, which could nudge France out of its protectionism into a more liberal mode. The difference in the description of the treaty by Erhard and Marjolin reflects the difference in ideology between France and Germany. What passed for liberalism in France appeared illiberal to Germans like Erhard. Whether there in fact was less governmental control over the economy in Germany than there was in France is a different issue, which economic historians can debate. The topic here is ideology more than practice.

In addition to the core provisions on the freeing of trade and the free movement of factors of production, one other part of the treaty represents an application of liberal ideology: the provisions with respect to competition policy. These articles (85 to 94) are a reflection of the belief that governments need to enforce the rules of liberal orthodoxy (Baskoy, 2004).

As for Christian democracy, it had been a prime influence at the time of the creation of the Coal and Steel Community. And so to the extent that the experiences of the ECSC influenced the creation of the EEC, Christian Democracy had an indirect influence on the EEC. But by 1956 the influence of Christian democracy in France had waned. The Mollet government did not include any MRP ministers. Christian democratic ideas had been influential during the early years of the Fourth Republic, but by 1955, only a few aspects of Christian democratic beliefs, such as that of social welfare and a strong family policy, continued to influence the governments of France. One of these ideas, that of the government's obligation to provide social welfare, continued to influence French politics and thus the Treaty of Rome. The only other hint of Catholic ideas during the negotiations comes in the occasional reference to the fact that decisions should be taken at the national level to the extent that this could be

---

1 *Auf dem Weg nach Europa. Erinnerungen und Ausblicke.*

effective, a foreshadowing of the idea of subsidiarity. The principle of subsidiarity constitutes an acknowledged offshoot of Catholic social thought (AA, Feb. 12, 1956; Comité, Feb. 13, 1957; Ministère, Feb. 17, 1956; Neunreither, 1991).

In Germany, a government which called itself Christian Democratic still governed, and indeed won the Federal Republic's only majority government in the October 1957 elections. But German Christian democracy (treating CDU and CSU as one party, which, of course, they were and are not) had become a label for 'catch-all' parties which included liberals such as Erhard, old-fashioned German conservatives, such as Strauss, and as Müller-Armack points out (1971:107-114), some genuine Christian democrats, such as Adenauer, Hallstein and Brentano. Christian democracy, however, shaped German policy on the EEC even less than it did that of France. As we shall, see, Adenauer's policy was the product of his European convictions and his geopolitical realism, more so than of his Christian convictions. It is noteworthy that when Küsters (1995) tries to make a case for the influence of Adenauer's Christian convictions on his European policies, he relies on a quotation from 1952.

Much more influential than the Christian tradition was the concept of Europe as a political objective. The majority of France and Germany's governing class believed firmly that it was their duty to build a supranational Europe which would overcome the nationalism which had brought Europe so much pain during the first half of the twentieth century. It was this idea, along with developments in the politics of the world, which carried the EEC project to its successful conclusion. The participants believed that they had to succeed, that failure would be an unacceptable derogation of duty (Küsters, 1982:255). This belief permeates not only their memoirs, but also shines through the discussions as revealed in the documentary record. The Italian delegation summed it up in one of its reports; the treaty, they wrote, satisfied the 'moral exigencies of Europeanism' (cited in Burgess, 2000:73).

Europeanism usually meant overcoming national sovereignty through the creation of supranational institutions. In his memoirs, Marjolin admits to discomfort with 'extreme European views', such as those of Monnet who advocated a United States of Europe, but Marjolin also writes of the need for supranational institutions to allow the community to function (1986:253 and 267-8). The lack of supranationality and, therefore, of perceived Europeanness, was the reason why the OEEC-wide free trade zone, which the British and Erhard tried to dangle before the negotiators, represented such a danger to the EEC negotiations (Küsters,

1982:294). Adenauer's memoirs (1967:254) express the determination to continue the integration of just six countries by any and all means and to the greatest degree possible. The Belgian, Baron Snoy et d'Oppuers, himself a participant in the negotiations, wrote of the need for majority voting within the community so as to induce the governments to 'assume their purely European responsibility'; he continued by advocating the creation of a 'community imperium', whatever that may mean (1965:194-5). The determination to create supranational institutions is a good illustration of the cross-cutting influence of ideas and interests (Parsons, 2000). Because they believed in a united Europe, participants decided to create supranational institutions. Because of the specific issues which needed to be resolved, they chose institutions designed to deal with these issues.

The determination to succeed and build Europe is also evident from discussions which took place at the time of the negotiations. Reporting on a conversation with Maurice Faure, Carstens pointed out how eager Faure was to continue the discussions and get results before the government in France might once again change (AA, Aug. 3, 1956). Writing to a journalist, who it seems had criticized the German government for making too many concessions of France, Hartlieb pointed out that there had been a revival of the European idea in France since the defeat of the EDC (AA, Jan. 11, 1957). Three weeks later, Ophüls, writing from Brussels where delegates were struggling with the details of the agricultural provisions and the association of the overseas territories, strongly advised against a postponement of the planned meeting of foreign ministers. That would be an admission of failure. There might be many issues still in dispute, but there must not be an impression of failure (AA, Feb. 1, 1957). Even Erhard told Maurice Faure that he, Erhard, believed in the 'European idea' and Franco-German reconciliation (Ministère, Sept. 16, 1956). The determination to give life to the European idea is as evident in the pages of the French documents as it is in the German, and surprisingly all of the references of this nature which I was able to find date from before the time when the Suez Crisis wound into its denouement. On February 11, 1956, Pineau, in a meeting with Brentano, said that 'it was vital for the future of the idea' (unspecified!) that the Brussels negotiations succeed (Ministère, Feb. 11, 1956). De Margérie, the French chargé in Bonn, made several references to Adenauer's and Faure's belief in the European idea (Ministère, Sept. 26, 1956). Indeed, French and German participants referred to the need to make 'sacrifices' to achieve this idea, an unusual word indeed for a politician to use when appealing to public opinion (Ministère, Feb. 11, 1956 and May 3, 1956; AA, [mid-January 1957]). Even more surprising, the German government was able to use its determination to pursue the European idea and its geopolitical concerns to persuade German agricultural groups to accept a treaty which was likely to lead to the creation of a common agricultural policy that would almost certainly result in less protection and lower prices for agricultural products produced by German farmers (Moravcsik, 1998:158).

Closely related to the European idea is the concept of Franco-German reconciliation (Burgess, 2000:184). During discussion leading to the negotiations, the idea that France and Germany had a special responsibility to cooperate and build Europe appears many times. When Pineau met Brentano in March 1956, shortly after Pineau had become foreign minister, they discussed difficult issues such as the Saar and the Moselle Canal, but they also expressed their determination to build a European community by resolving the differences which still separated France and Germany (Ministère, March 3, 1956). In October 1956, in a background document for the forthcoming Mollet-Adenauer meeting, a French civil servant wrote about the need to develop the habit of Franco-German cooperation. To that end, he suggested frequent bilateral meetings, supplemented by meetings with other European governments as the need arose (Ministère, Oct. 22, 1956). Writing from Paris, the German ambassador commented how in a vote on the delicate subject of the Saar, recently restored to Germany, the French National Assembly had displayed a willingness to improve relations with Germany (AA, Dec. 14, 1956). Reporting on the Adenauer-Mollet meeting of November 6, Carstens pointed out how the two leaders had expressed their determination to cooperate in the building of Europe (AA, Nov. 10, 1956).

What is missing from these declarations of devotion to the European idea and Franco-German reconciliation is the next logical step, which might have been a determination to create federalist institutions. While, as is evident from the previous chapter, there were many discussions of the issues on which the Council of Ministers should vote by majority or what the powers of the Commission and the Assembly should be, these discussions were linked to specific issues and interests. There was not a general determination to create supranational institutions for their own sake. So the idea of building a united Europe, by whatever means possible, had to some extent superseded the fascination with supranational institutions and the dream of a federal Europe, which had dominated the early days of post-war Europeanism up to and including the time of the founding of the European Coal and Steel Community. (Moravcsik, 1998:153).

Ideas and values other than the European idea also influenced the delegates. While nearly all knowledgeable Germans rejected the French idea of specific harmonisation of French and German social legislation, French and Germans did share a belief in ever rising standards of living and an expanding welfare state. This was a time before the concept of limits to growth had been invented. The Germans and the French disagreed on the means, not the end. Germans, including economic liberals such as Erhard, believed that economic growth was best achieved through free competition and that the resulting benefits were best distributed by means of collective bargaining between unions and management. With much weaker unions, and with the strongest union federation being the anti-establishment Communist-dominated *Confédération Générale du Travail*, French governments had chosen to distribute the benefits of growth primarily through social legislation such as laws setting the number of working hours and the minimum number of paid holidays. Nevertheless, all six delegations, regardless of their domestic social legislation, had no difficulty in resolving some of their differences by including in the treaty a profession of faith in rising standards of living and of expanding social security provisions.

A similar situation prevailed with respect to agriculture. While some German liberals, such as Erhard, were reluctant to accept a system that would force Germans to import European agricultural products in preference to those from elsewhere, the principle that agriculture embodied special values and needed to be protected was widely accepted in Germany as well as in France. There was a difference of degree. In Germany, trade unions and the Social Democrats were willing to sacrifice German agriculture to some extent, though that is not the terminology they would have used, whereas in France the mythology of the '*petit paysan*' and the values of agricultural life were so deeply ingrained that it would have been political suicide to question it. That the new community must have an agricultural policy was, therefore, self-evident to French and German negotiators. It only remained to work out the details, and that issue was postponed and left to the new institutions. The treaty itself only expressed a long list of desirable but somewhat contradictory aims for the future agricultural policy.

Ideas and values did not so clearly predominate when it came to the fourth of the topics selected for analysis in this book, that of the association of the overseas territories. Adenauer in his memoirs writes of the need to consult the peoples of the overseas territories and of the obligation to help them improve their standard of living. But he begins the discussion by referring to the raw materials to be found in those territories and the fact that the people there needed help in accessing and using and selling these materials (Adenauer, 1967:269-270).

A background paper written by a German official for a cabinet meeting in mid-January 1957 makes yet another point frequently found in the German discussions about the association with the overseas territories. It speaks of a German obligation to help in the economic development of these territories, a task which the colonial powers themselves could not afford. In this way, the territories would be 'drawn into the community of free Western nations' (AA, mid-January 1957). A letter from Brentano to Adenauer reporting on the progress of the Brussels negotiations was even more explicit. Brentano wrote of the earlier German request that the African territories be associated with Europe – there is no documentary record of such requests – and continues by mentioning a Western-Communist confrontation in Africa. Therefore, Brentano concludes, Germans should welcome the inclusion of the overseas territories in the European community (AA, Dec. 8, 1957).

Ophüls also supported the association with the overseas territories, but his reasons were somewhat different. He reasoned that if Germany would in any case be asked to contribute to the economic development of the underdeveloped countries, Germans should take this opportunity to concentrate aid on countries which were like to be friendly to Europe, whereas more scattered efforts might mean that aid would go to territories which were 'europafeindlich', a truly untranslatable term which suggests enmity to Europe as a concept (AA, Nov. 29, 1956).

In short, when German leaders and negotiators reflected on the association of the overseas territories they did feel some sense of obligation of helping what were then called the underdeveloped countries, but they also saw both economic and geopolitical advantages in this association. It is noteworthy that there is no record in the French archives of any such idealistic or even ideological or geopolitical justification for the association with the overseas territories. Though French leaders spoke of such factors in public (see Chapter 3), they do not occur in the records of the negotiations. There is no record of a French negotiator sitting down with a German one and saying, we are doing Europe such a service by helping to develop Africa; why do you not help us in this effort? Instead, the French negotiators were interested in the francs and marks of economic assistance and to a more limited extent with marketing the products of the overseas territories and with protecting their markets there (AA, March 19,

1957). They also wanted to retain for as long as possible whatever status France could derive from being an imperial power (Faure, 1984:205; Milza, 1992). The November 1954 beginning of the rebellion in Algeria, which became the eventually successful war of independence, is especially relevant in this respect. The slogan 'Algérie française' resonated across the French political spectrum, from right to left. In 1955 or 1956, very few French citizens could contemplate the idea of a France without Algeria.

In addition to ideas, the world geopolitical situation strongly influenced the negotiations, and indeed it is likely that without these geopolitical factors the treaties, and more especially the European Economic Community, would not have been created in 1957 (Parsons, 2000). Geopolitical factors were a necessary, if not a sufficient, condition for the creation of the EEC. Frequent references to world events, not only in the accounts of the participants but also in the documents detailing the negotiations, make this factor abundantly clear. On November 10, 1956, Carstens, in pleading with one of the frequent German interministerial meetings (see Chapter 5) not to attempt to alter the settlement he and Marjolin had reached after the Mollet-Adenauer meeting of November 6, said that 'the talks in Paris had been successful under the influence of the threatening world situation' (AA, Nov. 10, 1956). In joining the European Economic Community, according to Deighton, Germans chose the primacy of politics over the primacy of the economic (1995:44).

The Cold War had just passed its first peak between 1955 and 1957. In July 1955, President Eisenhower met First Secretary Khrushchev and Premier Bulganin in Geneva; Eisenhower made a daring 'Open Skies' proposal, whereby he offered the Soviet Union flights over the US in return for a reciprocal right for the US to over fly the USSR. What impressed European leaders about this meeting was the fact that they were sitting on the sidelines. Unlike at the last superpower summit, that at Potsdam in 1945, France and Britain were not major participants on this occasion, and Germany was not a factor at all, a feeling the counsellor in the American embassy in Bonn describes with empathy (Department of State, Jan. 8, 1957).

In a related development, Chancellor Adenauer travelled to Moscow in September 1955 to attempt to negotiate at least an attenuation of the division of Germany. His visit was almost totally unsuccessful. The soviet authorities were not willing to discuss the unification of Germany, and the only concession they were prepared to make to Adenauer was to release most of the remaining German prisoners of war, still in Soviet prison camps more than ten years after the end of World War II.

Adenauer's independent diplomacy reminded French leaders of the 1922 Rapallo Treaty, when Weimar Germany and Soviet Russia had signed a treaty of cooperation, with secret clauses which circumvented the disarmament of Germany mandated by the Treaty of Versailles. An independent neutral Germany, like that which signed the Treaty of Rapallo, was a nightmare no French government wished to see again.

The third world event, the one of the greatest importance to the negotiations in Brussels, was the Anglo-French attempt to retain control of the Suez Canal, a development which has already been described in Chapter 6. Another related development, not further discussed in this book, was the October 1956 Soviet invasion of Hungary. Hardly ever mentioned by the negotiators, it must have been on the mind of at least the German participants. While Hungary was outside NATO and the United States therefore had no obligation to defend it, the almost total inaction of the Western allies only underscored Adenauer's fears that the American governments might no longer be fully committed to the defence of Western Europe.

It would be wrong, however, to see the attempts to unite Europe as part of a Cold War effort to defend the West. While this factor existed, it was relatively unimportant. Adenauer's mentions it in his memoirs, but they, like most such testimonials, were written for public consumption (Adenauer, 1967:253). In private conversations, Adenauer more frequently spoke of the need to defend Western Europe against communism and a possible Soviet threat, but not in the context of an overarching Western alliance led by the US. In private, Adenauer expressed deep suspicions about the US, and he did so before and after the Suez and Hungarian crises.

In September 1955, at the Noordwijk conference, Hallstein told his colleagues that Adenauer had told him that détente between the superpowers intensified the need for the unification of Europe (AA, Sept. 6, 1956). The German record of the conference repeats this points and adds that détente was a reason to continue the policy of European unification and to practice the 'political, economic and cultural self-determination of Europe' (AA, Oct. 26, 1955). In September 1956, the French chargé in Bonn was surprised to hear Adenauer, who publicly appeared to be such a faithfully ally of the United States, express distrust of the United States, who, according to Adenauer, could not always be relied upon to 'link its fate with that of Europe' (Ministère, Sept. 26, 1956). On October 2, 1956, Mollet and Adenauer met to discuss bilateral issues. When the topic of European unity came up, Adenauer spoke of the United States becoming inward looking on the one hand, and relying on intercontinental defence on the other, leaving Europeans to defend themselves. Therefore, Europeans ought to respond 'drawing together and tightening the lines which bound them' (Ministère, Oct. 2, 1956). Later in October, Adenauer told the new French ambassador, Couve de Murville, that since the Geneva conference (that is since the meeting between Bulganin, Khrushchev and Eisenhower), he, Adenauer, had feared that the United States and the Soviet Union would come to an agreement, of which the Europeans would be mere objects (Ministère, Oct. 10, 1956). That is why Adenauer insisted on making his previously planned visit to Paris at the height of the Suez Crisis when several of his advisors counselled against an action that might identify Germany with French and British colonialism (AA, Nov. 2, 1956; Küsters, 1982:327). Adenauer wanted to create a sense of European solidarity in the face of external danger.

During his talk with Mollet on November 6, 1956, Adenauer expressed repeated suspicions of the US, and this was before Pineau was called out to receive the British ambassador's news of the British withdrawal because of American pressure. Adenauer told Mollet that an American vice-admiral had told him how the US was less interested than it had been in defending Europe; Adenauer promised to send Mollet a record of that conversation. Adenauer expressed mistrust of the US and, according to the French note taker, said that unifying Europe did not necessarily signify supranationality, but it did mean that the European countries would have to unite 'against the United States' ('*contre l'Amérique*'). America, Adenauer said, was responsible for the Suez Crisis, and American ignorance of Europe could make one cry. The Americans, Adenauer continued, wanted to come to an agreement with the Soviet Union, presumably at the expense of Europe (Ministère, Nov. 6, 1956). The Suez and Hungarian crises did more than intensify Adenauer's fears that the US might not defend Europe in times of need. It also convinced French leaders that their foreign policy objectives could not be achieved without the support of other European governments. The Suez Crisis, in Küsters's words, 'tipped the balance for the French government's decision in principle to join the Common Market' (Küsters, 1989:97-98). According to Deighton (1995:31), Mollet and Faure also believed that Europe needed to create a 'Third Force' between the superpowers, and the Suez Crisis must have intensified such a belief. Other developments also support this interpretation. As pointed out in Chapter 6, Mollet did not make concessions on social harmonisation until immediately after the Suez Crisis (see also Küsters, 1982:328-333).

An anonymous analysis of the effect of the Suez Crisis (found in the French foreign policy archives) credits the Suez Crisis with influencing the Belgians, the Luxembourgeois and the Italians to be more inclined to unify Europe, but says that the effect on the Germans and the Dutch has consisted of a certain degree of hostility toward France and Britain. This writer had obviously not spoken to Adenauer (Ministère, Dec. 5, 1956). Hallstein, writing many years later, said that the desire to create a European federation which could regain some of Europe's influence in the world was the most important motive for the creation of the European Economic Community, more so than lasting peace between France and Germany, which by then had been achieved (Hallstein, 1962).

As discussed in Chapter 6, geopolitical factors influenced the German decision to accept the costly association of the overseas territories. Adenauer in particular believed that growing Soviet influence in Africa could be countered by European support for the colonies there (Adenauer, 1967:269-270). Adenauer told Mollet that the Suez problem, then not yet a crisis, had demonstrated the degree to which 'the awakening of the peoples of colour' threatened Europe, and Mollet was said to have been in total agreement with this position (Ministère, Oct. 2, 1956). Brentano, in a letter to Adenauer, wrote that 'there could be no doubt that in Africa especially' was 'the scene of a confrontation between the communist states on one side and the Western community of nations on the other... It follows that we should not only accept but welcome the demand for an association of the overseas territories' (AA, Dec. 8, 1956). In January 1957, the anonymous writer of a lengthy cabinet background paper on the Brussels negotiations, wrote of the 'strategic importance of Africa' and of its 'economic reserves' now that its peoples were being emancipated. He continued: 'In the confrontation between the free West and the Soviet bloc, Africa cannot be surrendered' (AA, mid-January 1957).

A related geopolitical factor was the insistent belief by most Germans that their country should be, indeed had a right to be, reunified. No politician who hoped to be re-elected could speak out against this wish. Adenauer, in public as well as in private, insisted that a strong, unified western Europe was a necessary step toward the unification of Germany (Adenauer:1967:257). Neither Adenauer nor anyone else could explain just how a strong western Europe would lead to the unification of Germany, but events more than thirty years later proved that Adenauer and the CDU were right. In 1957, Germans insisted that what remained of German unity be enshrined in a special protocol to the treaty which gave both East Germany and the city of Berlin free trade access to the European Economic

Community, a concession the French made as much out of geopolitical logic as in return for the association of the overseas territories, as is generally supposed. Cold War logic held the Soviet Union responsible for the division of Germany, and not to allow East Germany access to the common market would have been a legitimation of the Soviet control of part of Germany.

French fears of Germany, not only as an economic but as a political and military rival, constituted another geopolitical factor. Küsters (1982:322) traces the degree to which the adoption of the German conscription law (1956) influenced the Mollet government to intensify its efforts toward European unity. Louis Joxe, the ambassador in Bonn, wrote to Pineau in February 1956 that, now that Germany 'had regained its rank as a great power', the European idea, which had been a help to German foreign policy, was becoming a hindrance (Ministère, Feb. 3, 1956). During February and March 1956, when Mollet, Pineau, Brentano and Adenauer held frequent talks to settle the details of the return of the Saar to Germany and of the canalisation of the Moselle which was part of that arrangement, the French participants felt compelled to say that all this was being done in a spirit of European unity and Franco-German cooperation (Ministère, Feb. 20, 1956). Most interestingly, in May 1956, when Pineau was in Moscow for talks with Bulganin and Khrushchev, Pineau told his Russian interlocutors that they had nothing to fear from European unification, that it was in no way directed against the Soviet Union, but rather that France, in a search for security, was attempting 'to insert Germany into a European community' (Ministère, May 18, 1956).

As for Germany as an economic power, as early as December 1955, an unsigned report from the central Europe division of the French foreign ministry warned of the new confidence of German industry and its spirit of initiative (Ministère, Dec. 12, 1955). Girault dates French concerns about German economic resurgence to an even earlier date, beginning in 1952 (Girault, 1992). An economic community was meant to share Europe's burdens, in Europe and Africa, and thus ensure that Germany's growth did not leap ahead of France's at too rapid a pace. Indeed, the French preoccupation with social harmonisation was to a large extent based on fear of economic competition from Germany. Instead of saying the Germans are more competitive than we, French business and political leaders preferred to say, we fear that we cannot compete because we are more generous than the Germans (Milward, 2000:44-45).

Another factor, which cannot be captured by any of the traditional frameworks for the study of European integration, but which has been evident as a motive for economic integration in the Western hemisphere, is the desire to promote or lock in domestic reforms both of a political and an economic nature (Mahant and De Vanssay, 1994; Mattli, 1999:46-50). When Prime Minister Brian Mulroney took Canada into free trade with the US, one of his motives was to ensure that no future Canadian government would be able to try to control the economy in the name of sovereignty, as he believed his predecessor Pierre Elliot Trudeau had tried to do (Mahant, 1993:46). Similarly, when President Bush Sr. eagerly accepted President Portillo's (later Salinas') offer of free trade with Mexico, Bush hoped to ensure that never again would the Mexican economy become as government-owned and government controlled as it had been (Mahant and Mount, 1999:184).

Domestic reforms were also a concern when the Treaty of Rome was being negotiated. Whereas the need to enshrine German democracy had been mentioned as a motive for the Coal and Steel Community and the Council of Europe, by the time of the discussions leading to the Treaty of Rome, reforms in France were a more frequent theme (Carstens, 1971:236). This is evident from some of the quotations from the MRP and the French *patronat* given in Chapter 3 above. The Belgian Snoy et d'Oppuers (1995) wrote of the need to create an 'indissoluble economic infrastructure', and Küsters (1982:365) mentions an agreement between the *patronat* and Mollet. The Mollet government would introduce economic reforms which would be to the *patronat's* liking and the *patronat* would support economic integration. By 1955, it was the Germans rather than the French who occasionally mentioned the need to consolidate German democracy or to prevent a renewed upsurge of German nationalism as a reason for anchoring the Federal Republic in Europe (Küsters, 1995). French leaders were more concerned about reforming France.

Missing almost entirely from the discussions among the governmental representatives is the idea that the common market would lead directly to economic prosperity and growth. The Spaak Report, in its introduction only, mentioned the benefits of longer production runs and rapidly advancing technology of which Europeans could not take advantage unless they created a larger market. As an example, the report added the fact that no European automobile manufacturer had a long enough production run to afford the technology Americans were using (Comité, 1956:9). The economic advantages of a larger economic area may have been assumed as being so obvious as not worth discussing, but this is not likely. French economists did try to measure the effects of integration and more development aid on the economy of the overseas territories. It is more likely that the political leaders who negotiated the European Economic Community believed the economic benefits that would result to be not only self-evident but also less important than the political advantages the common market was meant to produce. Besides, the leaders knew in their hearts that uniting Western Europe was the right thing to do.

Identifying the Birthmarks of Europe

It is time to examine the principal thesis of this book, the degree to which the motivations and policies which shaped the original European Economic Community continued to shape the European Union into the 1990s. I begin with a series of questions relating to the motivations of the Community's founders and continue with the ideas underlying the four policy areas examined in the last five chapters. In Chapter 8, I will then make a cursory attempt to determine the extent to which these birthmarks have continued to characterise the policy areas discussed earlier as well as three other events in the history of the European Community/Union: the Single European Market (also known as Europe 1992/93), the Single European Act and the Treaty of the European Union (also known as the Treaty of Maastricht).

The questions I shall be asking as I analyse each of these policies areas will be:

- To what extent has the idea that Europe should be united continued to influence the development of the European Union?
- To what extent has the wish to unite Europe as a Third Force against the superpower(s) continued to influence the development of the European Union?
- Have the ideologies of Christian democracy and liberalism continued to influence the development of the European Union?
- Has fear of Germany or the desire to anchor Germany in Europe continued to influence the European policies of the Union's member governments including that of Germany?
- To what extent have France and Germany continued to dominate and shape the policies of the European Union?
- Have the ideas that Europeans ought to adopt a progressive and expanding social policy which also ought to be harmonised across the

European Union continued to influence the making of European social policy?

- Have the ideas that agriculture is an industry which deserves special governmental support and that there should be one common European agricultural policy continued to influence the making of agricultural policy?
- To what extent have the ideas that Europeans have an obligation to give economic assistance to the peoples of the Third World (particularly those of Africa), and that they can rely on these countries as a source of raw materials and as markets, continued to influence the EU's policies toward the Third World?
- To what extent has the idea that Europeans have a special obligation to prevent the spread of unfriendly ideologies into the Third World continued to influence the EU's policies toward these countries?
- To what extent has the idea that a special relationship with former European colonies can help to enhance Europe's role as a world power continued to influence the EU's policies toward the Third World?

The next and last chapter will attempt an answer to some of the above questions by applying them to some of the developments in the history of the EU since its founding on January 1, 1958.

8 Birthmarks of Europe

As a kind of postscript to the rest of the book, this chapter makes an attempt to determine the extent to which the ideas and some of the interests which shaped the original Treaty of Rome have continued to influence the policies and the development of the European Union. It would not be sufficient to just pursue the four issues discussed in the earlier part of this book. Since 1958, the European Economic Community/Community/Union has expanded its tasks manifold and its institutions have become much more sophisticated and developed. Nevertheless, the basic institutional structure which the EEC adapted from the ECSC has remained in place, albeit with many accretions and variations. The two part executive representing, supposedly, the interests of the Community overall (the Commission) and the interests of the member states (the Council in its various guises) has remained in place. The most important change has been the election of a Parliament with some real authority. The projected European constitution may bring new and perhaps different institutional developments, though to date it seems to be mainly a compilation of existing practices.

By the turn of the century, some commentators were perceiving a decline of the Commission, as against the Council. The authority and prestige of Council and Commission has seesawed before. And each enlargement has brought pronouncements that the institutional structure must change or collapse. For now, however, the basic institutional framework would appear to have survived.

Rather than study the evolution of the Community's institutions, this chapter will examine three key developments in the history of the European Community as well as the continuation of the three policy areas studied earlier, with a view to determining the extent to which the basic ideas and interests which shaped the EEC in 1957 have survived over the years. The chapter will thus consist of a brief examination of the Single European Market program, the Single European Act and the Treaty on European Union as well as a brief examination of the EU's continuing policies with respect to social policy, agriculture and relations with developing countries. Intended more as a guide to further studies than a thorough analysis of the themes being discussed, the chapter will attempt a preliminary assessment of the degree to which institutional continuity, ideational continuity and enduring perceptions of subnational and national interests have marked the development of the EU.

Most of the examples date from before 1992, the date of the signing of the Treaty on European Union. This lack of contemporaneity is intentional. The author has a hunch that the reunification of Germany, the end of the Cold War in Europe and the imminent expansion of the Union to include many more East and South European countries may have forever altered the founding formulas on which the Union was based. However, to the extent that the policies studied, particularly agricultural policy and policy toward the developing world, continue into the 1990s and beyond, there are some intriguing hints that her hunch may be wrong. Only further studies at a future date will be able to determine the answer.

Social Policy

Social policy played an important part in the negotiations of the Treaty of Rome. Practically all participants believed in an expanding welfare state. The French negotiators sought harmonisation on their model of government legislated social benefits, as well as acceptance by the other governments of specific social benefits already enacted in France; this issue was primarily a Franco-German one. Lastly, the governments agreed on the need for some type of community financial assistance to those whose jobs were affected by technological developments or freer trade, and they agreed to help those whose skills needed upgrading to participate in the labour market.

Ideology has continued to shape European social policy. Christian democracy, the ideology which defined much of political life in postwar Europe, has faded into insignificance. There are still political parties with this or similar names, but these parties are moderate conservative parties. Therefore, Christian democracy as an ideology now has limited direct influence on European policy. On the other hand, some Europeans still find a European identity in their Christian traditions. As recently as 1997, the European People's Party (EPP) passed a resolution stating that Turkey did not share Europe's civilisation (Müftüler-Bac and McLaren, 2003). In 2003, the members of the European constitutional convention considered including Christianity as a European tradition in the preamble to the draft European constitution. However, in the end the secularists won the debate (K. Woodward, *New York Times*, June 17, 2003).

Liberalism has become the dominant ideology of the democratic world, and classical liberalism of a type found in the United States under the misleading label of conservatism and in Britain under Margaret Thatcher forms a part of the ideology of many continental political parties, including the German Christian Democrats, the French conservatives and even the formerly so statist French Gaullists. With respect to social policy, this has meant that the social policy espoused by the European Union now is Janus-like: it serves two purposes, one is social policy for its own sake, the other is social policy as an aspect of competitiveness (Roberts and Springer, 2001:28). While the context and the content of social policy has changed greatly since 1957, these were the two aspects of social policy included in the Treaty of Rome: social harmonisation, for the sake of fair competition, and a declaration of faith in social policy for its own sake. Indeed, the French preoccupation with social policy as an aspect of competitiveness returned in the 1990s in the guise of 'social dumping'.

The content of social policy now, however, has a very different emphasis from that which it had in 1957. At that time, social policy was conceived primarily in terms of benefits, such as paid holidays or subsidised housing. That aspect of social policy still exists, but much of the Union's social policy now deals with employment policy, work place health and safety and the inclusion into the labour force of the unemployed (Roberts and Springer, 2001:35-39). The social policy page of the EU's website clearly demonstrates these aspects of Union social policy. There are sections on benefits but also several discussions of 'inclusion' for the unemployed, the elderly, the disabled (http://www.europa.eu.int/scadplus /leg/en/s02206.htm June 15, 2003). Interestingly, the emphasis on gender equality has survived. Two topics on the list of the Union's explicit social policy competences include equal pay for men and women (apparently not yet achieved) and gender equality in the work force (Leibfried and Pierson, 2000). A new aspect of European social policy is a reflection of the German concept of co-determination and similar corporatist arrangements in some of the new member states (Austria, Sweden). There now is a European Works Council Directive as well as several directives requiring management to consult labour on issues such a major layoffs and company strategy (*Economist*, June 16, 2001; Leibfried and Pierson, 2000).

There is an emphasis, much greater than anyone could have imagined in 1957, on competitiveness and the single market. This includes mobility of workers and of social benefits. The initial exclusion of social policy from the single market program led to protests and then to the adoption of the purely declaratory European Social Charter (Dinan,

1999:423-5; van Velzen, 1991). The Treaty of Amsterdam clearly establishes social policy as one of the Union's responsibilities and establishes which aspects of social policy will be the subject of unanimous or weighted majority voting in the Council of Ministers (Leibfried and Pierson, 2000; Roberts and Springer, 2001:29-31).

Social policy is one aspect of Union affairs that is no longer clearly dominated by the Franco-German axis. For at last two decades Union social policy has been driven primarily by Franco-British disputes and Franco-British compromises, with most of the other governments supporting the French position. The British brand of Thatcher liberalism influenced the social policy aspect of the single market program, a British Conservative government prevented the inclusion of social policy in the Treaty of Maastricht, and a British Labour government reversed that position allowing social policy to be included in the Treaty of Amsterdam (Nugent, 1999: 337). Over roughly the same time period, a Socialist president in France (François Mitterrand) and a French Socialist President of the Commission (Jacques Delors) continued to keep social policy on the agenda of the Union (Dinan, 1999:421-2; Hoffmann, 1995:239-240). In 1996, a French conservative government (led by Alain Juppé) headed by a Gaullist President presented a memorandum on a 'new European social model' to the Council of Ministers; Europe, the memorandum stated, could not achieve the adherence of Europeans if it did not have a 'social and a human face' (*Le Monde*, March 26, 1996).

The European social fund still exists under that name, but it now has become a part of the Union's extensive regional development effort. The fund assists with retraining, but its aims now also include 'social inclusion' and 'adaptability and entrepreneurship' (*Economist*, Jan. 17, 1996: http://www.esfnews.org.uk/intro/index/shtml June 15, 2003). The fund provides 45 per cent of the funding of a project, as against the 50 per cent it provided during its first decades.

Thus social policy displays continuity as well as innovation. In spite of subsidiarity and the unwillingness of national and regional governments to give up control of a policy which benefits the people so directly, social policy has become increasingly a European activity. National and regional governments deliver social benefits with but very few exceptions, but the content of social policy is to a large extent driven by a European agenda. Though no longer accepted almost universally, the idea that Europe ought to be united has continued to drive the actions of the established elites, and social policy continues to be one aspect of the means by which this idea is implemented (van Oudenaren, 2000:150). The preamble to the Single European Act states the need to 'improve the economic and social situation by extending common policies and pursuing new objectives', the Treaty of Amsterdam states that the Union's objectives include 'economic and social progress and a high level of employment ... through the strengthening of economic and social cohesion', and the Lisbon European Council declaration of 2000 included the following objective: 'to modernise and improve social protection to respond to the transformation to the knowledge economy, change in social and family structures and build on the role of social protection as a productive factor'. Social policy has become a part of the *acquis communautaire.*

Agricultural Policy

For the first 25 years of the EEC's existence the Common Agricultural Policy (CAP) constituted the prime exhibit in the showcase of European integration. It was the one policy which was truly European. The Commission played a major role in both designing and implementing the CAP, and European-wide interest groups played an important role in the policy's formulation. But was it just bad luck or were there deeper reasons why three of the four industries which became the prime examples of European integration (coal, steel, agriculture and atomic energy) were also industries in decline, industries whose significance in the European economy shrank as European policy-making over them expanded (Sandholtz and Zysman, 1989)?

Since the time they first industrialised, European governments have, for the most part, chosen to support agriculture in the face of rising secondary and later tertiary industries (Rieger, 2000). Subsidising an entire industry is an expensive affair, but European governments were willing to make the sacrifice. By 1955, French agriculture was at a crossing point. Food shortages after World War II had begun to give way to surpluses (Ackrill, 2000:25 and 41; Delorme and Tavernier, 1969:102). This situation could have been resolved through various policy responses, such as export promotion, a campaign of consolidation, encouraging farmers to move off the land (a policy which would have been very much in line with the modernisation projects of the French national economic planning strategy), 'set asides' of agricultural land on the American model, or encouragement of farmers to grow food crops which would replace imports or non-food crops which could produce industrial raw materials or energy. Of all these possible options, the French government chose that of a European agricultural policy, one which various members of the French government had been advocating since the early 1950s. Fortunately for the government of France this was not only a French policy. In Chapter 6, we noted that German agriculture also needed protection and promotion, and Ackrill noticed that the agricultural objectives stated in the 1957 Treaty of Rome resemble those of the German agricultural law of 1955 (2000:42).

Books about the CAP are full of details on prices for wheat, beef, fodder, milk and so on, and about the specific interests of, for example, German, French and Dutch farmers. However, the choice of a European agricultural policy as a policy response was about more than such details. It was, to some extent, also a matter of timing, and more importantly, a reflection of a set of values and ideas. One idea was that of a united Europe. It was because this idea existed as a desirable goal that French policy-makers chose Europe as a solution for its potentially expensive agricultural surpluses, and it was because of the European belief in the value of the agricultural way of life that French policy-makers rejected most of the other possible options listed above. Leon Lindberg, in a book on the development of the CAP in which he specifically rejects the ideational explanation for the progress of European integration, comments on the '*apparent* disappearance of opposition to the principle of integration' and quotes the French minister of agriculture as saying of a European agricultural policy: 'We are condemned to succeed' (1963:108 and 269). In other words, uniting Europe, including its agricultural policies, had become a value in its own right.

What is true of France is even truer of Germany. For many years, Germans paid for the CAP. At the time that the initial CAP was being negotiated, that is from 1958 to 1961, it was obvious that the German government would need to pay many of the subsidies for farmers in other community countries, whereas German farmers might not continue to enjoy all the benefits the German government had provided for them. It is for this reason that Lindberg's detailed account of the negotiations is a story of (mainly) French demands and gradual German acquiescence (Ackrill, 2000:31; Gerbet, 1983:255; Lindberg, 1963: 249, 266-9, 275-7).

Why, however, would the government of Germany make such concessions on behalf of its taxpayers? The textbook truism that the European Economic Community was a deal between France on behalf of its agricultural exporters and Germany on behalf of its export-minded industrialists is simply not true (Ackrill, 2000:40-41). German industrialists opposed the agricultural policy. That is why the German government was so reluctant to accept it. Adenauer was Chancellor until 1963, when he was replaced by the free trade, free economy proponent Erhard. Adenauer was determined to continue the making of Europe, which was one of his government's many achievements, from having Germany admitted to the Council of Europe to the founding of ECSC and then the EEC and Euratom. Adenauer's belief in the building of Europe was so intense that he insisted on making all the concessions which were necessary to make a common European agricultural policy a reality. This was all the more true since the French government made the acceleration of the creation of the customs union, which most of its own industrialists wanted, dependent on the creation of the CAP (Lindberg, 1963:251). What a crowning achievement for Adenauer's career – an accelerating customs union linked to a common *European* agricultural policy; in short, a rapidly developing European Economic Community (Marjolin, 1986:319).

One could also speculate about Adenauer, Christian democracy and agriculture. The belief in the value of the rural way of life is an important component of the Christian democratic ideology, and it certainly formed a part of the program of both the CDU and the CSU, as against the SPD, which was more inclined to worry about the price of food for urban workers. This may be another reason why Adenauer insisted on the concessions needed to make the CAP a reality, but this is pure speculation. Adenauer did not write or speak about it. He was an urban person, a former city mayor and perhaps did not think too much about agriculture. To Adenauer, agriculture was one means to an end – a united Europe.

In 1962, when the negotiations were over and the new policy ready to be implemented, the British paper the *Financial Times* commented, incredulously, that the six governments 'were willing to gamble with votes at home rather than stand accused of blocking the advance toward closer unity' (cited in Lindberg, 1963:273). Once again a British commentator did not understand the importance of the value of a united Europe.

The common agricultural policy which came into force in 1962 had three main components: a single market, Community preference and financial solidarity (Dinan, 1999:335). By the mid-1970s this policy carried the seeds of its own destruction. It was not only that British participation brought in another government which paid in much more than it received and that the unexpectedly rapid industrialisation of Italy had converted that country into one which paid into rather than benefiting from the CAP. It was also the cost of the CAP itself, which rapidly grew to a point where it used up more than 60 percent of the Community's budget, even as the proportion of farmers in the European population decreased.

And there were the agricultural surpluses which became the laughing stock of the world, the mountains of wheat, the freezers full of butter and beef, the lakes of wine (Dinan, 1999:339).

The need for reform was obvious, and not only because Margaret Thatcher wanted her money back. Reforms began gradually in the mid-1980s, culminating in the McSharry reforms which capped the amount of some products, such a milk, for which the Community would pay full price, reduced the guaranteed prices of many products and began a program of direct assistance to low income farmers (Dinan, 1999:341-3; Rieger, 2000). The community also accelerated its efforts to help farmers retire, so as to consolidate farms and make them economically viable. Reform in the late 1980s and 1990s was driven by a new pressure from the United States, which practiced its own form of agricultural protectionism and wanted the Europeans to open their markets so as to relieve the US of some of its agricultural surpluses (Dinan, 1999:341).

The proposed enlargement to include East European countries, most of which have an agricultural sector of a size not seen in Western Europe since the 1940s, presents the CAP with new challenges. The Commission's 1997 proposal, 'Agenda 2000', was meant to deal with these challenges. It proposed further price cuts but included two aims also seen in the Treaty of Rome in 1957: stable incomes for farmers and a fair deal for consumers. However, the Agenda also reflects new concerns: environmentally friendly agriculture, safe food, an internationally competitive agricultural sector and alternative employment opportunities for farmers and their families (Dinan, 1999:347). The Council, meeting in Berlin two years later, accepted the objectives of the reform, but postponed reform of the basic structure of the CAP, that is the common prices and common financing of agricultural policy, to be reviewed in 2002. The Council also gave the CAP a new environmental and business gloss, both in the spirit of the times. There is to be investment in farm businesses and human resources as well as help to forestry and for farmers who use especially environmentally friendly farming practices (Ackrill, 2000:215-216; Rieger, 2000).

By 2002, the French and German governments, meeting separately before the Council meeting to deal with the postponed reform of the agricultural policy, decided to postpone reforms again, but also decided to keep costs down, meaning that in effect there would have to be further changes, especially once the East European countries with their large agricultural sectors join (*Economist*, Nov. 2, 2002).

For years the CAP was the most European of European policies, or at least that was its image. In fact, elements of national protection have crept back into the CAP ever since so-called Monetary Compensation Amounts in the 1970s allowed first the German and then other governments to compensate their farmers for currency fluctuations. The latest reforms, in an effort to reduce community costs while coping with the pressure of farmers who block roads and threaten to vote governments out of office, allow governments to subsidise their own farmers (Rieger, 2000). This, however, does not constitute the re-nationalisation of agricultural policy, which remains European with national and now regional elements (Nugent, 1999:414).

The rise and perhaps coming decline of the CAP illustrates the continuing power of the European idea and of other ideas on this much maligned policy. Delorme and Tavernier point out how the CAP helped to create a European identity among French, and one might add, Irish farmers (1969:119). Only the idea of Europe convinced Adenauer to impose sacrifices on his people for the sake of the CAP. And the idea of the value of the agricultural lifestyle has helped to persuade European taxpayers to continue to support the agricultural policy.

However, in recent years the values and ideas which underpinned the CAP have been joined by new ones. Environmentalism has come to the rescue of the CAP. Farming is said to be good for the environment; still, farmers are to avoid practices such as the genetic modification of food and intensive farming practices that lead to the spread of animal diseases and which may have caused BSE to spread from animals to humans. A look at the agricultural pages of the European Union's websites show as many headings which deal with food safety and environmental concerns as deal with traditional agricultural subjects. So although some new values and new ideas now infuse the CAP, the basic concept of preserving the agricultural life style remains.

Agricultural policy continues to be dominated by the Franco-German condominium. This is not to say that other governments have had no influence, only that the French and German governments continue to design and protect the principal structures of the CAP. While some things have not changed, others have. By aligning itself with environmentalism and regional development and by attempting to meet consumer demands for safe food, the Commission and others who favour a united Europe have succeeded in aligning themselves with some of the progressive forces in Europe (Ackrill, 2000:152). They have not been completely successful in these efforts – some European summit meetings have been the target of anti-globalisation protestors – but they have managed to stay on the progressive side of the values debate.

Policies Toward Former Colonies/Developing Countries

The provisions of the Treaty of Rome dealing with the overseas territories of the member states were a French initiative, which was somewhat modified as the result of German and Belgian input. The 1950s were the last decade of traditional European colonialism. By the early 1960s, most of the French and Belgian overseas territories became sovereign states. In 1973, Britain, which once had the largest colonial empire in history, became a member of the European Union. But that was in the past. By the turn of the 21st century only a few small territories still have colonial status. The largest of these are French controlled – New Caledonia, Tahiti and French Guyana.

From the beginning, that is from 1957, there were two primary justifications for the special relationship between the overseas territories and the European Economic Community. One was geopolitical, and in turn had two aspects. There was the concept of Europe as a Third Force between the superpowers; Europe could not be such a Third Force without the support, prestige and territorial extension of the overseas territories. The other geopolitical aspect of the argument was economic. In order to be an international power in its own right, Europe needed access to raw materials and, to a lesser extent, markets for its products. A preferential trading system with its former colonies would give Europe these advantages.

The other argument for the association was the altruistic argument that Europeans had an obligation to help the less fortunate peoples of their colonies and former colonies, not necessarily as an admission of guilt for former injustices (though that might be the case), but more generally as an obligation of the rich to help the poor. This was one of the arguments that won over Germans such as Adenauer and convinced them to pay for what at the time appeared to be the continuation of French colonialism.

So much has changed with respect to attitudes toward economic development since the 1950s that it is surprising that, through various successor agreements and arrangements, a special relationship between the European Union and some of the former colonies has survived to this day. The provisions of the 1957 treaty dealing with the overseas territories were succeeded by two inter-state agreements regulating the trade and development relationship between the European Economic Community and the former colonies (Yaoundé I in 1963 and Yaoundé II in 1969), to be succeeded, after Britain joined the Community, by four successive Lomé Conventions, spanning the period from 1975 to 2003. As of 2003, the Lomé conventions have been succeeded by the first Cotonou Agreement (signed in 2000; ratified by 2003).

Albeit in much altered form, the geopolitical purpose of the original agreement about the overseas territories has survived. European leaders see themselves as practitioners of an enlightened development policy and, without any need to say so, this means more enlightened than that of the former superpowers and now the United States. The Union's development policy is one way for it to gain prestige and an international presence. A Commission publicity pamphlet on the European Development Fund begins with the following statements:

> The European Union is one of the main actors in the field of development cooperation and poverty reduction. Its contribution to development aid has grown considerably and the range of beneficiaries has broadened... Today, the combined aid of the European Union and the member States represents nearly 55 per cent of public international development aid and more than two-thirds of grant aid (European Commission, 2002).

It is significant that the now 77 or more non-European signatories of the Cotonou agreement include the former African colonies of France, Britain, Belgium and Italy, most of the Caribbean states and some small Pacific territories. The larger, more populous or more developed ex-colonies (for example, India, Indonesia, Cambodia, Vietnam, Tunisia, Morocco) are excluded, as are the countries of Latin America. They all, singularly or in groups, have their own agreement with the EU. Yaoundé, Lomé and Cotonou are all agreements between one large and a large number of much smaller 'partners'. Suspicions that this was not meant to be an equal partnership intensified when the EU side suggested that the ACP group be broken up into smaller groups, such as, for example, the Caribbean states, so that the EU would become more selective in giving assistance (Dinan, 1999:506-7; ECDPM, 2001; Hylton, 2002).

As for the economic aspect of the geopolitical argument, this has become less important over time. At the time of the Suez Crisis and into the 1970s, the decade of the oil crisis, Europeans were concerned about access to raw materials. The special relationship with the overseas territories gave them some assurance of such an access (ECDPM, 2001;

Winters, 2001). This has changed. Raw materials have become less important as an economic input, and for most products there is an abundance or even an oversupply. This is especially true of tropical crops, such as rubber, sugar, cocoa and coffee. Trade with the ACP[1] countries has become less important to the EU over the years. Over the course of the Lomé agreements, the ACP's share of imports into the EU fell from 7 per cent in 1975 to 6 per cent in 1985 to 3 per cent in 1995. Worse yet for the ACP, their proportion of ACP imports declined more rapidly than did that from other developing countries. The tendency for the ACP countries to export labour-intensive primary products while the EU sells them capital intensive, high value added goods also has not changed (Babarinde, 1997). Indeed, the ACP countries, in spite of privileged access provisions in terms of tariffs, have struggled to maintain their access to European markets, where they have encountered competition from European farmers (rice, sugar) or traditional suppliers (bananas). The Cotonou Agreement includes a provision whereby the long-standing provisions for free access of the ACP countries to EU markets (for manufactured goods), available to the ACP countries without reciprocity, is to be replaced by a new system, to be in place by 2008, that would amount to a series of free trade areas (Regional Economic Partnership Agreements). While meant to be WTO-compatible, such a system is not likely to improve ACP access to European markets nor increase ACP influence in negotiations with the EU (ECDPM, 2001tres; Stevens, 2000).

The altruistic argument for development assistance and a special relationship with the former colonies has remained an important component of the justification for the EU's development policy. The Treaties of Maastricht and Amsterdam list the objectives of EU development policy as including sustainable development, 'the campaign against poverty,' the development of democracy and a commitment to the objectives of the United Nations (Article 177). While some elements have remained similar – the eradication of poverty is now one of the two primary objectives mentioned in the Cotonou Agreement – others have changed. Sustainable development is now the second objective mentioned in the agreement (ECDPM, 2001bis). The Cotonou Agreement provides for a development fund of 15.2 billion euros, as well as a carryover of the 10 billion that had not been taken up under the last Lomé Convention (ECDPM, 2001bis). Since the IVth Lomé Convention, Europeans have

---

1 African, Caribbean and Pacific, the official abbreviation for the non-European signatories of the Lomé and Cotonou agreements.

made the observance of human rights a condition of aid. In the Cotonou Agreement, progress toward gender equality and absence of corruption were added to the list of conditions for aid (ECDPM, 2001bis). Winters argues that the eradication of poverty and the geopolitical argument are connected, presumably because poverty could breed instability (2001).

The ideology underlying the agreements has also changed. Whereas in 1957 it was one of paternalistic Christian democracy, liberalism now governs. The Cotonou Agreement mentions private sector participation, emphasises the combating of corruption and talks about civil society, democracy and human rights (ECDPM, 2001bis; Stevens, 2000).

So in summary, the geopolitical argument, especially in its purely political manifestation, has remained an important component of the EU's development policy. The development policy, and more specifically the Yaoundé, Lomé and Cotonou agreements, are meant to enhance the EU's role in the world. The development policy has also taken on a new role, one it did not have at the time of the Treaty of Rome. As a part of the Union's common foreign policy, it is meant to contribute to the uniting of a Europe with state-like characteristics. That is why the EU development policy was incorporated into the Treaty of Maastricht and later Amsterdam (Van Reisen, 1999:37). While the EU's development policy is to be 'complementary' to that of the member states, it is nevertheless described as a Community policy (Article 177). Development policy has remained primarily a French interest with a considerable degree of German input, as it was in 1957. This has not changed much, but may with the membership of the Scandinavian states who have a strong tradition of development assistance. The altruistic justification has become more important over the years. It is now a principal component of the EU's development policy, whereas it played a secondary role in 1957.

The Single European Act (1987)

The Single European Act constituted the first major revision of the Treaty of Rome since the founding the European Economic Community.

The SEA's immediate antecedents are to be found in 1984, which not coincidentally was the last year of the first term of the directly elected European Parliament (first elected in 1979). Those of a European persuasion had seen the EEC, Euratom and the ECSC as only the beginning of a united European polity. Many of the elected members of the first European Parliament experienced a special sense of responsibility in this regard. Altiero Spinelli, for example, was a committed European of the early post-World War II days in Italy. As an elected member of the European Parliament, he sought to create a European federation, with a constitution which resembled that of the abortive European Political Community of 1953. In February 1984, the Parliament adopted Spinelli's plan by an overwhelming majority of 237-31, but the parliament had little real authority (Schmuck, 1989). The plan might have been forgotten had it not soon attracted a powerful supporter, President François Mitterrand of France. Addressing the Parliament in May, Mitterrand called for further discussions of the Spinelli Plan, as well as a revision of the 1966 Luxembourg Compromise, which had all but eliminated majority voting in the EEC's Council of Ministers (Mahant, 1985).

Mitterrand, like Spinelli, was a European of the post-World War II generation. The political party to which Mitterrand belonged before it merged itself into the newly created French Socialist Party in 1971 was called the UDSR. This party traced its roots to the Resistance against the Nazi occupation, and one of its hallmarks had been strong support for European unity. Mitterrand, however, had another reason to embrace accelerated European unification. As a new President in 1981, Mitterrand had tried to revive the French economy with typical Keynesian measures accompanied by a traditional socialist program of the nationalisation of major industries. These measures had been a failure, as the French economy failed to revive and the franc fell in the relation to the German mark. Mitterrand realized that national economies had Europeanised, perhaps even globalised, and that the kind of economic program he and many other French socialists wanted to implement would need to be both modified and carried out over an area which included several other states – certainly Germany and perhaps also Britain (Budden, 2002; Moravcsik, 1991).

A large majority from the European Parliament and the advocacy of President Mitterrand could not be ignored, especially when it came from the host country of the six monthly European Council (held in Fountainebleau on June 25-26, 1984). That Council appointed a committee, chaired by a former Irish foreign minister, James Dooge, to study both Mitterrand's and the Parliament's proposals. Though consisting of one representative per member state, this committee was said to be personal rather than intergovernmental, so that the members could study issues freely without committing their governments. In June 1985, the Milan heads of government meeting, after a long and acrimonious discussion and after the first ever majority, as against unanimous, decision at a heads of government meeting, which pitted the six original members of the EC against the more recent members, the Council appointed an Intergovernmental Conference (the first by that name – there have been many others since) to study amendments to the Treaty of Rome.

In December 1985, at a Council meeting held in Luxembourg, the heads of government adopted a revised version of the IGC's proposals, since known as the Single European Act (or SEA). The Act committed the member governments to three types of amendments to the Treaty of Rome: a commitment to complete the single market (on which see below), a commitment to revise the decision-making procedures of the European Community to provide for somewhat more majority voting and a larger role for the European Parliament, and the expansion of the activities of the EC to include new topics, such as the environment, regional development and technology, and more hesitantly also to take steps toward a common monetary and a common foreign policy (Nugent, 1999:49-51). Because it integrated political and decision-making in one treaty, this document became known as the Single European Act (Van Oudenaren, 2000:47).

The SEA constitutes a clear example of the wish to continue the unification of Europe. Milward ridicules it as an example of nostalgia, an attempt to apply the policies of the 1950s in the 1980s (Milward, 2000:431). But that is just the point. The political leaders of the post-war years were continuing policies they had been following for decades because they believed them to be the right policies. In the mid-1980s there were few geopolitical imperatives for such a policy – though the Reagan administration in the US made continental Europeans ever more aware of differences between European and American policies (Keatinge and Murphy, 1989). Chancellor Helmut Kohl and Mitterrand were geopolitically aware, but there were no immediate geopolitical pressures promoting the SEA. Nor were there any major developments which increased the neighbours' insecurities *vis-à-vis* Germany.

To the extent that the SEA was driven by interests as well as ideas, these interests were economic in nature, and they consisted as mentioned above, primarily of a French interest in reviving the French economy by means of a European wide policy of economic revival. European integration was by no means the only possible policy toward this goal. It was the European moral imperative which led to this choice (Moravcsik, 1998:377).

The negotiation of the SEA was also characterised by another factor that influenced later Treaty revisions. Mitterrand as the President of the Council in the second half of 1984 and Prime Minister Craxi in the same role in the first half of 1984 tied their prestige and, therefore, also to some extent that of their country to the success of the project undertaken (Budden, 2002; Moravcsik, 1998:343-346). And Mitterrand's influence carried forward into the second half of 1985 when Luxembourg chaired the Council.

The SEA was largely a French initiative carried through with German support. The Thatcher government was outmanoeuvred and outvoted as the Franco-German steamroller, supported by the other original member states, rolled on (Moravcsik, 1991). The SEA was also one of most clear-cut examples of the influence of individuals on European policy. Mitterrand was President of France, and his former finance minister, Jacques Delors, a strongly committed European, was President of the Commission in 1985. Together these two men were able to carry through measures based on ideas to the implementation of which they had dedicated much of their lives (Budden, 2002; Keatinge and Murphy, 1989). And because Delors was President of the Commission, the Commission and its staff played an important role in the drafting of the SEA (Budden, 2002).

Budden also credits the Christian Democratic group in the European parliament, the European People's Party, with a major role in the writing of the SEA, but he probably overestimates the role of the Parliament, let alone the role of anyone group in that Parliament. The Parliament has certainly been a strong advocate of further integration, but the major decisions as to the content of the SEA were taken by the IGC, which drafted a much less European program than that voted by the Parliament the previous year. The SEA did enhance the prestige of the Parliament by formally changing its name from Assembly to European Parliament (Corbett, 1989).

Liberalism was a much stronger influence in the 1980s, not on the SEA as such but on its sister agreement, the Single European Market.

The Single Market Programme or Europe 1992 (1993)

Often confused with the Single European Act, the Single Market Programme, also known as Europe 1992 (and in French as Europe 1993), consisted of a distinct policy initiative which began at roughly the same time as the SEA, but extended over a longer time period and had only a limited institutional connection to it.

An idea which has been adopted and then successfully implemented will inevitably have many putative parents. Thus the idea for the Single Market Programme has, jointly or in combination, been attributed to the European Parliament (Moravcsik, 1998:357), the European Commission and its staff (Moravcsik, 1998:330, 358 and 483; Sandholtz and Zysman, 1989; Young and Wallace, 2000), Lord Arthur Cockfield, an English peer who became a member of the European Commission on January 1, 1985 (Cockfield, 1990), Jacques Delors, President Mitterrand with the support of French industrialists (Moravcsik, 1998:336), a Franco-German initiative (Moravcsik, 1998:359), British Foreign Secretary Geoffrey Howe and the British government (Moravcsik, 1998:359), Prime Minister Margaret Thatcher (Moravcsik, 1998:325; Thatcher, 1993:546-7) and/or a coalition of European industrialists (Dinan, 1999:111; Sandholtz and Zysman, 1989; van Oudenaren, 2000:103). Not one of these claims is totally false. All of the actors mentioned played some role in the adoption of the Europe 1992 project.

The project consisted of a series of about 300 legislative measures, designed to eliminate physical, technical and fiscal barriers to free trade within the Community. The document outlining this project was drafted by a committee headed by Lord Cockfield and formally adopted by the European Council held at Milan in June 1985. Cockfield's White Paper, unlike the proposal for the Intergovernmental Conference that was to draft the SEA, was adopted unanimously. But what the Council at Milan adopted was not the actual 300 measures, but an agreement to implement these measures by December 31, 1992. The purpose was to create a truly barrier-free market in which goods and services could be sold and bought freely and throughout which people and money could move equally freely (though the movement of peoples was left to another intergovernmental initiative subsequently labelled the Schengen agreement).

The link between the Single Market Programme and the Single European Act was twofold. The SEA mentioned the SMP as an objective to be achieved, and the SEA simplified the procedure for adopting single market directives by providing for majority voting on many, but not all, of the directives the Council of Ministers would have to adopt in order to implement the SMP (Dinan, 1999:117-8; Gerbet, 1987:156; Moravcsik, 1998:365). (The Council of Ministers' adoption of these directives in most cases did not suffice to achieve a single, borderless market. In most cases, the measures needed also to be transposed into national laws, a procedure which, when multiplied by twelve, took the then membership of the European Community years – well beyond 1992 – to achieve, and which in some respects has not yet been completed (Nugent, 1999:323; Smith, 2001; http://www.europa.eu.int/scadplus/leg/en/lvb/l70000.htm July 29, 2003)).

The Europe 1992 project constituted a clear and unambiguous continuation of the idea that Europe should be united on the political as well as the economic level. Lord Cockfield's conclusions to his report are a ringing endorsement of European unity in the traditional language of the European idea:

> Europe stands at the crossroads. We either go ahead – with resolution and determination – or we drop back into mediocrity. We can now either resolve to complete the integration of the economies of Europe; or, through a lack of political will to face the immense problems involved, we can simply allow Europe to develop into no more than a free trade area (cited in Cockfield, 1990).

The Treaty of Rome had referred to a common market because the member governments intended to create more than just a customs union. They wanted to enact common policies and possibly continue with movement toward a European federation. But by 1984, the European market was still divided by many types of barriers to the movement of persons, goods and capital and to the provision of services and the establishment of businesses, and only a few common policies were in place. The Europe 1992 programme was an attempt to achieve some of the objectives of the original Treaty of Rome.

The 1992 programme implied more than just the elimination of barriers. There is evidence to suggest that both Mitterrand and Delors presented Europe 1992 as a programme of market liberalisation, all the time fully aware that the implementation of such a programme would require the strengthening of the European institutions which would need to supervise this implementation. Thus Delors and Mitterrand understood that liberalisation required European institutions which would implement that liberalisation (Dinan, 1999:109-110).

The Single Market Programme was also an expression of the idea that Europe could be a Third Force among the superpowers, though in this case the logic was not geopolitical but economic. By the late 1970s and early 1980s, many European leaders believed that the European economies had failed to compete successfully with those of the US and Japan, and particularly the latter. The US and Japan each enjoyed the advantage of a large internal market with few barriers to trade or competition. It followed, so some Europeans reasoned, that Europe should create a single market so as to be able to compete successfully with US and Japanese firms in economic sectors which were capital intensive or technologically advanced. The European Community could thus become an economic third force (Gerbet, 1987:155; Sandholtz and Zysman, 1989).

The SMP marks a turning point in the ideological development of the European project. For years, the European project had been dominated by Christian democratic ideas and influenced by social democratic thought (Thatcher, 1993:552). It is ironic that while two of the originators of the SMP (Mitterrand and Delors) were social democrats, the programme constitutes a clear turning away from Christian and social democracy toward economic liberalism, from the doctrines of Keynesianism to those of market economics. The irony is explained by the events which preceded the SMP. In 1981, President Mitterrand named his new cabinet, with Jacques Delors as Minister of Finance. For the next two years, this government tried to reverse the declining fortunes of the French economy by following a traditional European social democratic programme of social welfare spending, labour legislation and the nationalisation of major industries. The programme was a dismal failure. Not only did the French economy fail to revive, but the franc fell in relation to the German mark (and other currencies). This experience convinced both Delors and Mitterrand that they needed to accept at least some elements of the liberal credo if they were to achieve their social democratic objectives of economic growth and redistribution (Hoffmann, 1989; Moravcsik, 1998:317; Sandholtz and Zysman, 1989; Young and Wallace, 2000).

Though Hoffmann (1989) and Moravcsik (1991) stress the continuing importance of the Franco-German tandem in the adoption of the SMP, the SMP was more a Franco-British than it was a Franco-German initiative. Lord Cockfield, the British commissioner, appointed by Thatcher, drew up the list of the 300 measures which would be required to complete the single market. Though Cockfield did this at Delors's request, he had the support of both Thatcher and Foreign Secretary Geoffrey Howe (Moravcsik, 1998:362; Thatcher, 1993:547). The reasons for Thatcher's support are not clear. One explanation has her use the single market project as one additional means to shake up the British economy and make it competitive. Another explanation is that she wanted to tone down her image as Europe's nay-sayer, by contributing to a European project of which she approved (Hoffmann, 1989). A third explanation has her react to a Franco-German threat of exclusion from the single market (Moravcsik, 1998:374). The three explanations are not mutually exclusive, but the second and third ones are fascinating, for they suggest that even the committed British nationalist may not have been immune to the charms of the European idea. Thatcher's memoirs lend support to both of the last two explanations. She believed the single market to be the true European project, that of liberalisation, and she realised that she need to at least to appear to be European in some respect, if she was to negotiate successfully with Kohl and Mitterrand (Thatcher, 1993:548-553). In any case, the single market was not in itself a Franco-German project. Moravcsik (1998:327) suggests that, on the contrary, sectors of the German economy feared the single market.

It would appear that Mitterrand and Delors's apparent adoption of a liberal project marked a step away from the ideal of an expanding European social policy. Not so. Their experience in France during the years of the social democratic experiment (1981-83) had caused them to change the means, but not the goal. As the French franc fell while the mark continued to strengthen, Mitterrand and Delors convinced themselves that their project of a European welfare state could only be achieved at the European level and in the context of a common European monetary policy. But in 1984-85, other governments were not ready to accept such a common monetary policy, much less a European currency. So Delors sought to achieve the further unification of Europe to a stage where the need for a common currency would become the logical next step. Then, and only then, would it be possible to introduce a European social policy without fear of monetary disruptions (Moravcsik, 1998:372; Sandholtz and Zysman, 1989). In this respect, the single market project also includes *sous-tones*, though no more than that of the European project as a means of containing Germany. The might of the German currency had, however inadvertently, slain Mitterrand and Delors's social democratic project. A European market, followed by a European currency, might be able to tame that might.

The Treaty on European Union (also known as the Treaty of Maastricht)

The Treaty on European Union (TEU; also known as the Treaty of Maastricht) represented such a major step forward in the integration of Europe that it has become the subject of a large number of commentaries and studies. It is necessary to remember that large parts of this historic treaty have been superseded by the Treaties of Amsterdam and Nice. The

TEU nevertheless remains a striking illustration of the European imperative.

Even before the SEA was ratified, Jacques Delors renewed his efforts for a European monetary union, which he had failed to achieve with the SEA. In June 1989, five months before the fall of the Berlin Wall, Delors persuaded the European Council meeting in Madrid to take the first steps toward a European Monetary Union (*Economist*, Nov. 30, 1991; Dinan, 1999:128-129). And as had been the case since 1958, gradual reforms and movements toward further political integration continued, the more so since committed Europeans were disappointed with the unification provisions of the SEA (Mommsen, 1992:62; Nugent, 1999:59). But then in Delors's striking words, history accelerated and caused the Treaty of Maastricht to be negotiated in less than two years, from April 1990 to February 1992 (Dinan, 1999:128-129).

The TEU can only be understood in geopolitical terms. It was a Franco-German initiative in response to the process of German unification. This is not to say that no other interests were reflected in the treaty. Of course, they were. But geopolitical considerations dominated. This is abundantly clear from the records of the participants. Horst Teltschik was Chancellor Kohl's personal foreign policy advisor. He has published an edition of the diary he kept during the year of German unification (Teltschik, 1991). Teltschik is not an academic trying to prove any theory. His is just a story, but in that story the linking of German and European unification is a constant leitmotif. Examples from the book could fill pages. I cite just a few:

- on November 10, 1989, the day after the fall of the Berlin Wall, the foreign policy advisor to President Mitterrand issued a statement: it was time to build a stronger Europe (26);
- on December 5, 1989, days after announcing his ten point plan for German unification, Kohl writes Mitterrand to express his determination to continue the unification of Germany parallel to that of Europe (68);
- on January 4, 1990, at a private meeting in the French countryside, Mitterrand suggests a European confederation; Kohl assures him of his continued support for the Franco-German partnership; a united Germany, Kohl says, will be firmly anchored in the European Community (97-99);
- March 1, 1990, in a speech in Berlin, the French Foreign Minister Roland Dumas links the Franco-German friendship, European unity

> and the unification of Germany; a united Germany, says Dumas, will continue to be the partner of France's fate (164).

Many other commentators have noticed this connection which is too obvious to be denied. Mitterrand, to cite another example, did not commit himself firmly to agree to the unification of Germany, an agreement which was legally required, until after the East German election of March 1990, which showed overwhelming support for German unification. It was then that Franco-German planning for a further push forward of European unification began, culminating in the European Council decision of April 19, 1990, which created the IGC that was appointed to negotiate the Treaty on European Union (Dinan, 1999:133; Moravcsik, 1998:438). Hans-Dietrich Genscher, Germany' foreign minister, claims to remember Mitterrand telling him at a December 1989 NATO meeting that if 'the Germans helped to build Europe, then everything should be possible with respect to the German question' (Genscher, 1997:680). The Open University's Pim den Boer gives intra-European politics yet another angle. In order for France to be a leader of post-cold War Europe, it needed to work with Germany; Eastern Europe, Mitterrand said, should not be left to chance, which den Boer takes to mean Germany. But, the authors continue, this was not just a French policy. Kohl tried to ensure that German unification did not get ahead of European unification (though in the end it did) (den Boer, 1995:188-190).

Though the balance of power within Europe predominated, the world political situation also played a role. In January 1990, Mitterrand reluctantly consented to give provisional support to German unification, but wanted assurance from his two American interlocutors (Lawrence Eagleburger and Robert Gates) that the winding down of the Cold War would not mean that the US would withdraw from Europe (Teltschik, 1991:119). In discussing the TEU, Stanley Hoffmann says that both Germans and French 'remain convinced that America, the sole remaining superpower is ... more than ever a threat'. The Europeans, Hoffmann continues, hope to sustain their resistance against superpower dominance, a struggle which Americans consider to be no more than a 'pipe dream' (Hoffmann, 1995:56).

Furthermore, the TEU was a Franco-German initiative, indeed a Franco-German bargain, which the other member governments accepted with varying degrees of reluctance (Nugent, 1999:64). Since Jacques Delors had become president of the Commission, he had been promoting European monetary integration, and various Community committees had studied this issue since the mid-1980s. Delors, as one of Mitterrand's associates, was conscious of the limits of French monetary autonomy. The Mitterrand administration was determined to create a European monetary system. At the same time, Kohl believed that he could only justify German unification if that united Germany were firmly anchored in a European polity. Kohl did not expect the other European governments, nor the Soviet one, to accept a fully sovereign Germany. So he insisted on progress in political unification with almost as much determination as Mitterrand and Delors put into the monetary union. As a result of these complementary policies, the April 1990 European Council decision to create an IGC began with a Franco-German letter to the Council (Dinan, 1999:133-4; Nugent, 1999:62).

By the time of the TEU, liberalism was the dominant ideology in Europe and North America, and a particular aspect of this liberalism was reflected in the part of the treaty which laid down the timetable for the European Monetary Union. German monetary policy had been shaped by Ludwig Erhard, an economic liberal of the classical school. And it was German monetary policy which became the model for the European monetary policy mandated by the TEU (Hendriks and Morgan, 2001:68). This was a policy which identified a strong currency and the absence of inflation as well as, by implication, balanced budgets as the key to economic success and economic growth.

The TEU demonstrated an adherence to political as well as economic liberalism. In spite of the direct election of the European Parliament, European integration had remained largely an elite exercise (Hallstrom, 2003). The TEU tried to correct this by introducing elements of democratic decision-making. The powers of the Parliament were enhanced to a point where its agreement is now required for major community decisions. There was also to be a citizens' ombudsman reporting to the parliament. The treaty combined liberalism and Catholic social thought with the concept of subsidiarity. Expressed more elegantly in the preamble than in the body of the treaty, subsidiarity is intended to bring decision-making closer to the people.

Delors, and Mitterrand, tried to include the model of a European active social policy in the treaty. They succeeded only to the extent that social progress was given as one of the Union's aims. But in concrete terms the effort failed. The British government refused to participate; social policy was therefore put into a separate Social Charter, which the British government did not sign. Even then, the Social Charter was largely an empty framework, which made provision for a future European social policy (Moravcsik, 1998:454). Nevertheless, it did allow for majority voting on social policy recommendations and states specifically that harmonisation of social policy refers to an improvement, not a cutting, of benefits (Hamon and Keller, 1997:424-427). (The social policy did become a part of the Treaty of Amsterdam, signed after there was a change of government in Britain.) An active social policy has remained a part of the European identity, a characteristic which sets Europeans apart from the US.

As mentioned earlier, in the section on development policy, the concept of a special European relationship with the former colonies is also included in the TEU. It was the first time that the goals of a European development policy were specified in the body of a treaty and thus became part of the *acquis*.

Only agriculture was ignored. Once the star of European integration, the CAP had become an embarrassment. Agriculture did still command powerful political support within most member states; the agricultural myth had not died, but the CAP was in urgent need of a facelift, if not more radical surgery.

The Treaty on European Union is a clear expression of the European imperative. Geopolitical fears and wishes caused French and German leaders to seek revised policies. Europe was the answer closest to their hearts. Other leaders, such as the Italian foreign minister Gianni de Michelis, also responded to the changes over Europe with European enthusiasm. After the Maastricht conference, the *Economist* (Dec. 14, 1991) accused its British compatriots of failing to understand this sentiment:

> Not to see the romantic passion behind the prim Gallic exterior is itself a dangerous failure of imagination. Across most of the continent, the rhetorical vision has been listened to closely and has won support.

European unification has remained a goal that scarcely any continental political leader who wants to be taken seriously will deny. Only extremists, beyond the pale, the likes of Jean-Marie Le Pen, do that. Even those who have criticised the TEU and other specific projects claim to speak in the name of Europe.

Concluding Comments

The six policy areas examined in this chapter all bear the birthmarks of Europe, and most do so to a considerable extent.

The idea that Europe should be united and adopt common policies was a prime factor in the continuing development of each of the six policies examined here. The one possible exception would be agriculture, where some have identified a return to national policies. But, as we have seen, the national policies are only supplements to a continuing European policy.

The idea of Europe as a third (or second?) force as against the superpowers or superpower has also not only survived the Cold War, but continues to be an important factor in European policy-making on both economic and political issues. While the third force argument was overt in the case of the single market, the Single European Act and the Treaty on European Union, it is perhaps less obvious but nevertheless an important factor with respect to social policy, agriculture and policies toward the developing world. The European model of capitalism plus social policy sets Europeans apart from Americans. The EU continues to define a common policy toward many of the former colonies as a way of maintaining an economic and political sphere of influence. And agriculture is not only an issue which has caused many European-American confrontations. The traditional European rural life-style and its supposed virtues are, as is social policy, a source of European identity.

Christian democracy and liberalism have continued to be the defining ideologies of European integration, but over the last forty years, the emphasis as well as the content of the two ideologies has changed. Christian democracy is much less influential than it was at the time of the founding of the EEC, though elements of Catholic social thought have survived, for example, in the doctrine of subsidiarity and with respect to some aspect of social and agricultural policy and policies on third world development issues.

Liberalism has grown to a point where its influence has eclipsed that of Christian democracy. Politicians of nearly all political stripes in all EU member countries now mouth some of the doctrines of classical liberalism, and these doctrines have influenced many EU policies. Social policy is more about responsibility and less about redistribution than it used to be. Programs of economic aid for former colonies now include privatisation and democratisation as objectives. And the Single Market

Programme is an expression of almost pure economic liberalism, albeit with European touches.

Containment of Germany has continued to characterise the European policies of other and even German governments and seemed at first to take on new importance with the unification of that country in 1990. The Single European Act, the Single Market Programme and the Treaty on European Union show this policy in its purest form, but the desire to have German money to develop former colonies is also a way of anchoring Germany in Europe. That said, the policy of containing Germany has lost the overwhelming importance it had in the 1950s. On social policy, for example, the fear of social dumping expressed in France refers more to Britain or Ireland than it does to Germany. And with respect to agriculture, it is French and German governments together who have defended the existing policy against changes advocated by the governments of other member states, notably the UK. In the meantime, some of the more recent member states, such as Greece and Ireland, have developed a strong vested interest in the continuation of the CAP.

Indeed, the Franco-German dominance of most, though not all, Community policies has continued. Even in 2002 and 2003, it is primarily French and German leaders who are discussing the future of the agricultural policy of the fifteen member union. The SEA and the TEU were both French initiatives, enthusiastically endorsed by the German government and then presented to the remaining member states. Social policy presents a different picture in that it has become a common French and German (and Italian and Spanish) interest, which has at times become a matter of contention with British governments. One could also argue that cohesion policy represents a different type of social policy, extended to the southern member states.

The project of European integration, therefore, continues to be shaped by the marks its founders gave it at birth. These marks have been amazingly persistent, even as the world around Europe has changed.

9 Conclusions

Political science journals, especially those dealing with international relations, contain many articles which speculate as to the theories which provide the best fit for specific empirical studies. The problem is that theories which need to fit specific situations are not really worthy of that name, since theories are at the very least expected to explain a number of different types of developments and situations. On the other hand, so-called meta-theories arouse suspicion – and appropriately so – because universal explanations become the academic equivalent of religious fundamentalism.

As so many others before me, I shall, therefore, try to find a middle ground, the middle-level political theory or theories which best explain the process and progress of the European Community/European Union. Chapter 1 hypothesized that an 'additive model', including elements of constructivism, federalism, and consociationalism, would best explain this process.

The analysis presented in Chapter 7 demonstrates that even this wide ranging model is not sufficient to explain all aspects of the founding negotiations of the European Economic Community. To do so we need to reach for at least one of the traditional international relations theories, that of neo-realism. The French and German governments' decisions to persevere with the founding of the common market was influenced by geopolitical motives, a fact which even Moravcsik, an ardent neo-liberal, admits (1998:157). Adenauer in Germany and Mollet and Pineau in France were concerned about western Europe's position in a bilateral world, and they saw a united Europe as a means for Europeans to gain or maintain some autonomy in a world otherwise dominated by the two superpowers.

It is important to note that by 1955, and even more so by 1957, the effort to promote European unification was no longer a 'peace project' as Browning (2003) puts it – that is, an effort to prevent future wars among the West European countries. This factor had been important in 1950, when Robert Schuman called for the creation of the European Coal and Steel Community. But unlike some other ideas, it faded into the background when, in May 1955, the Federal Republic of Germany became a member of NATO, making France and Germany formal allies for the first time since the existence of the latter country.

By 1955, French fears of Germany were largely economic in nature. Weakened by two wars (Indochina and Algeria) and bedevilled by the falling value of its currency, many French men and women reacted to the German economic miracle with some concern. Tying Germany into Europe and getting Germany to share some of France's burdens were thus factors which motivated French policy-makers. Does a wish to benefit from and perhaps limit Germany's apparent economic prowess constitute an example of neo-realism in action? Not in the sense of traditional 'high politics', but in a context where economic competition has largely replaced military rivalry, perhaps it does. Neo-realists may need to revise their theories accordingly.

So if we add a little neo-realism, the additive model does quite well as a theoretical explanation for the founding of the European Economic Community. And among the components of the additive model, constructivism is the most important in this respect. By 1955, the European idea had become a norm to which the governing elites in France and Germany adhered in overwhelming majority. They identified with this policy as the right and proper one to follow, and, therefore, strove toward European integration in their search for a solution to other policy problems (Parsons, 2000), such as the surplus production of French agriculture. Indeed, the example of agriculture provides an almost perfect explanation for the additive model: a material policy problem for which policy-makers sought a solution by applying the norm of European integration.

Chapters 3 and 4 demonstrated the extent to which European elites had internalised the European norm, even during the years 1955 to 1957. Of course, interest group representatives defended the interests of their members, and political parties considered the electoral consequences of the position they took. But all, including the French Communists and Gaullists, claimed to be for a united Europe, even as they opposed the specific project presented to them. (The French Poujadists provide the only exception to this picture.) This rhetorical dedication to the uniting of Europe cast a common framework around the discussions and blunted some of the determination of interest groups, such as German agriculture and the French *patronat*, which represented usually very articulate economic interests.

As discussed in Chapters 1, 7 and 8, norms other than European integration influenced the negotiators. The three examples chosen for study in this book were the intrinsic value of the agricultural life style, the obligation to adopt a reasonably generous social policy and the obligation to help the peoples of Europe's former colonies. In all three cases, there were geopolitical or other material interests which caused governments to seek to put these issues on their policy agenda, but the values held greatly circumscribed the options available, and in some cases pointed in just one direction, that of European integration.

Federalism, on the other hand, provides a much less satisfactory explanation. The relationship between the actual process of European integration and the supposed end-product of a federal European state is an ambiguous one (Pentland, 1973:106-107). On the one hand, the advocates of a united Europe seem in many cases to be unable to think beyond the confines of the nation-state model. The most recent attempts to write a European constitution are an illustration of this line of thinking. On the other hand, advocates of a united Europe often feel compelled to emphasize that they do *not* wish to abolish the comfortably familiar nation-states. They want, so they say, to create institutions which may reduce the sovereignty of states without abolishing them while at the same time improving the lives of the people who live within these existing sovereign states. The irrelevance of Jean Monnet's 'Action Committee for a United States of Europe' during the 1955 to 1957 negotiations confirms the irrelevance of federalism as a valid explanatory approach. The 1957 treaty began with a commitment to 'an ever closer union', but few political leaders envisaged that union as a federal European state. In later years, political thinkers and leaders squared the circle of how to work towards both European federalism and bring government closer to the people by inventing multi-level governance (Hooghe, 1996).

The European project is consociational almost by definition. By creating an extra layer of authoritative decision-making geographically above and politically equal to, or in some cases also above, the national governments, European unification *ipso facto* places power in the hands of political elites. Hix's use of that most Canadian of terms, 'executive federalism', to describe the European political system is, therefore, especially apt (Hix, 1999:31). Such a system can function only as long as the objects of such policies trust the elites to make the right decisions most of the time. The elites, in turn, have a special obligation to consult and inform so as to maintain that trust.

It is the contention of this book that ideas, in many cases expressed through institutions, shape the policies of political systems for years after the material circumstances to which these ideas were originally linked may have changed. Thus I agree with Parsons (2000) that material interests may cause policy-makers to reach for certain policy solutions in preference to others. But I develop this idea one step further by arguing that such ideas, once they are expressed in institutions or have become established policies, take on a life of their own, even as material interests evolve or change.

Take the Franco-German dominance of the EU level policy-making process. As the membership of the Union expanded, the end of this dominance became a frequent prediction of pundits. But the predictions were not fulfilled. As the sample case studies in Chapter 8 demonstrate, Franco-German ideas and initiatives continue to shape EU policies. It is not that the policy preferences of the British or the Spanish or the Greek governments never matter, just as in 1955 to 1957 the policies of the Belgian or Italian governments sometimes made a difference. But overall, Franco-German initiatives and preferences have continued to dominate, and Franco-German meetings still usually provide much of the agenda for the next EU Council meeting (Hix, 1999:97). It does not take detailed case studies to show that the interests of the governments and people of the UK or Spain or Italy may in certain cases diverge sharply from those of the German or French governments and peoples. Nevertheless, other governments defer to these two, it would appear, natural leaders.

The norm of European integration has similarly survived and flourished. The European Community is an institution created in response to the European norm. So this creation in itself strengthened the support for the European idea. But it is not sufficient to justify the persistence of the European idea up to a point where it becomes widely accepted as an inevitability (Browning, 2003). The willingness of governments in at least two cases (Ireland and Denmark) to hold referendums a second time so as to get the right European answer suggests that the European norm has been so deeply internalised that it sometimes trumps that other supposed European virtue: participatory democracy.

An important contributing factor to the success of the European idea can be found in successful public relations. The European idea has been associated with other positive values which are widely accepted by the citizens of Europe: democracy, human rights, tolerance, caring, compassion, rationality, progress (especially scientific progress), a tradition of outstanding artistic achievement and most recently, a concern for nature and the natural environment. Underlying the association of a united Europe with positive values is an often hinted-at but seldom openly stated historical conceit. For centuries Europeans experienced wars and economic depressions. Since 1945, Western Europe has been free from wars, and economic conditions for nearly everyone are better than they have been throughout the continent's history. These changes occurred as

Europe united. Has the integration of Europe been wholly or partially responsible for this fortunate state of affairs? This is, of course, a question to which there can be no definitive answer. However, the integration of Europe has been part of a policy mix which appears to be responsible for this fortunate state of affairs. French and German elites especially have become so accustomed to treating the further integration of Europe as a basic policy, and to practising cooperation between their two governments a means to that end, that to even think of another policy may produce fear and anxiety, not to mention the difficulty of overcoming the bureaucratic inertia which accompanies an established policy. Policies can and, of course, sometimes do change, but it takes a dramatic turn of events or unusually strong leadership (or a combination of the two) to produce change in a long established policy.

Even the author of this book, who has long believed that sovereignty is much more fictional than real and that the concept of national self-determination is a dangerous illusion, believes that the reasoning which attributes Europe's fortunate condition to its unification is based on incomplete evidence. The concept of European integration may have been a bold and innovative idea in its time, its time being the 1940s and 1950s, and it may have served Europeans well since then. But how well it has served Europeans and the degree to which further integration and what type of integration may benefit Europeans, are questions which require empirical investigation, not ideological commitment.

Such scepticism has appeared even in the ranks of that most supranational of institutions, the Commission bureaucracy. Marc Abélès (as cited in Hooghe, 2001:97) cites a Commission official who claimed that mentioning the European idea would lead to disaster, presumably meaning that a person making such a comment would not be taken seriously. Yet Hooghe, who interviewed over one hundred Commission officials during the 1990s, found that dedication to supranational institutions was strong, to the point where even those who declared themselves to be intergovernmentalists advocated majority voting in the Council. A large proportion favoured additional powers for European institutions, such as the European Court and the Commission (Hooghe, 2001:77-81 and 92).

And the European idea is almost certainly not as dead as Abélès believed it to be. The citations from statements President Chirac and foreign minister Joschka Fischer made in 2000 (Chapter 1 of this book) display a great deal of European enthusiasm. In April 2003, on the occasion of the signing of the treaties which are to lead to the accession of ten new member states, Pat Cox, the President of the European Parliament, spoke enthusiastically about common European values, such as progress, unity and harmony (*Bulletin of the European Communities,* 22.04.2003, par. 331.592).

The ideas of the benefits of the agricultural way of life, the commitment to the European welfare state and the commitment to aid for the Third World, especially Africa, are also norms which have become a part of the institutional tradition of the European Union, as the case studies in Chapter 8 amply demonstrate. These norms have been linked to the European idea, to the point where they and others have become a part of the European identity.

But are these values European values, or are they values to be found among advanced, democratic industrial states more generally? There is little work done in this field, but what there is suggests that there are some differences in values between Europeans and Americans. The differences are major on some issues, such as the attitude to religion and the motivation for achievement; they are lower on other questions, such as willingness to demonstrate against a government or acceptance of labour-management cooperation as a desirable policy (Inglehart, 1997:364-387). What may matter as much as the actual difference in values is the fact that Europeans believe that there are distinct European values. One of Hooghe's respondents listed the following European values: 'solidarity, cohesion, local empowerment, empowering the citizen in region and localities'. He continued, 'We are defending a cultural model, neither the Japanese model nor the American model, but the social market economy, the Rhine model' (Hooghe, 2001:81).

This is not to deny the existence of transatlantic ideological and cultural influences. Apart from the common commitment to political democracy, which is the stock in trade of summit communiqués and NATO meetings, Europe has experienced an ideological shift from social and Christian democracy to classical liberalism, a trend which intensified during the Reagan years, and which influenced Europeans as it drifted across the Atlantic. The prime example is, of course, Margaret Thatcher, who had her own British tradition of liberalism to draw on, but the trend is evident in several other European countries, notably among French Gaullists, German Christian Democrats and the new breed of Italian conservatives.

If Adenauer and Mollet thought of Europe as a third force in geopolitical terms, and Delors and Mitterrand thought of Europe as a force in economic terms, an economic power which should be able to act independently of the US and Japan, is it not also possible to conceive of Europe as a force in terms of values and culture?

In spite of the plethora of theories on international relations and European integration, the boundaries between theories have been unnecessarily rigid, with but little allowance for the overlap which must occur. Hix (1999:16) helpfully points out that Moravcsik's neo-liberalism logically falls between neo-realism and liberalism in term of international relations theory. Sterling-Folker (2000) makes interesting connections between constructivism, neo-liberal institutionalism and neo-functionalism. But these are isolated examples in a world of theoretical rigidity. Neo-realism, with its emphasis on the concept of power, has been particularly resistant to change and adaptation, positing the permanence of nation-states and that of power based on military might. In neo-realist terms, economic and cultural power are subsidiary to political and military force (Hix, 1999:331-2 and 355-6).

Only very recently have advocates of the concept of 'soft power' offered an alternative concept of power (Hampson and Oliver, 1998). Power is, of course, central to the study of politics. It should, therefore, not be left out of the study of economic and cultural issues. Nor is power necessarily an attribute of only the nation-state. By definition, power is a component of every political system, and such power can be economic, cultural or military. The power of ideas has been a much neglected aspect of the study of international relations. Power exists within the political, military, economic and cultural spheres, and these spheres are related, but not subsidiary, one to another.

This book has argued that historical institutionalism or path dependency does not provide a sufficient explanation for the development of the European Union. Institutions need to be infused with a continuing supply of ideas and norms. The ideas which were major influences on the negotiations of 1955 to1957 – and this book has not studied all of them – have continued to influence the development of the European Community/Union. New ideas and values, such as environmentalism, have been added, while some ideologies, such as Christian and social democracy, have seen considerable changes. Many more case studies of the evolution of the European Union will be required to determine the extent to which the ideas of the founders have influenced the later development of the European Community. Even more work will be required to determine the influence of new ideas and values.

As it expands to cover almost the entire European continent, the European Union stands at a crossroads unprecedented in its history.

Europe's leaders may attempt to apply and adapt the ideas and institutions of the Community's founders to the new expanded Europe, and they may fail or succeed in that attempt, or they may attempt to develop new institutions and revised norms and ideas, another attempt in which they succeed or fail. Failure would mean the end of the European Union. Success would be its evolution to a post-modern model of multi-level governance. The next decade will be the one which will demonstrate the future path of this, one of the most innovative of the twentieth century's transnational institutions.

References

ABELSHAUSER, W. (1995) 'The Re-Entry of West Germany into the International Economy and Early European Integration.' In *Western Europe and Germany The Beginnings of European Integration 1945-1960*, edited by C. Wurm, 27-54. Oxford: Berg Publishers.

ACKRILL, R. (2000) *The Common Agricultural Policy*. Sheffield: Sheffield Academic Press.

ADENAUER, K. (1955) *World Indivisible with Liberty and Justice for All*, translated by E. Jackh. New York: Harper.

ADENAUER, K. (1965-68) *Erinnerungen*. Stuttgart: Deutsche Verlags-Anstalt.

ALMOND, G. A. (1955) *The Politics of German Business*. Santa Monica: The Rand Corporation.

ANDREWS, J. (1994) History matters. The past means different things to different people. *The Economist*, October 22, 16-19.

AXLINE, W. A. (1994) *The Political Economy of Regional Cooperation: Comparative Case Studies*. Madison: Fairleigh Dickinson University Press.

BABARINDE, O. (1995) Taking Stock of the Lomé Convention: A Panacea for Underdevelopment or a Grandiose Benevolence? Paper read at 38th Annual Convention of the International Studies Association, 18-12 March, at Toronto, Canada.

BASKOY, T. (2004) The Political Economy of EU Competition Policy: A Case Study of the Telecommunications Industry. Ph.D. Political Science, York University, Toronto.

BECKER, W. (1992) 'Views of the Foreign Policy Situation Among the CDU Leadership, 1945-1957.' In *Power in Europe? II Great Britain, France, Germany and Italy and the Origins of the EEC, 1952-1957*, edited by E. Di Nolfo, 351-371. Berlin: Walter de Gruyter.

BÉDARIDA, F. (1992) 'Frankreich und Europa - Von gestern bis heute.' In *Der lange Weg nach Europa, Historische Betrachtungen aus gegenwärtiger Sicht*, edited by J. W. Mommsen (Hrsg.), 1-38. Berlin: Edition q.

BOER, D., P. BUGGE, and O. WAEVER. (1995) *The History of the Idea of Europe*. New York: Routledge.

BONNAURE, P. (1996) A Brief History of European Union Research Policy. *Futuribles* 215:97-103.

BOSSUAT, G. (1995) 'The French Administrative Elite and the Unification of Western Europe, 1947-1958.' In *Building Postwar Europe. National Decision-Makers and European Institutions, 1948-63*, edited by A. Deighton, 21-37. New York: St. Martin's Press.

BRANDSTETTER, G. (1996) *Chronologisches Lexikon der europäischen Integration, 1945-1995*. Baden-Baden: Nomos.

BROWNING, C. S. (2003) Making Space for Marginality: The Inevitability of European Integration Reconsidered. Paper read at ISA Conference, 26-28 June, at Budapest.

BRUGMANS, H. (1969) *La Pensée politique du fédéralisme*. Leyden: A.W. Sijthoff.

BRUNET, J.-P. (1993) 'Le MRP et la construction européenne - 1955-1957.' In *Le MRP et la construction européenne*, edited by R. Rémond, 233-250. Bruxelles: Editions Complexe.

BUDDEN, P. (2002) Observations on the Single European Act and 'relaunch of Europe': a less 'intergovernmental' reading of the 1985 Intergovernmental Conference. *Journal of European Public Policy* 9: 76-97.

BÜHRER, W. (1993) 'The Federation of German Industry and European Integration 1949-1960.' In *L'Europe du patronat de la Guerre froide aux années soixante*, edited by M. Dumoulin, R. Girault and G. Trausch, 17-28. Berne: Peter Lang.

BÜHRER, W. (1995) 'German Industry and European Integration: 1947-1957.' In *Western Europe and Germany The Beginnings of European Integration 1945-1960*, edited by C. Wurm, 87-114. Oxford: Berg Publishers.

BURGESS, M. (1989) *Federalism and European Union. Political Ideas, Influences and Strategies in the European Community, 1972-1987*. New York: Routledge.

BURGESS, M. (1991) 'Innocents Abroad: Federalism and the Resistance between Party and Movement 1945-1947.' In *Shaping Postwar Europe. European Unity and Disunity 1945-1957*, edited by P. Stirk and D. Willis, 7-14. New York: St. Martin's Press.

BURGESS, M. (2000) *Federalism and European Union: The Building of Europe, 1950-2000*. New York: Routledge.

CARLYLE, M, ed. (1953) *Documents on International Affairs 1949-1950*. Toronto: Oxford University Press.

CARR, E. H. (1946) *The Twenty Years' Crisis: An Introduction to the Study of International Relations*. London: Macmillan.

CARRUBBA, J. C. (1998) A Formal Analysis of European Integration. Ph.D, Stanford University.

CARSTENS, K. (1971) *Politische Führung. Erfahrungen im Dienst der Bundesregierung*. Stuttgart: Deutsche Verlags-Anstalt.

CARSTENS, K. (1976) 'Das Eingreifens Adenauer in die Europa-Verhandlungen im November 1956.' In *Konrad Adenauer und seine Zeit*, edited by D. Blumenuitz, Stuttgart: Deutsche Verlags-Anstalt.

CARSTENS, K. (1993) *Erinnerungen und Erfahrungen*. Boppard Am Rhein: Harald Boldt Verlag.

CHIRAC, J. (2000) *Discours prononcés par Monsieur Jacques Chirac, Président de la République Française devant le Bundestag, mardi 27 juin* 2000 [cited June 28 2000. Available from http://www.elysee.fr/cgi-bin/aurac...r_file=discours/2000/ALLE0003.html.]

CHRYSSOCHOOU, D. (1997) New Challenges to the Study of European Integration: Implications for Theory Building. *Journal of Common Market Studies* 35:522-542.

CHRYSSOCHOOU, D. (2000) Meta-Theory and the Study of the European Union: Capturing the Normative Turn. *Journal of European Integration* 22: 123-144.

COCKFIELD, L. (1990) 'The Real Significance of 1992.' In *The Politics of 1992*, edited by C. Crouch and D. Marquand, Oxford: Basic Blackwell Ltd.

Comité national M.R.P. (1957) Le Marché Commun tel qu'on le parle. *Forces Nouvelles* 155.

'Communiqué on the talks between foreign ministers.'(1959) In *Documents on International Affairs 1956*, edited by N. Frankland, 695-6. London: Oxford University Press.

CORBETT, R. (1989) 'The 1985 Intergovernmental Conference and the Single European Act.' In *The Dynamics of European Union*, edited by R. Pryce, New York: Routledge.

DELORME, H. and Y. TAVERNIER. (1969) *Les paysans français et l'Europe*. Paris: Armand Colin.

DELZELL, C. F. (1960) The European Federalist Movement in Italy. *Journal of Modern History* XXXII.

DIEZ, T. (1999) Speaking 'Europe': The Politics of Integration Discourse. *Journal of European Public Policy* 6: 598-613.

DINAN, D. (1999) *Ever Closer Union. An Introduction to European Integration*. Boulder: Lynne Rienner Publishers, Inc.

Di NOLFO, E., ed. (1992) *Power in Europe? II Great Britain, France, Germany and Italy and the Origins of the EEC, 1952-1957*. Berlin: Walter de Gruyter.

ECDPM. *Cotonou Infokit: The Cotonou agreement at a Glance* 2001a [Available from www.oneworld.org/ecdpm/en/cotonou/02 gb htm.]

ECDPM. *Cotonou Infokit: History and Evolution of ACP-EU Cooperation* 2001b [Available from www.oneworld.org/ecdpm/en/cotonou/03 gb htm.]

ECDPM. *Cotonou Infokit: Innovations in the Cotonou Agreement* 2001c [Available from www.oneworld.org/ecdpm/en/cotonou/04 gb htm.]

EICKHORN, G. (1993) *Für ein föderales Europa. Beschlüsse der Bundeskongresse der Europa-Union Deutschland 1947-1991*. Saarbrücken: Europa Union Verlag.

ELLWOOD, D. (1990) 'The American Challenge and the Origins of the Politics of Growth.' In *Making the New Europe. European Unity and the Second World War*, edited by M. L. Smith and P. M. Stirk, 184-199. London: Pinter.

ETZEL, F. (1955) Die europäische Aufgabe der Wirtschaft. *Das Wirtschaftsbild*:2.

ETZIONI, A. (1963) *Political Unification: A Comparative Study of Leaders and Forces*. New York: Holt, Rinehart and Winston.

EUROPEAN UNION. (2001) *History of the European Union* [Website]. [Available from europa.eu.int/abc/history/index_en.htm.]

EUROPEAN UNION. (2003) [Cited June 15, 2003. Available from www.europa.eu.int/scadplus/leg/en/s02206.htm.]

European Union. (2003) *European Social Fund* [cited June 15, 2003. Available from www.esfnews.org.uk/introl/index/shtm.]

Ezra, E. (2000) The Undesired: Exclusion (and Inclusion) in Migration Policy-Making in Europe. *Revue des Affaires européennes*: 7-37.

Faure, E. (1984) *Mémoires II*. Paris: PLON.

Favell, A. (1998) 'We Are All Transnational Now'. Comparing Transnational Elites and Transnational Immigrants in the European Union. Paper read at International Sociological Association (ISA).

Fiddler, C. (2000) *Citizenship and the Euro: Perceptions and Attitudes to the Process of Socio-Economic Integration Between 1992 and 2002*. Sheffield: University of Sheffield.

Finnemore, M., and K. Sikkink. (1998) International Norm Dynamics and Political Change. *International Organization* 52: 887-917.

Fischer, J. (2000) Vom Staatenbund zur Föderation - Gedanken über die Finalität der europäischen Integration. Paper read at Berlin, 12 May 2000, at Humboldt-Universität. [Available from http://www.auswaertiges-amt.de/6_archiv/2r/000512a.htm].

Fontaine, P. (2000) *A New Idea for Europe. The Schuman Declaration - 1950-2000*. 2nd ed. Luxembourg: Office for Official Publications of the European Communities.

France. (1957a) *Journal officiel*, January 17th, 97.

France. (1957b) *Journal officiel*, July 4th, 3269.

Frank, R. (1992) 'The French Alternative: Economic Power through the Empire or through Europe?' In *Power in Europe? II. Great Briatin, France, Germany and Italy and the Origins of the EEC, 1952-1957*, edited by E. Di. Nolfo, 160-173. Berlin: Walter de Gruyter.

Friedrich, C. J. (1969) *Europe An Emergent Nation?* New York: Harper & Row.

Friend, J. (1994) Nationalism and National Consciousness in France, Germany and Britain: the Year of Maastricht. *History of European Ideas* 18: 184-198.

Fursdon, E. (1980) *The European Defence Community: A History*. London: Macmillan.

Gaffney, J. (1996) *Political Parties and the European Union*. New York: Routledge.

Garrett, G., and B. Weingast. (1993) 'Ideas, Interests and Institutions: Constructing the European Community's Internal Market.' In *Ideas and Foreign Policy. Beliefs, Institutions and Political Change*, edited by J. Goldstein and R. Keohane, 173-206. Ithaca: Cornell University Press.

Gebauer, B. (1980) *Europäische Integration. Werkbericht 6 herausgegeben im Auftrag der Konrad-Adenauer-Stiftung*. Melle: Verlag Ernst Knoth.

Genscher, H.-D. (1997) *Erinnerungen*. Munich: Wilhelm Goldmann Verlag.

Gerbet, P. (1983) *La Construction de l'Europe*. Paris: Imprimerie nationale.

Gerbet, P. (1987) *La Naissance du Marché Commun*. Brussels: Éditions Complexes.

Gerbet, P. (1975) 'Les Partis politiques et les Communautes européennes sous la quatrième République.' In *La France et les Communautés européennes*, edited by J. Rideau, P. Gerbet, M. Torrelli and R.-M. Chevallier, 77-100. Paris: Librairie générale de droit et de jurisprudence.

GERMANY. (1956) *Bundestag*, March 22nd, 7092.

GEYER, R. and D. SWANK. (1997) Rejecting the European Union: Norwegian Social Democratic Opposition to the EU in the 1990s. *Party Politics* 3: 549-562.

GIRAULT, R. (1989) 'La France entre l'Europe et l'Afrique.' In *Il rilancio dell'Europa e i trattati di Roma*, edited by E. Serra, 351-378. Bruxelles: Bruylant.

GIRAULT, R. (1992) 'Decision Makers, Decisions and French Power.' In *Power in Europe? II Great Britain, France, Germany and Italy and the Origins of the EEC, 1952-1957*, edited by E. Di Nolfo. 66-83. Berlin: Walter de Gruyter.

GIRAULT, R. (1993) 'Europe du patronat ou patrons européens?' In *L'europe du patronat. De la guerre froide aux années soixante*, edited by M. Dumoulin, R. Girault and G. Trausch, 12-15. Berne: Peter Lang.

GOLDSTEIN, J. (1993) *Ideas, Interests and American Trade Policy*. Ithaca: Cornell University Press.

GOLDSTEIN, J., and R. KEOHANE. (1993) 'Ideas and Foreign Policy: An Analytical Framework.' In *Ideas and Foreign Policy. Beliefs, Institutions and Political Change*, edited by J. Goldstein and R. Keohane, 3-30. Ithaca: Cornell University Press.

GOOD, T. (2000) A Missed Opportunity: Great Britain and the Foundation of the European Economic Community, 1954-1958. Ph.D, Bowling Green State University.

GOWLAND, D., and A. TURNER. (2000) *Britain and European Integration 1945-1998: A Documentary History*. New York: Routledge.

GRILLI, E. (1992) *The European Community and the Developing Countries*. Cambridge: Cambridge University Press.

GUAY, T. (1997) The European Union, Expansion of Policy-Making, and Defense Industrial Policy. *Journal of European Public Policy* 4: 404-421.

GUILLEN, P. (1992) 'Europe as a Cure of French Impotence? The Guy Mollet Government and the Negotiation of the Treaties of Rome.' In *Power in Europe? II. Great Britain, France, Germany and Italy and the Origins of the EEC, 1952-1957.*, edited by E. Di Nolfo, 505-516. Berlin: Walter de Gruyter.

GUILLEN, P. (1993) 'Le MRP et l'Union économique de l'Europe - 1947-mai 1950.' In *Le MRP et la construction européenne*, edited by R. Rémond, 131-148. Bruxelles: Editions Complexe.

HAAS, E. (1958) *The Uniting of Europe: Political, Economic and Social Forces*. London: Stevens.

HAAS, E. (1964) *Beyond the Nation-State: Functionalism and International Organization*. Stanford: Stanford University Press.

HAGLUND, D. (2001) Travels with Charlemagne: Metaphor, Myth and the Puzzle of Franco-German Security and Defence Cooperation after the Cold War, November 28, at the Canadian Centre for German and European Studies, York University, Toronto.

HALLSTEIN, W. (1962) *United Europe: Challenge and Opportunity*. Massachusetts: Harvard University Press

HALLSTROM, L. K. (2003) Support for European Federalism? An Elite View. *European Integration* 25: 51-72

HAMON, D. and I. S. KELLER. (1997) *Fondements et étapes de la construction européenne*. Paris: Presses universitaires de France.

HAMPSON, F. O. and D. F. OLIVER (1998) Pulpit diplomacy: a critical assessment of the Axworthy doctrine. *International Journal* LIII: 379-408.

HEDETOFT, U. (1993) National Identity and Mentalities of War in three EC Countries. *Journal of Peace Research* 30: 281-300.

HENDRIKS, G., and A. MORGAN. (2001) *The Franco-German Axis in European Integration*. Cheltenham: Edward Elgar.

HEUSER, B. (1998) The European Dream of Franz Josef Strauss. *Journal of European Integration History* 4: 75-104.

HIGGETT. R. (1998) 'The International Political Economy of Regionalism. The Asia-Pacific and Europe Compared.' In *Regionalism and Global Economic Integration: Europe, Asia and the Americas*, edited by W. D. Coleman and G. R. D. Underhill, 42-66. London: Routledge.

HITCHCOCK, W. (1997) France, the Western Alliance, and the Origins of the Schuman Plan, 1948-1950. *Diplomatic History* 21: 603-630.

HIX, S. (1999) *The Political System of the European Union*. New York: St. Martin's Press.

HOFFMANN, S. (1995) *The European Sisyphus, Essays on Europe, 1964-1994*. Boulder: Westview Press.

HOFFMANN, S. and R. KEOHANE, eds. (1991) *The New European Community: Decision-Making and Institutional Change*. Boulder: Westview Press.

HOFFMANN, S. (1989) The European Community and 1992. *Foreign Affairs* 68: 27-47.

HOLSTI, K. (1970) National Role Conceptions in the Study of Foreign Policy. *International Studies Quarterly* 14: 233-309.

HOOGHE, L. (1996) 'Introduction: Reconciling EU-Wide Policy and National identity.' In *Cohesion Policy and European Integration*, edited by L. Hooghe, 1-25. Oxford: Oxford University Press.

HOOGHE, L. (2001) *The European Commission and the Integration of Europe. Images of Governance*. New York: Cambridge University Press.

HYLTON, G. A. (2002) The Challenge of Integrating ACP States into the International Trading Regime: Venturing Outside the Lomé Framework. Paper read at CTA International Seminar, 27-29 November, at Brussels.

INGLEHART, R. (1997) *Modernization and Postmodernization. Cultural, Economic, and Political Change in 43 Societies*. New Jersey: Princeton University.

JÍLEK, L. (1997) 'Projet d'assemblée européenne en 1946-1948: rôle des associations de militants.' In *Jalons pour une histoire du Conseil de l'Europe*, edited by M.-T. Bitsch, 17-37. Bern: Peter Lang.

JONSSON, C. (1998) Negotiations in Networks in the European Union. *International Negotiation* 3: 319-344.

KEATINGE, P. AND A. MURPHY. (1989) 'The European Council's Ad Hoc Committee on Institutional Affairs (1984-85).' In *The Dynamics of European Union*, edited by R. Pryce, New York: Routledge.

Keesing's Contemporary Archives: 12932 (1953).

KEOHANE, R, and S. HOFFMAN. (1991) 'Institutional Change in Europe in the 1980s.' In *The New European Community: Decision-Making and Institutional Change*, edited by R. Keohane and S. Hoffman, 1-39. Boulder: Westview.

KEYNES, J. M. (1951) *The General Theory of Employment Interest and Money*. London: MacMillan and Co., Limited.

KIPPING, V. M. (1996) *Zwischen Kartellen und Konkurrenz*. Berlin: Duncker & Humblot.

KNIPPING, F. (1992) '"Firm with the West!" Elements of the International Orientation of West Germany in the Mid-1950s.' In *Power in Europe? II Great Britain, France, Germany and Italy and the Origins of the EEC, 1952-1957*, edited by E. Di Nolfo, 517-529. Berlin: Walter de Gruyter.

KORANY, B. (1974) Foreign Policy Models and their Empirical Relevance to Third-World Actors: a Critique and an Alternative. *International Social Science Journal* 26: 70-94.

KOURVETARIS, A. and G. KOURVETARIS. (1996) 'Attitudes toward European Integration: Ethnic and Cultural Dimensions.' In *The Impact of European Integration: Political, Sociological, and Economic Changes*, edited by G. Kourvetaris and A. Moschonas, Wesport, CT: Praeger.

KÜSTERS, H. J. (1982) *Die Gründung der Europäischen Wirtschaftsgemeinschaft*. Baden-Baden: Nomos.

KÜSTERS, H. J. (1989) 'The Treaties of Rome (1955-57).' In *The Dynamics of European Union*, edited by R. Pryce, 78-104. New York: Routledge.

KÜSTERS, H. J. (1995) 'West Germany's Foreign Policy in Western Europe, 1949-58: The Art of the Possible.' In *Western Europe and Germany. The Beginnings of European Integration 1945-1960*. edited by C. Wurm, 55-86. Oxford: Berg Publishers.

LADRECH, R. and P. MARLIERE. (1999) *Social Democratic Parties in the European Union: History, Organization, Policies*. London: Macmillan.

LEE, S. (1995) 'German Decision-Making Elites and European Integration: German "Europapolitik' during the Years of the EEC and Free Trade Area Negotiations.' In *Building Postwar Europe. National Decision-Makers and European Institutions, 1948-63*, edited by A. Deighton, 38-54. New York: St. Martin's Press.

'Le Marché commun tel qu'on le parle'. (1957) *Forces Nouvelles*: 5.

LEBLOND, L. (1997) *Le Couple franco-allemand depuis 1945. Chronique d'une relation exemplaire*. Paris: Le Monde Éditions.

LEIBFRIED, S. and P. PIERSON. (2000) 'Social Policy. Left to Courts and Markets?' In *Policy-Making in the European Union*, edited by H. Wallace and W. Wallace, 267-316. New York: Oxford University Press.

LETAMENDIA, P. (1993) 'La place des problèmes européens dans la vie interne du parti sous la IVe République.' In *le MRP et la construction européenne*, edited by R. Rémond, 103-114. Bruxelles: Editions Complexe.

LEVARD, G. (1957) Bilans de deux années de progrès dans des perspectives. Paper read at 29ème Congrès confédéral de la C.F.T.C., at Paris.

LIESHOUT, R. (1999) *The Struggle for the Organization of Europe: the Foundations of the European Union*. Northampton, Ma.: Edward Elgar.

LINDBERG, L. (1963) *The Political Dynamics of European Economic Integration*. Stanford: Stanford University Press.

LOTH, W. (1989) 'Deutsche Europa-Konzeptionen in der Grundungshpase der EWG.' In *Il Rilancio Dell'Europa E I Trattati Di Roma*, edited by E. Serra, 585-602. Bruxelles: Bruylant.

LOVETT, A. (1996) The United States and the Schuman Plan. A Study in French Diplomacy, 1950-1952. *The Historical Journal* 39: 425-455.

LYNCH, F. M. B. (1997). *France and the International Economy. From Vichy to the Treaty of Rome*. New York: Routledge.

MAHANT, E. (1969) French and German Attitudes to the Negotiations about the European Economic Community, 1955-1957. Ph.D, University of London, London.

MAHANT, E. (1985) Chronique d'Actualité. *Journal of European Integration*, 213-231.

MAHANT, E. (1993) *Free Trade in American-Canadian Relations*. Melbourne: Krieger.

MAHANT, E. and X. DE VANSSAY. (1994) The Origins of Customs Unions and Free Trade Areas. *Revue d'intégration européenne* 17: 181-210.

MAHANT, E. and G. MOUNT. (1999) *Invisible and Inaudible in Washington. American Policies toward Canada*. Vancouver: UBC Press.

MANIN, P. (1966) 'Le R.P.F. et les problèmes européens.' 78. Paris: Presses Universitaires de France.

MARCH, J. and J. OLSEN. (1998) The Institutional Dynamics of International Political Orders. *International Organization* 52: 943-969.

MARCUSSEN, M., T. Risse, D. Engelmann-Martin, H. J. Knopf, K. Roscher. (1999) Constructing Europe? The evolution of French, British and German nation state identities. *Journal of European Public Policy* 6: 614-633

MARGULIES, R . [no title]. *Freie Demokratische Korrespondenz*. (1957).

MARJOLIN, R. (1986) *Le travail d'une vie, Mémoires 1911-1986*. Paris: Éditions Robert Laffont.

MATTLI, W. (1999) *The Logic of Regional Integration. Europe and Beyond*. Cambridge: Cambridge University Press.

MAZZUCELLI, C. G. C. (1996) France and Germany at Maastricht: Politics and Negotiations to Create the European Union. Ph.D, Georgetown University, Georgetown.

'The Messina Conference and the Development of European Integration.' (1958) In *Documents on International Affairs 1955*, edited by N. Frankland, 163-169. London: Oxford University Press.

MILWARD, A. S. (2000) *The European Rescue of the Nation-State*. London: Routledge.

MILZA, P. (1992) 'Public Opinion and Perception of Power in France at the End of the Fourth Republic (1954-1958).' In *Power in Europe? II Great Britain,*

France, Germany and Italy and the Origins of the EEC, 1952-1957, edited by E. Di Nolfo, 462-476. Berlin: Walter de Gruyter.

MIOCHE, P. (1993) 'L'Adaptation du patronat de la sidérurgie française à l'intégration européenne de 1945 à 1967.' In *L'Europe du patronat. De la Guerre froide aux années soixante*, edited by M. Dumoulin, R. Girault and G. Trausch, 63-75. Berne: Peter Lang.

MOMMSEN, W. J. (1992) 'Einleitung VII.' In *Der lange Weg nach Europa, Historische Betrachtungen aus gegenwärtiger Sicht*, edited by J. W. Mommsen (Hrsg.), Berlin: Edition q.

MORAVCSIK, A. (1993) Idealism and Interests in the European Community: the French Referendum. *French Politics and Society* 11: 45-56.

MORAVCSIK, A. (1998) *The Choice for Europe. Social Purpose and State Power from Messina to Maastricht*. London: UCL Press.

MORAVCSIK, A. (1991) Negotiating the Single European Act: national interests and conventional statecraft in the European Community. *International Organization* 45: 19-56.

MORGAN, R. (1994) European Integration and National Interests. *Government and Opposition* 29: 128-134.

MUFTULER-BAC, M. and L.M.MCLAREN. (2003) Enlargement Preferences and Policy-Making in the European Union: Impacts on Turkey. *Journal of European Integration* 25: 17-30.

MÜLLER-ARMACK, A. (1971) *Auf dem Weg nach Europa. Erinnerungen und Ausblicke*. Tübingen: Rainer Wunderlich.

MUUS, P. (2001) International Migration and the European Union, Trends and Consequences. *European Journal on Criminal Policy and Research* 9: 31-49.

NEUNREITHER, K. (1991) Euphoria about Subsidiarity? The Constitutional Debate in the European Community. *Political Science and European Unification*.

NOBLE, A. (1996) *From Rome to Maastricht: the Essential Guide to the European Union*. London: Warner Books.

NUGENT, N. (1999) *The Government and Politics of the European Union*. Durham: Duke University Press.

NUTTING, A. (1972) *Nasser*. London: Constable.

OPPERMAN, T. (1997) Du Plan Schuman au Traité d'Amsterdam: la coopération franco-allemande, moteur de l'intégration européenne. Paper read at La Coopération Franco-allemande en Europe à l'Aube du XXIe Siècle. Colloque du quarantième Anniversaire du Jumelage Aix-Tübingen, 26-27 juin, at Aix-en-Provence.

OUDENAREN, J.VAN. (2000) *Uniting Europe. European Integration and the Post-Cold War World*. New York: Rowman & Littlefield Publishers, Inc.

PAKASLAHTI, J. (2001) The Social Dimension of the European Union: Studies on the Impact of Integration. Doctorate in Social Science, Department of Social Policy, University of Helsinki, Helsinki.

PALAYRET, J.-M. (1997) 'De l'espoir à la désillusion: le mouvement européen et le Conseil de l'Europe (1949-1952).' In *Jalons pour une histoire du Conseil de l'Europe*, edited by M.-T. Bitsch, 99-132. Bern: Peter Lang.

Parsons, C. (2000) Domestic Interests, Ideas and Integration: Lessons from the French Case. *Journal of Common Market Studies* 38: 45-70.

Parsons, C. (2002) Showing Ideas as Causes: The Origins of the European Union. *International Organization*: 47-84.

Paterson, W. E., and R. Gaffney. (1996) 'The German Christian Democrats.' In *Political Parties and the European Union*, 53-70. New York: Routledge.

Paterson, W. E. (1974) *The SPD and European Integration*. Farnborough: Saxon House - Lexington Books.

Pedersen, T. (1998) *Germany, France and the Integration of Europe: A Realist Interpretation*. London: Pinter.

Pegg, C. H. (1952) Die Resistance als Träger der europäischen Einigungsbestrebungen in Frankreich während des zweiten Weltkriegers. *Europa-Archiv*. Vol. VII. 5197-5206.

Pentland, C. (1973) *International Theory and European Integration*. New York: Free Press.

Perez-Diaz, V. (2000) The Role of Civil Nations in the Making of Europe. *Social Research* 67: 957-988.

Pierson, P. (1966) The Path to European Integration: A Historical Institutionalist Analysis. *Comparative Political Studies* 29: 123-163.

Pineau, C. and C. Rimbaud. (1991) *Le grand pari: l'aventure du traité de Rome*: Paris: Fayard.

Preuss, U. (1998) Migration. A Challenge to Modern Citizenship. *Constellation* 4: 307-319.

Rabier, J.-R. (1989) 'L'Opinion publique et l'intégration européenne dans les années 50.' In *Il Ralancio dell'Europa e il trattai di Roma*, edited by E. Serra, 561-584. Bruxelles: Bruylant.

Reisen, M. van. (1999) *EU 'Global Player': the North-South policy of the European Union*. Utrecht, the Netherlands: International Books.

Reynaud, P. (1951) *Unite or Perish. A Dynamic Program for a United Europe*. New York: Simon and Schuster.

Rhenisch, T. (1994) Die deutsche Industrie und die Gründung der Europäischen Wirtschaftsgemeinschaft, Abteilung Geschichte und Kulturgeschichte, Europäisches Hochschulinstitut, Florence.

Rhodes, M. (1999) 'An Awkward Alliance: France, Germany and Social Policy.' In *The Franco-German Relationship in the European Union*, edited by D. Webber, 131-147. London: Routledge.

Rieger, E. (2000) 'The Common Agricultural Policy. Politics Against Markets.' In *Policy-Making in the European Union*, edited by H. Wallace and W. Wallace, 179-210. New York: Oxford University Press.

Riekmann, S. P., G. Hosking, and G. Schopflin, eds. (1998) *The Myth of European Unity. Myth and Nationhood*. New York: Routledge.

Rittberger, B. (2001) Which institutions for post-war Europe? Explaining the institutional design of Europe's first community. *Journal of European Public Policy* 8: 673-708.

Ritter, G. (1958) *The German Resistance*. London: George Allen & Unwin Ltd.

RIVOIRE, J. (1993) 'Le Crédit Lyonnais de 1945 à 1970: une lente ouverture à l'Europe.' In *L'Europe du patronat. De la guerre froide aux années soixante*, edited by M. Dumoulin, R. Girault and G. Trausch, 139-164. Berne: Peter Lang.

ROBERTS, I. and B. SPRINGER. (2001) *Social Policy in the European Union. Between Harmonization & National Autonomy*. Boulder, Colorado: Lynne Rienner.

ROBYN, R. (2000) Forms of Attachment to the European Union: A Study of French Conceptions of Identity in the Context of a Changing Europe. Ph.D, Kent State University.

ROEDERER, C. (2000) Popular Struggle and the Making of Europe's Common Agricultural Policy: Farm Protest in France, 1983-1993. Ph.D, University of South Carolina.

ROSENAU, J. (1980) *The Scientific Study of Foreign Policy*. New York: Nichols Publishing.

ROSS, G. (1995) *Jacques Delors and European Integration*. New York: Oxford University Press.

RUANE, K. (2000) *The Rise and Fall of the European Defence Community. Anglo-American Relations and the Crisis of European Defence, 1950-1955*. New York: St. Martin's Press.

RUGGIE, J. G. (1998) What Makes the World Hang Together? Neo-utilitarianism and the Social Constructivist Challenge. *International Organization* 52: 855-885.

SANDHOLTZ, W. AND J. ZYSMAN. (1989) 1992: Recasting the European Bargain. *World Politics* 42: 95-128.

SCHMIDT, V. (1997) Economic Policy, Political Discourse, and Democracy in France. *French Politics and Society* 15: 37-48.

SCHMUCK, O. (1989) 'The European Parliament's Draft Treaty Establishing the European Union (1979-84).' In *The Dynamics of European Union*, edited by R. Pryce, 188-216. New York: Routledge.

SCHREINER, R. (1993) 'La Politique européenne de la CDU relative à la France et au MRP des années 1945-1966.' In *Le MRP et la Construction européenne*, edited by S. Berstein, J.-M. Mayeur and P. Milza, 273-290. Bruxelles: Editions Complexe.

'The Schuman Plan.' (1953) In *Documents on International Affairs*, edited by M. Carlyle, 315-317. London: Oxford University Press.

SCHWABE, K. (1988a) 'Konrad Adenauer und der Schuman-Plan. Ein Quellenzeugnis.' In *Die Anfänge des Schuman-Plans 1950/51. The Beginnings of the Schuman-Plan*, edited by K. Schwabe, 131-142. Baden-Baden: Nomos.

SCHWABE, K. (1988b) 'Ein Akt konstruktiver Staatskunst - die USA und die Anfänge des Schuman-Plans.' In *Die Anfänge des Schuman-Plans 1950/51. The Beginnings of the Schuman-Plan*, edited by K. Schwabe, 211-240. Baden-Baden: Nomos.

SEWELL, J. P. (1966) *Functionalism and World Politics: a Study Based on United Nations Programs Financing Economic Development*. Princeton: Princeton University Press.

SHIELDS, J., and J. GAFFNEY. (1996) 'The French Gaullist.' In *Political Parties and the European Union*, 86-109. New York: Routledge.

SIMMONS, H. G. (1996) *The French National Front*. Colorado: Westview Press.

SIMONIAN, H. (1985) *The Privileged Partnership: Franco-German Relations in the European Community 1969-1984*. Oxford: Clarendon Press.

SMITH, M. P. (2001) In pursuit of selective liberalization: single market competition and its limits. *Journal of European Public Policy* 8: 519-540.

SNOY et D'OPPUERS, J-C. (1965) 'Des Traités de Rome à l'Europe politique.' In *Zur Integration Europas: Festschrift für Carl Friedrich Ophüls aus Anlass seines siebzigsten Geburtstages*, edited by W. Hallstein, Karlsruhe: C. F. Müller.

SOETENDORP, B. (1999) *Foreign Policy in the European Union: Theory, History and Practice*. New York: Addison Wesley Longman.

SPAAK, P. H. (1971) *The Continuing Battle: Memoirs of a European 1936-1966*, translated by H. Fox. Boston: Little Brown.

SPINELLI, A. (1966) *The Eurocrats: Conflict and Crisis in the European Community*. Translated by C. Grove Haines. Baltimore: Johns Hopkins Press.

SPINELLI, A. (1972) *The European Adventure: Tasks for an Enlarged Community*. London: C. Knight.

Statute of the Council of Europe March 11.2002 2002 [Available from http://conventions.coe.int/treaty/en/Treaties/Html/001.Int.]

STERLING-FOLKER, J. (2000) Competing Paradigms or Birds of a Feather? Constructivism and Neoliberal Institutionalism Compared. *International Studies Quarterly* 44: 97-119.

STEVENS, C. (2000) 'Trade With Developing Countries.' In *Policy-Making in the European Union*, edited by H. Wallace and W. Wallace, 401-426. New York: Oxford University Press.

STIRK, P. (1996) *A History of European Integration Since 1914*. New York: Pinter.

STRANGE, S. (1996) *The Retreat of the State: the Diffusion of Power in the World Economy*. New York: Cambridge University Press.

SWEDBERG, R. (1994) The Idea of 'Europe' and the Origin of the European Union-A Sociological Approach. *Zeitschrift für Soziologie* 23: 378-387.

TEITGEN, P.H. (1957) Common Assembly. *ECSA*, March 15th, 277.

TELTSCHIK, H. (1991) *329 Tage: Innenansichten der Einigung*. Berlin: Siedler.

THATCHER, M. (1993) *The Downing Street Years*. New York: Harper Collins.

THIEMEYER, G. (1998) Supranationalität als Novum in der Geschichte der internationalen Politik der fünfziger Jahre. *Journal of European Integration History* 4: 5-21.

Treaty Establishing the European Economic Community and Connected Documents. (1962). Luxembourg: Publishing Services of the European Communities.

VELZEN, W. VAN. (1991) The Community's Labour Pains. *European Affairs*: 63-65.

Voices of Europe. A Selection of Speeches Delivered before the Parliamentary Assembly of the Council of Europe 1049-96. (1997). Strasbourg: Council of Europe Publishing.

YOUNG, A. R. AND H. WALLACE (2000) 'The Single Market.' In *Policy-Making in the European Union*, edited by H. Wallace and W. Wallace, 85-114. New York: Oxford University Press.

WEBBER, D. (1999) Franco-German Bilateralism and Agricultural Politics in the European Union: the Neglected Level. *West European Politics* 22: 45-67.

WEBER, H. (1986) *Le Parti des patrons le CNPF (1946-1986)*. Paris: Éditions du Seuil.

WILLIAMS, P. M. (1964) *Crisis and Compromise Politics in the Fourth Republic.* London: Longmans.

WINTERS, L. A. (2001) 'European Union Trade Policy: Actually or Just Nominally Liberal?' In *Interlocking Dimensions of European Integration*, edited by H. Wallace, 25-44. Basingstoke: Palgrave.

ZUBOK, V. M., and K. PLESHAKOV. (1996) *Inside the Kremlin's Cold War: from Stalin to Khrushchev.* Mass.: Harvard University Press.

'Zwei aussenpolitische Memoranden der deutschen Opposition'. (1957) *Vierteljahrshefte für Zeitgeschichte* V.5. 388-401.

Archival References

Ad Hoc Assembly Instructed to Work out a Draft Treaty Setting up a European Political Community. Constitutional Committee. Session of January 1953. Report of the Constitutional Committee. Paris, December 20, 1953. Document 1.

Auswärtiges Amt, Bundesminister des Auswärtigen, Politisches Archiv, Abt.2. [Section 923], Band 5, File 225-30-02, Dec 8, 1956 (letter from Brentano to Adenauer).

Auswärtiges Amt, Bundesminister des Auswärtigen, Politisches Archiv, Abt.2. [Section 923], Band 5, File 225-30-02, Jan. 1957, Kabinettvorlage.

Auswärtiges Amt, Konsulat der Bundesrepublik Deutschland, Dakar, March 4, 1957, Parteikongress der B.P.S. (Politisches Archiv, Abt. 2. [Section 917], Band 9, File 225-30-01, Bonn.

Auswärtiges Amt, Politisches Archiv, Abt. 2. [Section 901], Band 2, File 225-10-01, June 15, 1955, Aktenvermerk von Hädrich an Ophűls, Kurzprotokoll űber die Ressortbesprechung.

Auswärtiges Amt, Politisches Archiv, Abt. 2. [Section 901], Band 3, File 225-10-01, June 20, 1955.

Auswärtiges Amt, Politisches Archiv, Abt. 2. [Section 902], Band 3, File 225-10-01, July 25 and Aug. 12, 1955. [untitled document].

Auswärtiges Amt, Politisches Archiv, Abt. 2. [Section 903], File 225-10-02, Sept. 2, 1955, [untitled document].

Auswärtiges Amt, Politisches Archiv, Abt. 2. [Section 901], Band 3, File 225-10-01, Sept. 3, 1955, Konferenz vom 6. September.

Auswärtiges Amt, Politisches Archiv, Abt. 2. [Section 902], Band 3, File 225-10-01, Sept. 3, 1955 [memo from Ophűls to Calmes].

Auswärtiges Amt, Politisches Archiv, Abt. 2. [Section 899], File 225-00, Sept.. 6, 1955, 6.9.1955 Noordwijk.

Auswärtiges Amt, Politisches Archiv, Abt. 2. [Section 899], File 225-00, Sept. 29, 1955, Integration.

Auswärtiges Amt, Politisches Archiv, Abt. 2. [Section 904], File 225-10-03 and 04, Oct. 26, 1955, An das Sekretariat des Regierungsauschusses eingesetzt von der Messinakonferenz, Oct. 26, 1955.

Auswärtiges Amt, Politisches Archiv, Abt. 2. [Section 899], File 225-00, Nov. 8, 1955, Integration.

Auswärtiges Amt, Politisches Archiv, Abt. 2. [Section 899], File 225-00, Nov. 9, 1955, Aufzeichnung [2 different documents with the same title].

Auswärtiges Amt, Politisches Archiv, Abt. 2. [Section 899], File 225-00, Nov. 9, 1955, Kabinettvorlage.

Auswärtiges Amt, Politisches Archiv, Abt. 2. [Section 904], Band 2 File 225-30-01, Feb. 12, 1956 [letter from Brentano to Adenauer].
Auswärtiges Amt, Politisches Archiv, Abt. 2. [Section 910], Band 2 File 225-30-01, May 18, 1956, Französische Haltung gegenüber den Brüsseler Vorschlägen auf Bildung eines gemeinsame Marktes.
Auswärtiges Amt, Politisches Archiv, Abt. 2. [Section 910], Band 2 File 225-30-01, May 23, 1956, Hinweise auf die voraussichtliche Haltung der französischen Regierung (signed Müller-Roschach).
Auswärtiges Amt, Politisches Archiv, Abt. 2. [Section 910], Band 2 File 225-30-01, June 7, 1956 [untitled document on letterhead of ECSC].
Auswärtiges Amt, Politisches Archiv, Abt. 2. [Section 910], Band 2 File 225-30-01, June 23, 1956, Brüsseler Konferenz (signed Ophüls).
Auswärtiges Amt, Politisches Archiv, Abt. 2. [Section 910], Band 2 File 225-30-01, June 30, 1956, Brüsseler Integrationskonferenz.
Auswärtiges Amt, Auswärtiges Amt, Politisches Archiv, Abt. 2. [Section 910], Band 2 File 225-30-01, June 21, 1956, Aufzeichnung.
Auswärtiges Amt, Politisches Archiv, Abt. 2. [Section 910], Band 2 File 225-30-01, June 21, 1956, Brüsseler Konferenz.
Auswärtiges Amt, Politisches Archiv, Abt. 2. [Section 922], Band 4 File 225-30-02, June 21bis, 1956, Brüsseler Integrationskonferenz.
Auswärtiges Amt, Politisches Archiv, Abt. 2. [Section 910], Band 2 File 225-30-01, June 23, 1956, Brüsseler Konferenz.
Auswärtiges Amt, Politisches Archiv, Abt. 2. [Section 910], Band 2 File 225-30-01, June 30, 1956, Ressortbesprechung.
Auswärtiges Amt, Politisches Archiv, Abt. 2. [Section 910], Band 2 File 225-30-01, June 1956 [day not specified], letter from Adenauer to Fritz Berg.
Auswärtiges Amt, Politisches Archiv, Abt. 2. [Section 910], Band 2 File 225-30-01, July 5, 1956, Kurzprotokoll.
Auswärtiges Amt, Politisches Archiv, Abt. 2. [Section 910], Band 2 File 225-30-01, July 5, 1956, 47. Tagung des wirtschaftlichen Beirats des Bundeswirtschaftsministerium.
Auswärtiges Amt, Politisches Archiv, Abt. 2. [Section 910], Band 2 File 225-30-01, July 16, 1956, Kurzprotokoll.
Auswärtiges Amt, Politisches Archiv, Abt. 2. [Section 910], Band 2 File 225-30-01, July 23, 1956, Gemeinsamer Markt.
Auswärtiges Amt, Politisches Archiv, Abt. 2. [Section 910], Band 2, File 225-30-01, July 25, 1956, Gemeinsamer Markt/Besprechung BWM.
Auswärtiges Amt, Politisches Archiv, Abt. 2. [Section 910], Band 2 File 225-30-01, Aug, 3, 1956, Kurzprotokoll über die Ressortbesprechung vom 27.7.1956.
Auswärtiges Amt, Politisches Archiv, Abt. 2. [Section 887], File 224-24-00. Aug. 16, 1956, Gemeinsamer Markt.

Auswärtiges Amt, Politisches Archiv, Abt. 2. [Section 910], Band 2 File 225-30-01, Aug. 22, 1956, Bericht über die bei der Brüsseler Integrationkonferenz bisher aufgetretene Hauptprobleme.

Auswärtiges Amt, Politisches Archiv, Abt. 2. [Section 887], File 224-24-00, Aug. 24, 1956, Vermerk.

Auswärtiges Amt, Politisches Archiv, Abt. 2. [Section 887], File 224-24-00, [date unspecified], Gesprächsunterlage für Unterhaltung des Herrn Bundeskanzlers mit Herrn Mollet [probably Sept. 1956].

Auswärtiges Amt, Politisches Archiv, Abt. 2. [Section 887], File 224-24-00. Sept. 7, 1956, Brüsseler Integrationskonferenz.

Auswärtiges Amt, Politisches Archiv, Abt. 2. [Section 887], File 224-24-00, Sept. 11, 1956, Gemeinsamer Markt.

Auswärtiges Amt, Politisches Archiv, Abt. 2. [Section 887], File 224-24-00, Sept. 13, 1956, Brüsseler Integrationskonfeenz.

Auswärtiges Amt, Politisches Archiv, Abt. 2. [Section 922], Band 4 File 225-30-02, Sept. 5, 1956, untitled telegram from Botschaft der Bundesrepublik Deutschland.

Auswärtiges Amt, Politisches Archiv, Abt. 2. [Section 887], File 224-24-00, Sept. [29], 1956, Ausschuss der Delegationsleiter.

Auswärtiges Amt, Politisches Archiv, Abt. 2. [Section 943], Oct. 2, 1956, Kabinettsvorlage.

Auswärtiges Amt, Politisches Archiv, Abt. 2. [Section 907], File 225-10-06, Oct. 3, 1956, Kabinettsvorlage.

Auswärtiges Amt, Politisches Archiv, Abt. 2. [Section 943] File 225-10-06, Oct.3bis, 1956, Brüsseler Integrationskonferenez.

Auswärtiges Amt, Politisches Archiv, Abt. 2. [Section 943] File 225-10-06, Oct. 5, 1956, Der Bundesminister für Ernährung, Landwirtschaft und Forsten.

Auswärtiges Amt, Politisches Archiv, Abt. 2. [Section 907], File 225-10-06, Oct. 6, 1956, Ergebnisprotokoll über die Ressortbesprechung.

Auswärtiges Amt, Politisches Archiv, Abt. 2. [Section 907], File 225-10-06, Oct. 8, 1956, Brüsseler Regierungskonferenz.

Auswärtiges Amt, Politisches Archiv, Abt. 2. [Section 907], File 225-10-06, Oct. 18, 1956, Aussenministeronferenz.

Auswärtiges Amt, Politisches Archiv, Abt. 2. [Section 907], File 225-10-06, Oct. 19, 1956, Aufzeichnung.

Auswärtiges Amt, Politisches Archiv, Abt. 2. [Section 907], File 225-10-06, Oct. 22, 1956, Diplogerman für Staatssekretär.

Auswärtiges Amt, Politisches Archiv, Abt. 2. [Section 943] File 225-10-06, Oct. 22bis, 1956, untitled document.

Auswärtiges Amt, Politisches Archiv, Abt. 2, microfiche A9078,

-Oct. 23, 1956 – note by Hartlieb (AA)

-Oct. 29, 1956 – memo from Carstens (AA) to Minister of Food, Agriculture and Forestry and others

- Nov. 6, 1956 – note by Thossen (AA)

- Jan. 1957 [day unspecified], draft reply to Deutschen Bauernverband

- Jan. 7, 1957 – letter from Rehwinkel of the Deutsche Bauernverband to Chancellor Adenauer
- Jan. 17, 1957 – note by Hartlieb
- Feb. 2, 1957 – Ophüls to Chancellor's Office.

Auswärtiges Amt, Politisches Archiv, Abt. 2. [Section 922], Band 4 File 225-30-02, Oct. 26, 1956, Tagung der Aussenminister der Staaten der Montan-Gemeinschaft in Paris.

Auswärtiges Amt, Politisches Archiv, Abt. 2. [Section 918], Band 10, File 225-30-01, Nov. 2, 1956, Besuch des Herrn Bundeskanzlers in Paris [note to Hallstein signed by Fechter].

Auswärtiges Amt, Politisches Archiv, Abt. 2. [Section 918], Band 10, File 225-30-01, Nov. 7, 1956, Brüsseler Regierungskonferenz.

Auswärtiges Amt, Politisches Archiv, Abt. 2. [Section 914], Nov. 10, 1956, Ergebnisprotokoll über die Ressortbesprechung.

Auswärtiges Amt, Politisches Archiv, Abt. 2. [Section 914], Nov. 12, 1956, Aufzeichnung.

Auswärtiges Amt, Politisches Archiv, Abt. 2. [Section 914], Nov. 17, 1956, Brüsseler Integrationskonferenz.

Auswärtiges Amt, Politisches Archiv, Abt. 2. [Section 914], Nov. 17, 1956, Stellungnahme.

Auswärtiges Amt, Politisches Archiv, Abt. 2. [Section 914], Nov. 19, 1956, Vermerk.

Auswärtiges Amt, Politisches Archiv, Abt. 2. [Section 907], File 225-10-06, Nov. 20, 1956, Vermerk.

Auswärtiges Amt, Politisches Archiv, Abt. 2. [Section 914], File 225-10-06, Nov. 23, 1956, Brüsseler Integrationskonferenz .

Auswärtiges Amt, Politisches Archiv, Abt. 2. [Section 914], Nov. 24, 1956, Ergebnisprotokoll über die Ressortbesprechung.

Auswärtiges Amt, Politisches Archiv, Abt. 2. [Section 914], Nov. 26, 1956, Gemeinsamer Markt/Überseegebiete.

Auswärtiges Amt, Politisches Archiv, Abt. 2. [Section 914], File 225-10-06, Nov. 29, 1956, Brüsseler Integrationskonferenz

Auswärtiges Amt, Politisches Archiv, Abt. 2. [Section 914], Dec. 1, 1956, Ergebisprotokoll über die Ressortbesprechung.

Auswärtiges Amt, Politisches Archiv, Abt. 2. [Section 914], Dec. 7, 1956, Gemeinsamer Markt.

Auswärtiges Amt, Politisches Archiv, Abt. 2. [Section 887], File 224-24-00, Dec. 10, 1956, letter from von Welck to Erhard.

Auswärtiges Amt, Politisches Archiv, Abt. 2. [Sections 915 & 916], Band 7, File 225-30-01, Dec. 3, 1956, Stand der Arbeiten im Ausschuss Gemeinsamer Markt.

Auswärtiges Amt, Politisches Archiv, Abt. 2. [Sections 915 & 916], Band 7, File 225-30-01, Dec. 3, 1956, Aufzeichnung.

Auswärtiges Amt, Politisches Archiv, Abt. 2. [Sections 915 & 916], Band 7, File 225-30-01, Dec. 5, 1956, Beihilfen.
Auswärtiges Amt, Politisches Archiv, Abt. 2. [Sections 915 & 916], Band 7, File 225-30-01, Dec. [day unspecified], Das Problem der Landwirtschaft.
Auswärtiges Amt, Politisches Archiv, Abt. 2. [Sections 915 & 916], Band 7, File 225-30-01, Dec. 8, 1956, Gemeinsamer Markt.
Auswärtiges Amt, Politisches Archiv, Abt. 2. [Sections 915 & 916], Band 7, File 225-30-01, Dec 14, 1956, [note by Carstens].
Auswärtiges Amt, Politisches Archiv, Abt. 2. [Sections 915 & 916], Band 7, File 225-30-01, Dec 17, 1956, [note by Hartlieb].
Auswärtiges Amt, Politisches Archiv, Abt. 2. [Sections 915 & 916], Band 7, File 225-30-01, Dec. 17, 1956, [letter from Lűbke to several other cabinet ministers].
Auswärtiges Amt, Politisches Archiv, Abt. 2. [Section 922], Band 4, File 225-30-02, Paris, Dec. 14bis, 1956, Innenpolitische lage Frankreichs [telegram from German ambassador Maltzan].
Auswärtiges Amt, Politisches Archiv, Abt. 2. [Sections 915 & 916], Band 7, File 225-30-01, Jan. 5, 1957, Brűsseler Integrationskonferenz. Delegationskonferenz vom 4. Jan. 1957.
Auswärtiges Amt, Politisches Archiv, Abt. 2. [Section 943], File 225-30-01, [mid-January 1957], Kabinettsvorlage.
Auswärtiges Amt, Politisches Archiv, Abt. 2. [Sections 915 & 916], Band 7, File 225-30-01, Jan. 7, 1957, Kabinettsvorlage Regierungskonferenz fűr den Gemeinsame Markt.
Auswärtiges Amt, Politisches Archiv, Abt. 2. [Sections 915 & 916], Band 7, File 225-30-01, Jan. 8, 1957, Weisung des Bundeskabinetts and die deutsche Delegation.
Auswärtiges Amt, Politisches Archiv, Abt. 2. [Sections 915 & 916], Band 7, File 225-30-01, Jan. 11, 1957, Herrn Dr. Janicke, Gemeinsamer Markt.
Auswärtiges Amt, Politisches Archiv, Abt. 2. [Section 923], Band 7, File 225-30-02, Jan. 11bis, 1957, Brűsseler Verhandlungen.
Auswärtiges Amt, Politisches Archiv, Abt. 2. [Sections 915 & 916], Band 7, File 225-30-01, Jan. 14, 1957, Kabinettvorlage.
Auswärtiges Amt, Politisches Archiv, Abt. 2. [Sections 915 & 916], Band 7, File 225-30-01, Jan. 16, 1957, Gemeinsamer Markt./Euratom.
Auswärtiges Amt, Politisches Archiv, Abt. 2. [Sections 915 & 916], Band 7, File 225-30-01, Jan. 16bis, 1957, Gemeinsamer Markt/Űberseeische Gebiete.
Auswärtiges Amt, Politisches Archiv, Abt. 2. [Sections 915 & 916], Band 7, File 225-30-01, Jan. 18, 1957, Gemeinsamer Markt./Euratom (memo signed by Hartlieb).
Auswärtiges Amt, Politisches Archiv, Abt. 2. [Sections 915 & 916], Band 7, File 225-30-01, Jan. 24, 1957, Brűsseler Verhandlungen.
Auswärtiges Amt, Politisches Archiv, Abt. 2. [Section 908], File 225-10-017, Jan. 27, 1957, Dem Herrn Bundeskanzler vorzulegen (letter from Brentano to Adenauer).

Auswärtiges Amt, Politisches Archiv, Abt. 2. [Sections 915 & 916], Band 9, File 225-30-01, Jan. 30, 1957, Gemeinsamer Markt/Euratom Sachstand.

Auswärtiges Amt, Politisches Archiv, Abt. 2. [Sections 917], Band 9, File 225-30-01, Feb. 1, 1957, Brűsseler Integrationsverhandlungen.

Auswärtiges Amt, Politisches Archiv, Abt. 2. [Section 917], Band 9, File 225-30-01, Feb. 5, 1957, Brűsseler Regierungskonferenz, Anpassungsfonds.

Auswärtiges Amt, Politisches Archiv, Abt. 2. [Section 917], Band 9, File 225-30-01, Feb. 8, 1957, Erklärung der deutschen Delegation.

Auswärtiges Amt, Politisches Archiv, Abt. 2. [Section 917], Band 9, File 225-30-01, Feb. 8bis, 1957, [letter from Foreign Minister Brentano to Finance Minister Schäffer].

Auswärtiges Amt, Politisches Archiv, Abt. 2. [Section 917], Band 9, File 225-30-01, Feb. 9, 1957, Brűsseler Integrationsverhandlungen.

Auswärtiges Amt, Politisches Archiv, Abt. 2. [Section 917], Band 9, File 225-30-01, Feb.13. 1957, Brűsseler Regierungskonferenz hier Sozialpolitik.

Auswärtiges Amt, Politisches Archiv, Abt. 2. [Section 917], Band 9, File 225-30-01, Feb. 14, 1957, Gemeinsamer Markt, finanzielle Fragen.

Auswärtiges Amt, Politisches Archiv, Abt. 2. [Section 917], Band 9, File 225-30-01, Feb. 14, 1957, Marokko und der Gemeinsame Markt.

Auswärtiges Amt, Politisches Archiv, Abt. 2. [Section 917], Band 9, File 225-30-01, March 10, 1957, Brüsseler Integrationsverhandlungen.

Auswärtiges Amt, Politisches Archiv, Abt. 2. [Section 917], Band 9, File 225-30-01, March 11, 1957, Gemeinsamer Markt./Offene Fragen.

Auswärtiges Amt, Politisches Archiv, Abt. 2. [Section 917], Band 9, File 225-30-01, March 11bis, 1957, Gemeinsamer Markt./Offene Fragen.

Auswärtiges Amt, Politisches Archiv, Abt. 2. [Section 917], Band 9, File 225-30-01, March 12, 1957, Brüsseler Regierungskonferenz.

Auswärtiges Amt, Politisches Archiv, Abt. 2. [Section 917], Band 9 File 225-30-01, March 15, 1957, untitled telegram from Botschaft der Bundesrepublik Deutschland, Paris.

Berg, F. (1956) Letter to the German Chancellor Adenauer. Archives of Auswärtiges Amt. Altena. Classification # 241. May 28th.

Brűsseler Integrationskonferenz, Delegationsleiter, Sept. 13, 1956, anonymous document included with Auswärtiges Amt, Politisches Archiv, Abt. 2. [Section 887], File 224-24-00.

Comité intergouvernemental, créé par la Conférence de Messine, July 21, 1955, Conférence sur la Relance de l'Idée européenne. (CM31/NEGO 036) (hereinafter Comité intergouvernementale), Florence.

Comité intergouvernemental: Commission du Marché commun, July 18, 1955, Note de la délégation allemande (CM3/NEGO 034).

Comité intergouvernemental: Commission du Marché commun, Sept. 28, 1955, Remarques de la délégation française (9CM3/NEGO 038).

Comité intergouvernemental, Oct. 14, 1955, Mémorandum de la délégation française (CM3/NEGO 039).
Comité intergouvernemental, Oct. 24, 1955, Première note pour les chefs des délégations (CM3/NEGO O4O).
Comité intergouvernemental, Nov. 6, 1955, Document de Travail, No. 6.
Comité intergouvernemental, Nov. 8, 1955, Document de Travail No 5. (CM3/NEGO 030).
Comité intergouvernemental, Nov. 9, 1955, Procès-verbal de la réunion des chefs de délégations tenue à Bruxelles le 7 novembre 1955 (CM3/NEGO 030).
Comité intergouvernemental: réunion des chefs de délégation, Feb. 11-12, 1956 [untitled document].
Comité intergouvernemental, Feb. 13, 1956, Annexe au document No. 6 sur les Institutions.
Comité intergouvernemental, Feb. 18, 1956, Document de Travail No. 9 Problèmes d'harmonisation.
Conférence de Bruxelles, Nov.23, 1956, Réunion du comité des chefs de delegation du 22 novembre, 1956 (Document found in German foreign ministry archives).
Conférence des Ministres des Affaires étrangères, Venise, May 29-30, 1956 (European Archives).
Conférence des Ministres des Affaires étrangères. Secrétariat, June 8, 1956, Projet de Procès-verbal. (CM3/NEGO 092).
Conférence des Ministres des Affaires étrangères, Paris, Oct. 20-21, 1956, Projet de procès-verbal (European Archives File CM3/NEGO095).
Conférence des Ministres des Affaires étrangères, Bruxelles, Jan. 26-28, 1957, Projet de procès-verbal (European Archives File CM3/NEGO098).
Conférence des Ministres des Affaires étrangères, Bruxelles, Feb. 4, 1957, Projet de procès verbal. (CM3/NEGO 096).
Conférence des Ministres des Affaires étrangères, Paris, Feb. 18, 1957. Conférence des chefs de gouvernement et des ministres des affaires étrangères, Paris, Feb. 18-20, 1957, Principales questions traitées. (European Archives File CM3/NEG 097)
Conférence intergouvernementale pour le Marché commun et l'Euratom: comité des chefs de délégation, Sept. 19, 1956, Note présenté par la délégation française. (hereinafter Conférence intergouvernementale), Bruxelles.
Conférence intergouvernementale, Chefs de délégation, Réunion restreinte, Jan. 21, 1957, L'Association des Pays et Territoires d''Outre-Mer.
Conférence intergouvernementale: comité des chefs de délégation, Bruxelles, Nov. 21, 1956, Projet de procès-verbal.
Conférence intergouvernementale: comité des chefs de délégation, Bruxelles, Dec. 10, 1956, Projet de procès-verbal (European Archives file PU 54).
Conférence intergouvernementale: comité des chefs de délégation, Bruxelles, Jan. 11, 1957, Projet de procès-verbal (Uri papers, Folder 54), Florence.
Conférence intergouvernementale: comité des chefs de délégation, Bruxelles, Jan. 21, 1957, Projet de Protocol. (CE3/NEGO181).

Conférence intergouvernementale: comité des chefs de délégation, Bruxelles, Jan. 25, 1957, Projet de Procès-verbal (CE3/NEGO121).
Conférence intergouvernementale: comité des chefs de délégation, Bruxelles, Feb. 27, 1957, Projet de procès-verbal (European Archives, Uri papers, folder 54).
Conférence intergouvernementale: comité des chefs de délégation, Bruxelles, March 7-8, 1957, Projet de procès-verbal (European Archives, Uri papers, folder 54).
Conférence intergouvernementale: documents non numérotés, Nov. 9, 1956, Note rapide au sujet de l'accord franco-allemand en matière du marché commun, Bruxelles.
Conférence intergouvernementale: réunion du groupe du marché commun, July 12-13, 1956, Proposition française 'comparaisons des coûts', Bruxelles.
Conférence intergouvernementale: réunion des chefs de délégation, Bruxelles, Jan. 18-20, 1957, Projet de procès-verbal (CM3/NEGO 122).
Conférence intergouvernementale: réunion des chefs de délégation, Bruxelles, Feb. 1, 1957, Projet de procès-verbal (CM3/NEGO 122).
Conférence intergouvernementale: réunion des chefs de délégation, Bruxelles, Feb.28-March 3, 1957, Projet de procès-verbal (CM3/NEGO 128).
Conférence intergouvernementale: réunion des chefs de délégation, Rome, March 24, 1957, Projet de procès-verbal (CM3/NEGO 130).
Conférence intergouvernementale: réunion du groupe du marché commun, Sept. 24-26, 1956, Projet de procès-verbal, Bruxelles.
Conférence intergouvernementale: réunion des chefs de délégation, Bruxelles, Oct. 22, 1956, Projet de procès-verbal (European Archives file CM3/NEGO 112).
Conférence intergouvernementale: réunion des chefs de délégation, Bruxelles, Nov. 22, 1956, Projet de procès-verbal (European Archives file CM3/NEGO 112).
Conférence intergouvernementale: réunion des chefs de délégation, Bruxelles, Jan. 23-24, 1957, Projet de procès-verbal (European Archives file CM3/NEGO122).
Conférence intergouvernementale: réunion des chefs de délégation, Bruxelles, Feb. 8-9, 1957, Projet de procès-verbal (CM3/NEGO125).
Conférence intergouvernementale: réunion du groupe du marché commun, Bruxelles, June 17, 1956, Mémento interne.
Conférence intergouvernementale: réunion du groupe du marché commun, Bruxelles, Oct. 9, 1956, Projet de Procès-verbal (CM3/NWGO 112).
Conférence intergouvernementale: réunion du groupe du marché commun, Bruxelles, Jan. 31,-Feb. 9, 1957, Approbation de la rédaction des articles concernant la politique sociale (CM3/NEGO153).
Conférence intergouvernementale: secrétariat, July 28, 1956, Procès-verbal, Bruxelles.

Conférence intergouvernementale: secrétariat, Sept. 19, 1956, Note présentée par la délégation française (document found in German foreign ministry archives), Bruxelles.
Conférence intergouvernementale: secrétariat, Nov.30, 1956, Projet de procès-verbal de la réunion des chefs de délégation, le 29 novembre 1956 (Uri papers).
Conférence intergouvernementale: secrétariat, Dec. 10, 1956, Projet de procès-verbal de la réunion des chefs de délégation, le 6 décembre 1956 (Uri papers).
Couve de Murville. (1957) Letter to the French Minister of Foreign Affairs. Archives du Quai d'Orsay. Bonn. February 8th.
Deutscher Gewerkschaftsbund. (1957) Letter to the President of the Foreign Ministers Conference at Brussels. Archives of the Auswärtiges Amt. Düsseldorf, Classification #102, January 3rd.
Gabriel Sedlmayr Spaten-Franziskaner-Bräu. (1957) Letter to the Secretariat of the German Delegation at the Brussels Conference. Archives of the Auswärtiges Amt. Munich, Classification #250, February 7th.
Inudstrie-Gewerkschaft Metall. (1956) Letter to the President of the Foreign Ministers Conference at Brussels. Archives of the Auswärtiges Amt. Frankfurt. Classification # 110, December 17th.
Internationaler Bund der Christlichen Gewerkschaften. (1957) Letter to the German Minister of Foreign Affairs. Archives of the Auswärtiges Amt. Brussels. Classification # 112, January 12th.
Konferenz der Regierungschefs, Sekretariat, Feb. 20, 1957, Zusammenfassung der Beschluesse der Regierungschefs (document found in German Foreign Ministry Archives, Politisches Archiv, Abt. 2 [Section 917], Band 9, File 225-30-01, March 11, 1957).
Ministere des Affaires Étrangères, Cabinet du ministre. 1955, Projet de procès verbal de réunion des ministres des affaires étrangères des États membres de la C.E.C.A. à Messine, Paris.
Ministere des Affaires Étrangères, Nov. 12, 1955, De la part de la Délégation française [telegram from de Margerie in Geneva], Florence.
Ministere des Affaires Étrangères, Feb. 20, 1956, Compte-rendu de la première réunion tenue le 20 février 1956 (document found in European Archives, Florence, MAEF, 381).
Ministere des Affaires Étrangères, March 3, 1956, [untitled document recording conversation between Pineau and Brentano] (document located in European Archives Florence).
Ministere des Affaires Étrangères, Sept. 16, 1956, [untitled telegram from de Margérie] (Série Europe, 1956-1960, Sous Série Questions internationales), Florence.
Ministere des Affaires Étrangères, Oct. 10, 1956, [untitled telegram from Couve de Murville describing his first call on Adeanuer] (Série Europe 1944-1960, Sous-série Allemagne), Florence.

Ministere des Affaires Étrangères, Ambassade de France, Bonn, Feb. 3, 1956, Intégration européenne et intérêts nationaux (document located in European Archives, Florence, MAEF 629-30).

Ministere des Affaires Étrangères, Ambassade de France en Belgique, Bruxelles, July 20, 1955, Diplomatie Paris (document located in European Archives, Florence MAEF 630-631).

Ministere des Affaires Étrangères, Ambassade de France en Belgique, Bruxelles, Dec.28, 1956, M. Raymond Bousquet à Son Excellence Monsieur Christian Pineau (document located in MAEF, Série E 1944-1960, vol. 185, Marché commun).

Ministere des Affaires Étrangères, Ambassade de France en Belgique, Bruxelles, Nov. 27, 1956, M. Raymond Bousquet à Son Excellence Monsieur Christian Pineau (document located in MAEF, Série E 1944-1960, vol. 185, Marché commun).

Ministere des Affaires Étrangères, Ambassade de France en Belgique, Bruxelles, Jan. 7, 1957, M. Raymond Bousquet à Son Excellence Monsieur Christian Pineau.

Ministere des Affaires Étrangères, Ambassade de France en Belgique, Bruxelles, Jan. 29, 1957, M. Raymond Bousquet à Son Excellence Monsieur Christian Pineau.

Ministere des Affaires Étrangères, Ambassade de France en Belgique, Bruxelles, Jan.29, 1957, M. Raymond Bousquet à Son Excellence Monsieur Christian Pineau (Quai d'Orsay Archives, Série Europe 1956-1960).

Ministere des Affaires Étrangères, Ambassade de France en Belgique, Bruxelles, Feb. 6, 1957, M. Raymond Bousquet à Son Excellence Monsieur Christian Pineau.

Ministere des Affaires Étrangères, Direction Générale Politique, Dec. 9 and 28, 1956, M. Raymond Bousquet à Monsieur Christian Pineau (European Archives File EU 38).

Ministere des Affaires Étrangères, vol. 307, Wormser papers, Note Pour le Président, Oct. 10, 1955 (Document located in European Archives, Florence).

Ministere des Affaires Étrangères, vol. 307, Wormser papers, Oct. 11, 1955, Note Pour le Président (Document located in European Archives, Florence).

Ministere des Affaires Étrangères, vol. 381, March-Feb. 1956, Compte-rendu de la réunion tenue le 3 mars 1956 (Document located in European Archives, Florence).

Ministere des Affaires Étrangères, Bonn, May 3, 1956, Untitled letter from Louis Joxe to Christian Pineau (Dcoument located in European archives, Florence).

Ministere des Affaires Étrangères, vol. 613, Présidence du Conseil, Réunion interministérielle de 3 juillet 1956.

Ministere des Affaires Étrangères, vol. 613, Aug. 8, 1956, [untitled telegram from du Fournier in Brussels to ministry in Paris] (document found in European Archives, Florence).

Ministere des Affaires Étrangères, vol. 629-30, Sept. 16, 1956, Conversation entre M. Maurice Faure et M. Erhard, Berlin (document found in European Archives, Florence).

Ministere des Affaires Étrangères: Le Cabinet du Secrétaire de l'État, Nov. 8, 1956 Note à l'attention de M. Jorgenson.

Ministere des Affaires Étrangères: Le Cabinet du Secrétaire de l'État, Dec. 22, 1956, [untitled document].

Ministere des Affaires Étrangères, Sécrétariat Général, vol.381, Sept. 16-17, 1956, Conversations franco-allemandes.

Ministere des Affaires Étrangères, vol. 381, Sept. 17, 1956, De la part de M. Maurice Faure.

Ministere des Affaires Étrangères, Sécrétariat Général, Dec. 9, 1956, Bruxelles, M. Raymond Bousquet à Son Excellence Monsieur Christian Pineau (document located in European Archives, Florence).

Ministere des Affaires Étrangères, Sécrétariat Général, Jan. 7, 1957, Bruxelles, M. Raymond Bousquet à Son Excellence Monsieur Christian Pineau (document located in European Archives, Florence.)

Ministere des Affaires Étrangères, Bruxelles, Feb. 5, 1957, [untitled telegram from Bousquet to ministry], (Document found in European Archives, Florence).

Ministere des Affaires Étrangères, vol. 629-30, March 16, 1957, [untitled telegram from Couve de Murville in Bonn].

Ministere des Affaires Étrangères, 1958, [undated, unsigned history of the EEC negotiations based on other French documents and found in the ministry archives].

Ministere des Affaires Étrangères, Direction Générale des Affaires Économiques & Financières, Service de Coopération Économique, Feb. 2, 1956, Note, Le Marché commun.

Ministere des Affaires Étrangères, Direction Générale des Affaires Économiques & Financières, Service de Coopération Économique, Feb. 17, 1956, Réunion des six ministres des affaires étrangères (Wormser Papers).

Ministere des Affaires Étrangères, Direction Générale des Affaires Économiques & Financières, Service de Coopération Économique, Vol. 613, note pour le cabinet du Sécretaire d'État, March 26, 1956.

Ministere des Affaires Étrangères, Direction Générale des Affaires Économiques & Financières, Service de Coopération Économique, vol. 613, Note, March 30, 1956.

Ministere des Affaires Étrangères, Direction Générale des Affaires Économiques & Financières, Service de Coopération Économique, vol. 613, Note, April 21, 1956.

Ministere des Affaires Étrangères, Direction Générale des Affaires Économiques & Financières, Service de Coopération Économique, vol. 613, Note, April 25, 1956, [title illegible].

Ministere des Affaires Étrangères, Direction Générale des Affaires Économiques & Financières, vol. 613, Note pour Monsieur Maurice Faure, May 3, 1956 (document located in European Archives, Florence).
Ministere des Affaires Étrangères, Direction Générale des Affaires Économiques & Financières, Service de Coopération Économique, vol. 613, Note, May 12, 1956 (Document located in European Archives, Florence).
Ministere des Affaires Étrangères, Direction Générale des Affaires Économiques & Financières, vol. 613, June 23, 1956, Note, (Document located in European Archives, Florence).
Ministere des Affaires Étrangères, Direction Générale des Affaires Économiques & Financières, vol. 306, July 23, 1956, Note pour Monsieur Maurice Faure (Wormser Papers).
Ministere des Affaires Étrangères, Direction Générale des Affaires Économiques & Financières, Service de Coopération Économique, vol. 306, June 23, 1956, Harmonisation sociale et mécanismes de sauvegarde (Wormser papers).
Ministere des Affaires Étrangères, Direction Générale des Affaires Économiques & Financières, Service de Coopération Économique, vol. 613, Feb. 24, 1956, Marché commun européen.
Ministere des Affaires Étrangères, Direction Générale des Affaires Économiques & Financières, Service de Coopération Économique, vol.306, Nov. 9, 1956, [untitled document with the hand-written notation 'M . Wormser'].
Ministere des Affaires Étrangères, Direction Générale des Affaires Économiques & Financières, Service de Coopération Économique, vol. 613, Aug. 30, 1956, M. Wormser [title] [signed X].
Ministere des Affaires Étrangères, Direction Générale des Affaires Économiques & Financières, Jan. 8, 1957, Note, (Wormser Papers).
Ministere des Affaires Étrangères, Direction Générale des Affaires Politiques, Direction d'Europe centrale, Paris, Oct. 22, 1956, Note sur l'ordre du jour de la rencontre Mollet-Adenauer.
Ministere des Affaires Étrangères, Sécrétariat d'État des Affaires Économiques. Direction des Relations Économiques extérieures, Feb. 24, 1956, Marché commun européen.
Ministere des Affaires Étrangères, vol. 306, Wormser papers, Untitled document dated Feb. 8, 1956 (Document located in European Archives, Florence).
Ministere des Affaires Étrangères, vols. 630-631, June 18, 1955, Telegram from Rivière in Brussels to MAEF (document located in European Archives, Florence).
Ministere des Affaires Étrangères, vols. 629-630, Conversation entre M. Maurice Faure et M. Erhard, Sept.16, 1956 (Document located in European Archives, Florence).
Ministere des Affaires Étrangères, Le Cabinet du Secrétaire de l'État, Nov. 8, 1956, Note à l'attention de M. Jorgenson.

Ministere des Affaires Étrangères, Direction Générale des Affaires Économiques & Financières, Wormser papers, Note, Sept. 27, 1956.

Ministere des Affaires Étrangères, Direction Générale des Affaires politiques, Europe, Nov. 7, 1956, [untitled telegram addressed to seven embassies].

Ministere des Affaires Étrangères, Direction générale politique, Sous-direction des affaires européennes, Relance européenne et prochaines réunions ministérielles.

Ministere des Affaires Étrangères, Europe, Sous-direction d'Europe, Dec. 12, 1955, Note pour Monsieur Jurgensen.

Ministère des Affaires Étrangères, Secrétariat générale, Entretiens et Messages, Feb. 11, 1956, [untitled].

Ministere des Affaires Étrangères, Secrétariat générale, Sept. 16-17, 1956, conversations franco-allemandes.

Ministere des Affaires Étrangères, Secrétariat générale, Oct. 2, 1956, [untitled telegram by Louis Joxe to diplomatic missions summarising talks between Mollet and Adenauer], (document found in European Archives, Florence).

Ministere des Affaires Étrangères, Secrétariat générale, vol. 381, Nov. 6, 1956, Procès-verbal de l'entretien du 6 novembre 1956.

Ministere des Affaires Étrangères, Secrétariat générale, Moscow, May 18, 1956, Conversations franco-soviétiques, 16-19 mars 1956 (document located in European Archives, Florence, MAEF 381).

Ministere des Affaires Étrangères, Service de Coopération économique, vol. 613, Oct. 30, 1956, Les Ministres des Affaires Étrangères à Monsieur l'Ambassadeur de France (document located in European Archives, Florence).

Ministere des Affaires Étrangères, 1956-58, Série: Cabinet du Ministre, Sous-série: Christian Pineau, April 12, 1957, Letter from Comité National Française de l'Artisanat et des Petites et Moyennes Entreprises.

Ministere des Affaires Étrangères, 1956-58, Série: Cabinet du Ministre, Sous-série: Christian Pineau, May 16, 1957, Untitled notes of a meeting with Léon Gingembre of the CGPME.

Ministere des Affaires Étrangères, Série Europe 1944-1960, Sous Série Allemagne, Télégramme à l'arrivée, Couve de Murville, Jan. 23, 1957.

Ministere des Affaires Étrangères et du Commerce Extérieur [Belgium], Sept. 24, 1956, Note, (document included in Ministère des Affaires Étrangères [France], vol. 613).

Movement républicain populaire. (1957) Compte rendu sténographique des Congrès nationaux. In Reproduction de Documents appartenants aux Archives du M.R.P. 13 Congrès National à Biarritz. Paris: Fondation nationale des Sciences politiques.

Pinay, A. (1955) Letter to Adenauer. Archives du Quai d'Orsay. Paris. Classification # 389. 7th of April 1955.

Regierungskonferenz für den Gemeinsamen Markt und Euratom, Sekretariat, Ad Hoc-Gruppe fuer die Ueberseeischen Gebiete, Dec. 20, 1956, Bericht (located in German foreign ministry archives, Bonn).

Regierungskonferenz für den Gemeinsamen Markt und Euratom, Sekretariat, Ausshuss der Delgationsleiter, Nov. 14, 1956, Französisch-Belgischer Bericht, (Auswärtiges Amt, Politisches Archive, Abt. 2, Band 914, File A9052-9055).

Regierungskonferenz für den Gemeinsamen Markt und Euratom, Sekretariat, Ausschuss der Delegations leiter, Nov. 16, 1956, Erklärung der französischen Delegation betreffend die Einbeziehung der Überseeischen Gebiete, (Auswärtiges Amt, Politisches Archive, Abt. 2, Band 916, File A9052-9055).

Réunion des Ministres des Affaires étrangères, Secrétariat, Bruxelles, Sept. 28, 1955, Projet de procès-verbal de la réunion des Ministres étrangères, Noordwijk, 6 septembre 1955.

Richter, W. (1957) Letter to the President of the Foreign Ministers Conference at Brussels. Düsseldorf.

United States, American Embassy, Bonn, Elim O'Shaughnessy, Counsellor of Embassy German policy regarding West European Integration from September-December 1956, 8 January 1957.

Index